QUESTIONS AND ADMISSIONS

Questions and Admissions

Reflections on
100,000
Admissions
Decisions at
Stanford

JEAN H. FETTER

.

Stanford University Press, Stanford, California

Stanford University Press

Stanford, California

© 1995 by the Board of Trustees of the
Leland Stanford Junior University
Printed in the United States of America

CIP data are at the end of the book

Stanford University Press publications are
distributed exclusively by Stanford
University Press within the United States,
Canada, Mexico, and Central America;
they are distributed exclusively by Cambridge
University Press throughout the rest of the world.

Original printing 1995
Last figure below indicates year of this printing:
05   04   03   02   01   00   99   98   97   96

Preface

WHILE THERE IS SOMETHING psychologically unsettling about beginning with the admission of what-this-book-is-not, the approach has the immediate virtue of saving time for the prospective reader. This is not, then, a book about how to "get into" Stanford or any other selective college. It is true I have been assured that such a topic would guarantee many readers; after completing seven enormously challenging years as dean of undergraduate admissions at Stanford University, it is also true that I could perhaps provide some helpful guidance and advice to such would-be readers. This is not the place for the reader to find specific advice, although I hope that most of this book will provide an informative view of the college admissions process at selective institutions. The descriptions are (or at least were) true for Stanford University; other selective colleges and universities conduct somewhat different processes, although the fundamental principles are similar.

Having said what this book is not, I believe it is important to state what (I hope) this book is. Although it is primarily a case study of the process for selecting undergraduates at Stanford, written by a primary source, only the first two chapters (and not all of them) describe specifically what takes place at Stanford. The six subsequent chapters are relevant to the process of admitting undergraduates at a range of four-year colleges and universities in the United States. Some of the chapters (such as Chapter 4, "Special Talents, Special Considerations") apply only to the more selective and private colleges; the role of varsity athletics (Chapter 6) is more relevant to

Division I-A institutions (those engaged in the NCAA's highest competitive level for football) than to others, although almost every college in the country has athletics teams engaged in some form of competition. In addition, every college and university in the country is, or should be, concerned about affirmative action (Chapter 5) and ethical dilemmas (Chapter 7), as they are about changes ahead (Chapter 8). In short, the case study of Stanford presented here is applicable to the process of selecting any class of undergraduates. Consequently, the book should be of interest beyond the Stanford community—to prospective college and university students, their parents, teachers, and guidance counselors, not to mention those involved directly in the college admissions process.

The question of what gained an applicant admission to Stanford was not the one that presented the most difficult dilemmas and challenges of my job. One of the major surprises for me when I became dean of undergraduate admissions in 1984 was how ill-informed were the participants in the college admissions process. Parents, for example, were often surprised to learn that many selective colleges practice need-blind admissions (that is, each member of the freshman class is selected without consideration of his or her ability to pay for a college education; instead, the college or university guarantees to meet the computed need of every admitted student). High school seniors, particularly in large public and rural high schools, were not familiar with the options of Early Action or Early Decision or, in many cases, did not know a more basic fact: the application deadlines of the colleges they planned to apply to. Well-meaning alumni were reported to proliferate myths about the selection process: purported quotas for states or high schools; supposed geographic disadvantages; the weight of unsolicited letters of reference. One evening at dinner in a San Francisco restaurant, where the tables were so intimately placed as to impose enforced eavesdropping, my husband and I listened aghast as a Stanford alumnus, obviously unaware of the identity of his better-informed neighbors, described to an out-of-town visitor his almost totally incorrect interpretation of the selection process for Stanford undergraduates. Miss Manners's etiquette books offer no guidance on how the eavesdropper should react in such circumstances, and I opted for the perhaps cowardly path of not spoiling anyone's dinner. I have had some regrets.

On another occasion, I overheard a high school teacher at a conference tell one unsuspecting senior that he needn't bother applying to Stanford because the school admitted only the children of alumni and other wealthy families. Fortunately, I was one of the speakers at this event and therefore could offer some advice on how to obtain the correct information. In any case, it is a Sisyphean and frustrating exercise constantly to counteract myths, and each summer the admissions staff diligently revised the office's publications to increase the number of facts we distributed about the admissions process at Stanford. Alas, as all deans know, facts face hard times in counteracting myths. For those disappointed that this book does not provide what they were looking for, I hope that one fact is reassuring: almost every college and university in the United States will provide, usually free of charge, a publication that answers the fundamental questions about the college and its admissions process. All it takes is a postcard with your name and address along with a straightforward question or request. The quality of the response can often provide a revealing first impression of the college or university in which you are interested. If your question is not answered in the publication you receive, don't hesitate to telephone and ask it again. All admissions officers would rather provide you with the facts than have you accept secondhand or incorrect information.

My purpose here is to attempt to inform and enlighten prospective college applicants and their parents, teachers, and guidance counselors, as well as interested faculty and alumni, about some fundamental philosophical and ethical issues and how they apply to the selection of any college freshman class. College admissions professionals will immediately recognize the dilemmas, just as they will acknowledge the lack of time to discuss and debate them during the relentless pressures of regular business of the academic year—an interesting irony when the undebated topics play such a significant role in the selection process. A Stanford faculty member once asked me, in all innocence, what I did outside the months of January to

April, when we tackled the 15,000 or so freshman applications. The answer was to visit four high schools a day in the fall (our staff of twelve annually visited close to 700 high schools nationwide); attend three or four national and regional meetings a year; give numerous invited talks to alumni, counselors, parents, and students; help read 1,200 applications from students wanting to transfer to Stanford from other colleges and universities; manage an office staff of close to 30; participate in the annual revision of all our publications; answer a never-ending flow of mail, approaching 45,000 letters a year; and fill in the remaining time with committees, dorm dinners, office appointments, and freshman advising—along with many other duties that are unspecified in the job description of a dean of undergraduate admissions. Needless to say, this assignment cannot be completed single-handedly, and I was blessed with a talented, hardworking, and committed staff from whom I learned a great deal. But the internal workings and management of the office are also the material for another book, not this one.

Because I set myself a deadline for finishing the manuscript for this book, hard choices characterized my selection of topics. Consequently, I have not addressed some important matters, such as financial aid; although concerns about the costs of attending college loom large for students, their parents, and everyone in Undergraduate Admissions, the omission here seemed sensible because the Office of Financial Aid operates independently of admissions in Stanford's need-blind selection process. Some colleges and universities have, alas, already departed from the practice of need-blind admissions, which is an increasingly expensive undertaking (in 1990 Stanford spent close to $30 million on undergraduate scholarship aid alone, contributing to the educational costs of almost 60 percent of the freshman class), and in times of extreme financial pressures, the future of need-blind decisions remains uncertain. I have not made the arguments here about the unfortunate consequences of abandoning a need-blind admissions process; I would be remiss, however, not to regret in the strongest possible terms such a necessity, for which the federal and state governments must undoubtedly accept some responsibility.

Some of the topics I have included merit books of their own, and I readily admit to not having done some subjects full justice; affirmative action and varsity athletics are two obvious candidates for such a disclaimer. Fortunately, other authors have recently tackled those topics, and I am grateful to be able to refer interested readers to more comprehensive discussions of these subjects elsewhere. My decision here was to present a survey of the most challenging questions and dilemmas in selecting Stanford's undergraduates; this approach is necessarily more superficial in its analysis than a comprehensive examination would be, but it does have the advantage of bringing an array of the most critical questions to some unaccustomed light.

This is an appropriate place to comment that everything written here is based on my personal experience in undergraduate admissions at Stanford between 1984 and 1991; it does not claim to reflect on the work of the office during the times of either my predecessor or my successor. A final, and apologetic, disclaimer is owed to my great and former colleagues at Stanford: the views here may have been influenced by their thinking, but what the reader will find, for better or for worse, are my personal impressions and opinions rather than any official institutional policies and procedures of the Office of Undergraduate Admissions or Stanford University. Where the stated policies are, in fact, "official," I hope that I have made that clear. (This disclaimer is based, of course, on the dubious premise that any office or institution has a unanimous or collective viewpoint. A simple test of this statement is to pose a question—for example, "Should Stanford use the grade of F?"—to any random sample of Stanford's approximately 1,300 faculty or 6,500 undergraduates.) But since my staff and I took pride in our focus on the *individual,* not on any groups or representatives of groups, in the selection of the freshman and transfer classes, I am not about to begin to apologize for appreciating the value of independent thought.

My experience working in Undergraduate Admissions at Stanford provided all that any human being could ask for in a job: an important, if somewhat terrifying, responsibility; a first-rate university in a glorious setting; extraordinarily talented students; committed,

hardworking, and stimulating colleagues; enthusiastic and supportive faculty and staff; thoughtful, encouraging, and demanding
trustees; and loyal alumni and alumnae. (Well, there were some
memorable exceptions to all the above categories, but the accolades
are, for the best part, overwhelmingly accurate.) My position unquestionably presented the most challenging professional assignment that I have ever tackled, but it was also the most exhilarating.
I cannot, in honesty, claim to have loved every minute of it; there
were some miserably low moments, but the gains certainly exceeded the pains by a large margin. As Stanford celebrates the beginning of its second century, I appreciated the opportunity of my
sabbatical year to reflect on undergraduate admissions in the latter
part of its first century. I am sorry that I won't be around to see how
things compare in another one hundred years, but may "the winds
of freedom" continue to blow long and hard through Stanford's
quadrangles and classrooms.

Acknowledgments

AS I ACKNOWLEDGED PUBLICLY on numerous occasions between 1984 and 1991, no dean of undergraduate admissions could select a freshman class single-handedly; many share the credit for such an effort. Similarly, while this book carries only my name on the cover, I am indebted to significant friends and colleagues for their contributions to the work found inside the covers.

The primary words of thanks go to all my colleagues, past and present, in the Office of Undergraduate Admissions at Stanford. In the course of seven years, their tough questions clarified my thinking, their comments often determined my judgments, and their support made possible the seemingly impossible. In particular, former assistant director of undergraduate admissions Shellye McKinney has earned my gratitude for the invaluable help she provided as my editorial assistant in producing both the second and third (and final) drafts of the text. I doubt that this book would have been finished without her. Other colleagues were generous in the time they spent to review and comment on the first draft: John Bunnell, Jon Reider, Holly Thompson, all of Stanford, and Christiane Neuville at University High School in San Francisco. Muriel Bell, senior editor at the Stanford University Press, offered gentle but firm and experienced guidance and sage comments at a critical stage. In the final, important stages, no detail escaped the keen eye of associate editor Lynn Stewart. I am grateful for her intelligence and constructive questions and for her perceptive reading of the manuscript. The responsibility for the final product, however, is entirely mine.

Other Stanford faculty and colleagues were helpful in a range of different ways: professors Bliss Carnochan, Carl Degler, and Herant Katchadourian about writing and publishing; Maggie Kimball and Pat White for providing access to archival materials; and Christian Rowcliffe for giving computer support to a relative novice. Provost James Rosse made possible the time to write by granting a sabbatical year, albeit one that was interrupted by interesting service on Stanford's Presidential Search Committee. Dean Mike Smith of the School of Education gave me a warm welcome and an office to write in.

Last, but far from least, thanks to Sandy, Anne, and Andrew, who provided perennial support and encouragement in ways that only family can. I am grateful to them all.

Contents

1. Admissions from the University's Founding, 1

2. Decisions: Selecting the Freshman Class, 16

3. Can Selectivity Be Justified? 41

4. Special Talents, Special Considerations, 61

5. Affirmative Action, 88

6. The Role of Varsity Athletics, 146

7. Ethical Dilemmas, 193

8. The Changing Scene, 229

Epilogue, 249

Notes, 257

Bibliography, 265

Index, 271

Tables

TABLE 1   Profile of Applicants, Admitted Students, and Enrolled Students in the Stanford Freshman Class, 1991   14

TABLE 2   Admissions to the Freshman Class at Stanford University, 1960–90   71

TABLE 3   Ethnic Breakdown of Freshmen Admitted to Stanford, 1986 and 1991   90

TABLE 4   Breakdown by Race of California's Population of 15–19-Year-Olds, 1985 and 1990   90

TABLE 5   Freshman Admission Data for Targeted Minorities at Stanford, 1970–90   94

TABLE 6   Minority Freshmen at Six Universities, 1986–88   95

TABLE 7   Asian-American Freshmen at Stanford, 1982–90   96

TABLE 8   Matriculated Undergraduates at Stanford, 1991   100

TABLE 9   Graduation Rates at Selected Division I-AA and I-A Institutions, 1989   166

■

QUESTIONS AND ADMISSIONS

1

Admissions from the University's Founding

Admissions will be able to stand firm much more easily if the faculty are actively engaged in the admissions process. After all, it is primarily the responsibility of the faculty to set the academic purpose and tone of the institution. If there is not to be a mismatch between the types of students admitted and those that the faculty prefer to teach, the faculty must make their preferences known.
—Herant Katchadourian, *Careerism and Intellectualism Among College Students*

STANFORD BEGINNINGS

One of the first documents I was given as a "green dean" of undergraduate admissions in 1984 was a historic publication presented to me by an engaging, elderly alumna. Written by the registrar of Leland Stanford Junior University, O. L. Elliott, in the early 1890's, it was entitled "Recommendation for Exemption from Entrance Examinations." This document was to be completed by the applicant's high school principal to verify that the applicant had satisfactorily completed a specified amount of work in 10 subjects from a list of

26, including English, algebra, geometry, botany, zoology, freehand drawing, English history, Grecian and Roman history, Latin, and Greek. For those high school seniors who were not certified to be exempted, the first entrance examinations for Stanford University were held in Los Angeles on July 7, 1891, when twelve boys and one girl took the tests. "Some of my thirteen are very poorly prepared, I fear," reported a university official.[1]

Among the required subjects in those early days, item 24, Latin, specified the completion of "Cicero's orations, *pro Archia Poeta* and *pro Lege Manilia*; the first six books of Virgil's Aeneid, including prosody; and the translation into Latin of a passage of connected English based on Cicero." It was duly noted that "excellence in writing Latin will often compensate for deficiencies in other parts of the examination." The English requirement specified, in addition to essay writing, spelling, and punctuation, the reading of "Shakespeare's Merchant of Venice and Julius Caesar; Scott's Lady of the Lake; Whittier's Snow-Bound; Longfellow's Evangeline; Irving's Sketch-Book; Thackeray's English Humorists; The Sir Roger de Coverly Papers from the Spectator; Scott's Antiquary; Macaulay's Essay on Addison; Macaulay's Life of Johnson." In addition to recommending exemption from the entrance exams, the applicant's high school principal was also required to sign beneath the statement, "And I further recommend h.. as a person of good moral character." Applicants were told that to ensure "consideration in season, all associated certificates should be forwarded to the Registrar at least as early as the middle of August." A further requirement, imposed at some point in the 1890's, was that candidates were to be at least sixteen years of age. On October 1, 1891, the first Stanford class of 559 students enrolled, one-fourth of them women, to constitute the largest collegiate enrollment in the western United States; no tuition was charged.

The comparative simplicity and directness of the admissions process from those founding days leaves much to be envied, as any contemporary high school senior, anxious parent, or overworked college guidance counselor will attest. As Stanford University expanded over the next 50 years, the admissions process continued to be handled through the registrar.

Some notable differences developed in the treatment of men and women. By 1899, as the enrollment of women approached 40 percent, one of the founders, Jane Stanford, grew alarmed that Stanford might turn into a women's college and thus be inappropriate as an institution founded in memory of her beloved son, and she subsequently amended the university's charter to limit the number of women students at any one time to 500. This limitation remained in effect until 1933, when the Board of Trustees adopted a resolution to maintain the same proportion between men and women that had existed in 1899. At that time, the number of men had increased to about 2,800 and the limitation of women to 500 was considered "socially undesirable"; in addition, the necessary rejection of many qualified women applicants was generating much ill will. The total enrollment grew from just over 2,000 in 1916 to over 5,000 in 1941.[2] Limited dormitory accommodations for women held their number to about 30 percent until the policy was upset by World War II.

A report on admissions applicants in the January 1958 edition of the *Stanford Alumni Magazine* listed 3,000 applications from men for 720 openings, and 1,750 applications from women for 420 openings—similar ratios of applicants to openings for men and women, but far fewer places for the women. The limit on the number of women at Stanford persisted until 1972, when the Committee on Undergraduate Admissions and Financial Aids recommended that:

1.) The Board of Trustees take whatever steps are necessary to remove limitations imposed by the 1933 Board of Trustees resolution on the proportions of men and women and by the amendment to the Founding Grant in 1899 which allots a maximum number of 500 places for women.

2.) The University eliminate pre-set targets which determine the ratio of men to women in the freshman classes. That ratio should be determined by the nature of the applicant pool, with due regard for specific University strengths.

The Senate of the Academic Council fortunately accepted this recommendation in June 1972. From that time until now, there have been no limitations on the enrollment of women at Stanford, and a typical entering freshman class since the early 1980's has been nearly 45 percent women, about the same percentage of women as in the applicant pool. The question why, in a time when women nationally earn 52 percent of the undergraduate degrees, Stanford is slightly behind the national representation is an interesting one. Some have suggested that Stanford's perceived focus on the sciences and engineering may encourage more applications from men, but that seems to me a simplistic explanation. While this is a time when opportunities for women are unequaled in the history of the United States, the professional aspirations of women generally remain more modest than those of men. Combine this situation with women's lesser confidence in their abilities (as documented by the work of Harvard School of Education professor Carol Gilligan, among others) and women's ongoing struggle to balance their personal and professional lives, and the result is that women are still far from reaching their potential and from equal representation at elite institutions. (Unlike Stanford, many of these were founded for men, and the admission of women began only about twenty years ago.)

Pearce Mitchell, former Stanford chemistry professor and registrar from 1925 to 1945, described the changing admissions requirements for Stanford undergraduates up to 1940. Of particular interest was the introduction in 1920–21 of an aptitude test to supplement the fifteen units of "recommending" grade required to enter the university. (The "recommending" grade was defined by the preparatory school but was at least 5 percent above the lowest passing grade.) The Committee on Admission found that the combination of aptitude scores and school grades gave a better correlation with university grades than did either criterion alone. The committee also devised a point-distribution scheme for making admissions decisions based on a maximum rating of ten points.

These ten points were distributed on the following basis: three for the school record on a strictly mathematical scale; three for the score on the aptitude test, using a scale based on experience with the correlation between the score on the test and the subsequent academic record; and four points for the Committee's judgment regarding the student's personal qualities, general promise, and so on. Two members of the Committee read and scored all the applications and averaged the results.[3]

The two primary hazards of such a process were readily admitted: outstanding applicants from small, obscure high schools might be overlooked in favor of those from better-rated or more distinguished schools; a hazard of a different kind was "the antisocial, maladjusted youth whose only recourse was booklearning—regardless of his high scores and grades, he should be avoided." Presumably, young women were exempt from such social maladjustments. "A personal interview with each applicant was not undertaken because of the inherent difficulties in finding someone to pass judgment."[4] On such considerations were admissions decisions made for Stanford undergraduates from 1921 to 1941.

During the years of World War II, the Committee on Admission and Advanced Standing had discretion to adjust entrance requirements for individuals enlisted in the armed services. As a consequence, about one hundred men were admitted after the successful completion of three years of high school rather than the usual four. They performed as ably as students admitted under normal circumstances, although it was reported that "they looked too young; acted too young; . . . and did not fit into the University student body."[5] (Ironically, of course, these young men were not considered too young to die for their country.) By 1948, the responsibilities of the registrar had grown so large that a new position, director of admissions, was created to relieve him; a professor of English, Dr. Alfred Grommon, was the first appointee.

Between 1950 and 1991, the following common elements were required for admission, approved by a faculty oversight committee: evidence of a strong academic record in high school; the results of standardized tests; and three recommendation letters to confirm qualities of "character, citizenship, and initiative." An examination of the details, however, reveals some significant differences (in addition to the fact that in 1964, for example, it cost only $10 to apply to Stanford and $1,410 for three quarters of tuition). As late as 1969, the academic requirements were quite specific: a minimum of fifteen units of college preparatory course work, including three units of English, two units of foreign language, two units of mathematics, and one unit of laboratory science. More vaguely, applicants were to demonstrate the "highest academic and personal qualifications." Transfer applicants (students applying to Stanford after a year or two at another college) were expected to show previous college work "at least the equivalent of a Stanford C average," a record that would certainly not gain a student admission ten years later. The only hint of interest in ethnic diversity appeared in the mention of international students. The applications of the 1960's posed some personal questions that would be considered insensitive or even illegal today. Applicants in 1969 were asked to rate their eyesight and hearing and whether they had any speech or physical "handicaps." The personal recommendation form filled out by high school teachers and counselors went so far as to ask, "What is your impression of his appearance?" Sexist language was clearly a phrase yet to be invented; the freshman admissions brochures of this period were written entirely with the male pronoun, a feature jarringly outmoded today.

As late as the mid-1980's, applicants were asked for their height and weight. This latter information was eliminated by general agreement of my staff as irrelevant. A more controversial decision during my term was discarding the request that applicants provide "a small unmounted photograph." Some admissions staff members argued that a photograph lent a personal touch to the Stanford application; others argued that looks were irrelevant in the selection of a freshman class. I elected to eliminate the request after seeking the advice of a distinguished professor of psychology, who told me of the persuasive studies demonstrating that people tend to perceive that "beautiful is good."

Much more substantive changes came after 1968, when the university undertook a comprehensive study of itself, which resulted in a series of ten reports under the general title *The Study of Education at Stanford*. One volume, devoted to undergraduate admissions and financial aid, was published in December 1968.[6] It not only confirmed the selection of students on a need-blind basis, but also included a series of eighteen overarching recommendations concerning publications, selection criteria and procedures, and minority students. This document formally outlines Stanford's early efforts to recruit and enroll minority undergraduates.

Only three successors to Dr. Grommon held the position of director of admissions, subsequently renamed dean of undergraduate admissions, between 1950 and 1991: Rixford Snyder (1950–69), Fred Hargadon (1969–84), and I (1984–91). My successor, Stanford alumnus James Montoya, is in his third year as dean as I write. The declining length of time in office may reflect the increasing complexity of the assignment. I resigned from the position at the end of 1991, after seven years in office. Change is healthy both for institutions and for individuals. I do not think my predecessors worked in quite the same way I did, nor do I expect my successor to maintain all the processes and procedures of 1984–91.

Institutional circumstances differ and so, understandably and advantageously, do the ways of deans. The rest of this book, however, is predicated on some understanding of how the selection of Stanford freshmen worked in the period 1984–91. For simplicity, I limit the discussion throughout to freshmen, although about 100 students enter Stanford each year as transfer students from other four- and two-year colleges. These transfer students provide a welcome infusion of talents and perspectives different from those of freshmen, notably by virtue of an age range of roughly 20 to 45 and a wide range of life experiences.

In the first three decades of Stanford's existence, there was no need to raise the question of financial aid or to mention the process of need-blind admissions; in those times, there was no charge for tuition. By 1920, however, "the unwelcome but necessary step" was taken of imposing a tuition fee of $40 per quarter.[7] Today the Stanford admissions process remains need-blind; that is, except for students who are citizens of other countries, applications are reviewed without consideration of the ability of the applicants and their families to meet the costs of attending the university. If a student is admitted, the university guarantees to meet what is called the demonstrated need. A need-blind admissions process is an increasingly expensive undertaking for any institution, and a decreasing number of colleges and universities find themselves able to maintain such a financial commitment.

Although the following reflections are based on my experience at Stanford, I think it is fair to say that they are generally applicable to any of the private American colleges and universities that are able to select no more than 30 percent of their applicants for admission. There are about 35 such selective institutions in the United States. For a comparison with policies and procedures at a selective public university, a 1989 report on the University of California makes interesting reading.[8]

THE CRITERIA FOR ADMISSION

Perhaps the most frequent question asked by high school seniors of admissions officers is, "What do I have to do to get in?" Although I would prefer a different kind of question, such as, "How can I best prepare for a college education?" admissions materials should answer the question of criteria explicitly. If they do not, prospective applicants should not hesitate to ask. When I became dean, I asked the Committee on Undergraduate Admissions and Financial Aids to approve an unambiguous statement on the criteria for admission for two primary reasons: to allow the Undergraduate Admissions staff to carry out their responsibilities most effectively and to inform prospective applicants of our expectations. Here is what the current Stanford publication for undergraduate applicants states under the heading "Criteria for Undergraduate Admissions":

Stanford University was founded, in 1885, "to advance learning, the arts and sciences, and to promote public welfare." It seeks undergraduates of varied ethnic, social, cultural, and economic backgrounds: women and men whose talents, achievements, and character suit them for leadership. It offers students a broadly based liberal education with "the hope and trust that they will become thereby of greater service to the public."

Stanford's diverse undergraduate community is drawn from throughout the United States and from many foreign countries. It includes men and women whose abilities, intellectual interests, and personal qualities will allow them to benefit from the University's wide range of teaching and research programs in the humanities, the sciences, and engineering. The University admits students with highly developed skills in particular areas as well as those with versatility in a number of fields. A comprehensive financial aid program aims to promote broad socioeconomic representation. Admissions are decided without regard to an applicant's economic resources; the University guarantees to meet the need of every admitted student. No one should fail to apply because of financial concerns. Affirmative action programs promote equality of opportunity for minorities; there are no restrictive quotas of any kind. Admissions practices conform to the University's policies on non-discrimination. Specific criteria for admission accord with the general goals and policies outlined above.

The primary criterion for admission is academic excellence: a compound of exceptional capacity, scholastic performance in relation to available opportunities, and promise of intellectual growth. A secondary criterion is personal achievement outside the classroom in a range of pursuits including academic activities, the creative and performing arts, community service and leadership, athletics and other extra-curricular areas. Persistence and marked effectiveness in one or more distinct areas of personal achievement count for more than scattered involvement but initiative, curiosity, and vigor are significant. The consideration of applicants for admission centers on: scholastic performance (including grades, honors, and substantiality of program); scores on standardized national tests; documented perseverance and attainment in activities outside the classroom; quality of conception and writing in the personal statement; and strength of recommendations from the secondary school. The University bases its overall judgment of each application on these criteria.

A few categories of applicants receive special consideration provided they meet the basic requirements of academic excellence and personal achievement. Stanford University is committed to a substantial representation of Blacks, Mexican Americans, and Native American Indians in the undergraduate student body. Children of Stanford graduates receive preference in choices among applications of approximately equal qualifications. Children of eligible Stanford faculty and staff receive favorable consideration, once again provided they meet basic requirements. The Department of Athletics may designate outstanding athletes for special attention. The Dean of Undergraduate Admissions retains final authority over all admissions.

The admissions process at Stanford is sensitive to individual circumstances and the effect they may have on the record of any applicant and the available resources. While all applicants receive careful consideration, in reviewing applications we take note both of extenuating circumstances and a variety of cultural and economic situations including ethnic backgrounds, recent immigration to the U.S., and students who are the first in their families to attend college or are from economically disadvantaged backgrounds.

Stanford expects students to adhere to the principles of its Fundamental Standard: "To show both within and without the University such respect for order, morality, personal honor, and the rights of others as is demanded of good citizens." Traits of honesty, good judgment, and magnanimity are consonant with this rule.

On the whole, then, Stanford wants undergraduates who will benefit most from the University's resources, contribute to its community, finish well, and proceed to a lifetime of intellectual, personal, and societal accomplishment.

These criteria clearly invite comparisons with those of 100 years ago. Two of the basic criteria are fundamentally unchanged: first, and not surprisingly, an emphasis on the quality of academic preparation, achievement, and promise; and second, a concern with personal qualities of the applicants. The latter is important in an institution that has always been residential, and in which a Fundamental Standard for student conduct has existed since the days of Stanford's first president, David Starr Jordan.

In 1990, we did not list 26 subject areas from which an applicant must qualify in 10, but we did recommend a basic course of study in high school that best prepares a student for the challenges of a liberal arts education. This information is distributed in a special, free publication to high schools throughout the country and to students or parents who request it.[9] The recommended course of study for grades ten through twelve includes at least three years of English (with significant emphasis on writing and literature); three years of mathematics; two or more years of laboratory science; three years' study of one foreign language; one year of study in the creative and performing arts; and computer literacy. No minimum requirements are set for grade-point average or rank in class; these numbers are a function not only of student achievement but also of the quality of the program and the high school. The level of course detail (or more accurately, *lack* of detail) in 1990 provides a notable contrast to the specific curriculum outlined in the application materials of the 1890's.

Another notable difference is in the role of extracurricular activities. In the period 1980–90, and probably earlier, it was impossible to select an entering class of 1,550 solely on the primary criterion of academic achievement and promise. In any given year, more than 3,000 out of roughly 15,000 applicants presented straight-A high school transcripts, and more than 75 percent of the applicants placed in the top tenth of their high school graduating class. Clearly, some screening mechanism beyond the academic one was necessary. Even without an explicit admissions criterion related to extracurricular activities, Stanford had always attracted multitalented students: there has been a student-run daily newspaper since the university's opening day; the Encina and Roble Glee Clubs led the singing groups; four special drama clubs showed vigorous growth and ambitious productions; Stanford's first football game against California was played in 1892 (Stanford won, 14–10); the first Stanford intercollegiate tennis match was played in that same year, and all the other outdoor sports followed as playing fields and facilities were developed. In short, student activities at Stanford were energetic from opening day.

A more fundamental difference in the selection criteria from those early days appeared in the early 1970's when considerations of ethnicity came into play. The role of affirmative action in the undergraduate admissions process continues to raise important questions and is discussed at length in Chapter 5. The question of preference for applicants who were the children of alumni was moot in the 1890's because there were no alumni with college-age children. This subject was of more significance in later years, as it remains today, and it merits a special section in Chapter 4.

Many people mistakenly think of today's dean of undergraduate admissions as omnipotent, a person who can single-handedly determine the criteria for admission and then apply them in the selection of the freshman class. Such is not the case. All policies governing both admissions and financial aid are recommended by a standing committee of the Senate of the Academic Council comprising eight faculty and three student members (and not surprisingly called the Committee on Undergraduate Admissions and Financial Aids); the dean of undergraduate admissions and the director of financial aid are ex-officio members of the committee. The policies recommended by this committee require subsequent approval by the 54 members of the Senate, an elected body of the Academic Council. An annual report is presented to the Senate by the chair of the committee, an occasion when faculty senators may ask any questions they wish concerning admissions and financial aid. Since the minutes of all Senate meetings are published in the weekly newspaper, *Campus Report*, all this information is readily available to any interested member of the Stanford community.

Before I was interviewed for the position of dean of undergraduate admissions in early 1984, I read all I could find about the office and its policies and procedures. One of the items in my reading file was the charge to the Committee on Undergraduate Admissions and Financial Aids, as amended in 1973, which included the following statement:

The Committee shall receive recommendations of the Dean of Admissions and shall make the following determinations: The number of students to be admitted whose admission is influenced by preferences resulting from characteristics which deviate from the established standards, such as students whose parents graduated from Stanford, provided that the Committee shall first inform itself of *the number of students to be admitted by decision of the President of the University.* [The emphasis is mine.]

When the opportunity came for me to ask the interview committee some questions, I inquired what, exactly, the last proviso meant; the faculty were at a loss to explain it except to suggest that it was historical accident. Indeed, after my appointment, the charge was amended to remove the troublesome clause—at least it was troublesome for the incoming dean. At the Senate meeting where the change was subsequently passed, some faculty joked with

President Donald Kennedy that he might want to reserve the privilege. I believe that such a presidential privilege still exists in some colleges.

At Stanford, then, the criteria for admission are very much under the control of the faculty, and rightly so. It is true that the dean of undergraduate admissions has considerable leeway in the application of these criteria, especially since, at Stanford, faculty play a minimal role in the actual reading of applications. During my seven-year term, the only applications reviewed by faculty were those of applicants with extraordinary aptitude in mathematics who intended to pursue majors in math or math-related fields. (This is an opportune moment to note that freshmen at Stanford are selected with no consideration given to a predetermined major; although we ask a question about preliminary academic interests on the application form, all undergraduates are selected without an eye to intended discipline, and they are allowed until the start of their junior year to declare a major.) The consideration of special talents in mathematics and the creative and performing arts is taken up in Chapter 4.

Once they understand the criteria for admission, prospective applicants predictably go on to ask about their chances for admission. It is impossible, of course, to answer this question precisely, but each year we publish basic academic profiles of applicants, the students we admitted, and enrolling students. We do not cite mean SAT scores, believing that such numbers are misleading and put undue emphasis on standardized test scores. Instead, we publish ranges of SAT scores and ranges of high school rank in class. Table 1 is the profile of the last class for which I was responsible, the freshmen who enrolled in the fall of 1991.

Even the data we do publish can be misleading; for example, they cannot distinguish the rigor of an applicant's academic program, an important consideration when we review an application. In addition, an individual applicant may be in the top range of one set of measures and in the middle or bottom of another. The data also reveal no information about achievements outside the classroom,

TABLE 1
Profile of Applicants, Admitted Students, and Enrolled Students in the Stanford Freshman Class, 1991

BACKGROUND DATA

	Applicants	Applicants admitted		Students enrolled
		No.	Pct.	
Male	7,668	1,468	19%	816
Female	5,862	1,247	21	731
Total	13,530	2,715	20	1,547
Secondary school[a]				
Public	9,574	1,950	20	1,119
Private	3,956	765	19	428

ACADEMIC PROFILE

	Percentage of applicants meeting criterion	Percentage of applicants meeting criterion who were admitted	Percentage of admitted class meeting criterion
High school rank in class			
Top decile	76%	26%	91%
Top quintile	90	23	98
SAT verbal score (% of national test takers)			
700–800 (1%)	13	48	30
600–699 (6%)	37	27	48
500–599 (18%)	32	12	18
Below 500 (75%)	18	4	4
SAT math score			
700–800 (4%)	46	28	64
600–699 (14%)	34	17	29
500–599 (25%)	15	9	6
Below 500 (57%)	5	3	1

SOURCES: Percentages of national test takers from College Board, Admissions Testing Program, National Data for 1991 (annual publication of College Board). Other data from Stanford Office of Undergraduate Admissions.

[a] 4,174 secondary schools were represented in the pool of applicants, 1,525 in the pool of applicants admitted, and 1,038 in the pool of students enrolled.

an applicant's personal qualities, or the quality of the references. All of these factors, along with the written essay, come into play in the review of an application. One of my colleagues once aptly said that admissions officers admit for life, not for freshman grades; the only trouble with that approach is that it is difficult to get a handle on life's criteria.

2

Decisions:
Selecting the Freshman Class

> One cannot tell by looking at a toad how far he will jump.
> —B. Alden Thresher, director of admissions emeritus, MIT

APPLYING THE CRITERIA: THE SELECTION PROCESS

A completed application for freshman admission consists of the following *required* information:

1. an official high school transcript
2. standardized test scores (either the SAT or the ACT, and any Achievement Test results. We highly recommend that at least three Achievement Tests be taken.)
3. a self-presentation (including basic background information, an essay, a summary of activities, and summer or school-year jobs)
4. a secondary-school report and reference from the guidance counselor or principal
5. two teacher references from grades ten through twelve

This material is supplemented in the winter quarter by a mid-year report from the high school to provide information on academic progress in the senior year. Applicants are also given the opportunity to provide an optional reference from a third teacher, an employer or coach, or someone else who knows them well enough to address the criteria for admission.

Once all this material is assembled in an applicant's file (a task easier said than done with close to 15,000 applicants returning all this information in separate envelopes), the admissions staff is almost ready to begin reading. Before that, however, they review the high school transcript to compute a grade-point average for the tenth and eleventh grades, using only the grades from academic courses. This means eliminating, for example, driver's education, typing, band, physical education, and similar courses, so that the focus is on the academic preparation for college work. This recomputed grade-point average is noted on the so-called work-card, a yellow card where information pertinent both to the criteria for admission and to the required credentials is summarized. The work-card is inserted in the front of each applicant's file and serves as the primary means of communication between readers of the application.

At this point, the files are ready for distribution among the readers. It would be cumbersome and confusing to describe every nuance of the process, but the following outline should provide sufficient detail to give a very good idea of how a reading period works.

The reading of applications usually begins around January 10, when a sufficient number of files are complete and the grade-point averages have been calculated. The senior associate dean makes a preliminary first review of the academic credentials of each applicant and eliminates those that are significantly below the norm of admitted students (for example, an applicant with a grade-point average lower than 3.0 and SAT scores each below 500). In a highly selective pool, such applicants stand a low probability of admission and reading time is more productively spent on applicants who better meet the primary criteria for admission.

In a typical year, the readers in the Office of Undergraduate Admissions consist of twelve full-time directors (including the dean and two associate deans), supplemented by six to eight part-time readers. The latter are usually former admissions officers who (for personal reasons) wish to work part-time, and doctoral students who either have had experience teaching Stanford undergraduates or have worked in an admissions office at another selective college. The completed files are distributed at random among these readers, and each reader is given a weekly allotment of folders to read, as either first reader or second reader. First readers have several key tasks to complete: they must read carefully every document in the file; summarize, using the traditional blue-ink pen of first readers, the content of the file on the work-card; write a summary evaluation; recommend a rating based on the two primary criteria (which are discussed below); and, finally, recommend the action to be taken on that file. The choices for recommended action are "admit," "deny," or "swim" (the last means to defer the decision for another round of readings). There are, however, severe constraints on these choices. Over the total reading period (and, roughly, over any given week), first readers may recommend "admit" on no more than 20–25 percent of the files read, and they may recommend "swim" on no more than 30–35 percent of the files read. This means they must recommend "deny" on close to 50 percent of the files read. These limitations are necessary because (1) only a specified number of students can be admitted, (2) there must be some flexibility in making decisions (the "swims") and time to assess the quality of the total pool; and (3) it is important to face immediately the difficult fact that almost 75 percent of the applicants must finally be denied admission. A quick glance back at the academic profiles in Table 1 will confirm the challenges inherent in making recommendations on final action.

After the first reading is completed, the files are randomly redistributed among the second readers and the exercise is repeated with a different color pen (so that the comments of the two readers can be distinguished by subsequent readers). In a small number of cases, where an experienced reader determines that an application is clearly an "admit" or a "deny," the first reader may choose to route the file directly to a dean and skip the second round of reading. In any case, the dean and the two associate deans (and in some years, a very experienced assistant dean) are the third readers on all the files (or the second readers on a special, clear-cut subset). These senior staff have the authority to make a final decision based on the recommendations of the previous readers. For example, if both the first and second readers recommend "deny," the third reader will probably concur—but not always. There may be circumstances related to the high school or student that are not known to the first two readers but are known to the dean, and the dean has the authority to overrule. For instance, the dean may have received correspondence from the principal of a high school complaining of apparent inconsistencies in decisions on prior applications to Stanford. In such a case, the dean may be reluctant to deny, in a first-round reading, the valedictorian from that high school even though the applicant may be considered less compelling than other applicants reviewed by a new first reader. Alternatively, it may be clear from the summary paragraphs of the first two readers that both were wavering on the edge of a "swim" recommendation, and then the dean may tip the balance and place the file in the "swim" set after the first three readings. Once a file is signed off by a dean for the "deny" set, that file is never reviewed again, so the action is disconcertingly definitive; we want to be close to certain that we are making the best call that is humanly possible. At the other end of the decision spectrum, recommendations of "admit" by the first and second readers will generally yield the same decision from the third reader, especially if the summary paragraphs are unambiguously enthusiastic, such as "Just admit!" or "I'm not going to this high school again if we don't take!" or simply "Next!" Those are the lovely files, what I once described as the "jump-for-joy" cases, when I wanted to run out of my office in sheer delight at the prospect of this student as a Stanford undergraduate and to share the decision with everyone in the office. Sometimes I did just that.

The first round of evaluations, involving the three readings per file, usually ends in early to mid-March. At this point, we typically have admitted close to 1,600 applicants, placed about 3,000 in the "swim" set, and denied the remainder. In the years 1984–91, the provost's staff gave Undergraduate Admissions a target number for enrolling freshmen of between 1,550 and 1,600. (The variation depended on the estimated number of graduating seniors so that the total undergraduate enrollment at Stanford remained stable at 6,550.) Obviously, we do not aim to limit the number of admitted students to this target number, because most students offered admission to Stanford will also be offered admission to other colleges and can of course attend only one. In a typical year, most applicants admitted to Stanford applied to six to eight colleges and received offers of admission to four to six of them, with most of the variation attributed to the decisions made at the highly selective institutions. The number of students who *accept* an offer of admission divided by the total number of students actually offered admission is called "the yield." Fortunately, the institutional historical record provides some helpful information in estimating the yield, although there can be some notable, and inexplicable, variations from year to year. The yield in recent years, when (to cite one factor) the number of high school seniors has been declining, has become more uncertain—a cause for some nail biting among admissions officers. At Stanford the yield, over almost two decades, ranged from 60 to 64 percent; in the most recent and most competitive years, the yield was closer to 58 percent, a drop attributable partly to the Bay Area earthquake of 1989, but complicated by such other factors as national demographic changes and family economic concerns.

This brief aside on the question of "yield" is necessary to explain the next stage in the reading process. In order to enroll a freshman class of around 1,550, we needed to admit approximately 2,600 applicants. By mid-March, we had admitted 1,600; the remaining 1,000 needed to be selected from the 3,000 "swimming" files. All of the reading process is difficult, but this stage is among the toughest. Any applicant in the swim pool was there because, all other things being equal, we had good reasons for wanting to admit her or him, but at this stage we could select only one in three from this set. Since we aimed to mail admissions decisions the first week in April, we had about fifteen days to complete the next grueling round of reading. Taking yet a different color pen—brown was usual at this stage—we embarked on the fourth reading of the files, repeating the review exercise described above. This time, however, we had the advantage of detailed knowledge of the total pool of applicants, as well as some detailed information on the 1,600 students already admitted. For example, this was the time to review the geographical distribution of applicants, admits, and swims—were there any states where we had both applicants and swims, but no admits? (During my first few years as dean, there was a running joke that the freshman class had representatives from every state except one. North Dakota had the distinction of appearing on this list twice, but the honor of omission was shared with West Virginia, Delaware, and Maine, which had small numbers of applicants in our pool.) This was also the time to acknowledge recommendations from the faculty in the departments of art, music, drama, and dance to ensure that we would be bringing in some fine talent in the creative and performing arts. At this point we also reviewed the distribution of men and women in the admitted and swim sets. In summary, this round of reading allowed some fine-tuning in the makeup of the freshman class.

With these considerations in mind, we turned to the fourth reading of the files. As in the first round, folders were randomly distributed among all the readers, and the fourth reader was able to see, on the work-card, the comments of the three previous readers. This was neither the time nor the place for pride or stubbornness on the part of the hardworking and, at this point, exhausted reader. Because the folders were distributed randomly, the fourth reader sometimes would also have been the first reader. Judgments can change with greater knowledge and the benefit of time to reflect, so it was not unusual for such readers to admit that they had changed their mind and now leaned toward a "deny." Alternatively, the early reading may have been too tough, causing the fourth reader to decide upon rereading that an applicant was now clearly an admit. In the most difficult cases the applicant still appears to sit in the middle of the "swims"; at this stage, though, the luxury of indecisiveness is not permitted. The fourth reader must recommend "admit," "deny," or (a new category of sort-of-final decision) "wait list." As in the first round of readings, there were specific targets for the decision sets: in this case the numbers were roughly one-third for each call of "admit," "deny," and "wait-list." After the unenviable fourth reader completed the reading, the file then passed again to a dean for final decision. Near the end of March, all the files had been read between two and five times, and the final decisions were made. Approximately 2,600 applicants received thick envelopes with offers of admission, 400–500 received letters offering them a spot on the waiting list, and the remaining 10,000 or so, alas, received letters guaranteed to make them unhappy.

Lest this reading process sound too heartless, let me assure the reader that we are constantly reminded that we are very much involved with human beings. The high school teachers, for example, who spend hours each fall writing those required college references, provide not only invaluable information, but some great, sometimes unintentional, laughs. "I would lend John my best hunting dog, but probably not my Stradivarius," wrote one. "Frank arrived in U.S. History with a reputation for not participating in class discussions, and he lived up to it," offered another. A prize for telling-it-like-it-is goes to the following: "Mike is a big friendly kid who might be overrating his abilities a bit. He tried really hard but regularly makes ticky-tacky mistakes. He comes back to retake exams and does ultimately grasp the material." The runner-up prize goes to the teacher who challenged us thus: "Believe me, you have a real opportunity to develop her full potential. If you don't, you're courting disaster in the same fashion as the master of the Titanic." How could any reader not enjoy this job?

Before I review some of the more subtle aspects of this complex and demanding process, three topics mentioned in the section above need further discussion: the "ratings" recommended by readers; the handling of international applications; and the meaning and purpose of a waiting list. As the statement on criteria in Chapter 1 attests, there are two primary criteria for the selection of the freshman class: academic achievement and potential, and achievements outside the classroom. In an attempt both to simplify the review of 15,000 freshman applications and to keep track of the strength of the pool over time, a system was devised (well before my time as dean) to quantify these achievements using a numerical *rating scale*. (At Stanford the personal qualities criterion was not assigned a comparable rating, although I know that some schools do assign it to such a scale; as a subjective element, it seems to me to resist quantification.) The system about to be described here, with some minor modifications, was used throughout the period 1984–91.

Although the scales for the two ratings—for academic achievement and potential and for extracurricular achievement—are discrete, the assessment process that underlies the ratings is rather more subjective, and new readers inevitably found it hard to master the guidelines for assigning a rating. Often the ratings recommended by two readers differed by one point (on a scale of 1 to 5). Here again, the third-round reader, one of the deans, had the responsibility of making the final call. It is important to emphasize that admissions decisions were not made simply by selecting applicants with the highest ratings on both scales. The reading process would be formulaic and hence a good deal simpler if that were all there was to a class. Not surprisingly, students with ratings at the upper end of the scales, especially on the academic side, tended to have the highest rates of admission. But an entering class was made up of students who received a range of ratings, with both the upper and lower ends represented. As we often repeated to one another, "We don't admit by the ratings."

We used a five-point scale for both criteria, with 1 the highest designation and 5 the lowest. On the academic criterion, a rating of 1 was recommended for applicants with a 4.0 grade-point average in the strongest program of courses available to them, with both verbal and math SAT scores above 700, and with a ranking in the top 1–2 percent of their high school class. By comparison, and to show the narrowness of the scale, a rating of 3 was assigned to applicants with a 3.8 grade-point average, verbal and math scores between 600 and 650, and a ranking in the top 4–5 percent of their class. Many an applicant with an academic rating of 5 was no slouch. Each year, however, if we had selected the freshman class solely on the basis of academic achievement and potential, we could have more than filled it

with applicants having academic ratings of 1 and 2! Applicants with
4.0 transcripts but more modest test scores might be surprised to
find themselves at the lower end of the academic rating distribution.
The same could be said for applicants with SAT scores above 700
(putting them in the top 1 percent of national test takers), but with
a scattering of B's in a not-very-demanding program on their high
school record. Some problems inherent in this rating system are
immediately apparent, as in the preceding example. Students' academic records do not always fall into the neat categories assumed by
the rating system. High test scores are not always accompanied
by high grades or vice versa. Some high schools assign no rank in
class. High schools use widely varying grading systems, some much
tougher than others. The demands of available course work also
vary considerably across the 26,000 high schools in the United
States. Most international schools have systems completely different
from that of their American counterparts. The list could go on but,
whatever its limitations, the assignment of ratings is one way of
amalgamating quantitative (and some qualitative) measures in order
to distinguish between the many thousands of applications.

On the scale for extracurricular achievement, the rating of 1 was
reserved for applicants who had earned recognition at a national
level (for example, an author of a published novel, a Westinghouse
Science Prize winner, or an Olympic medalist—all real examples
from the Stanford applicant pool). A rating of 3 was for applicants
who had been recognized at a regional level (for example, a student
who had been selected as a member of a mayor's task force on drug
abuse or team captain for a regional academic bowl, or who had
won unusual distinction in athletics). Here again, the limitations of
the rating scale are apparent. Although we were more impressed
with energy exhibited in sustained activities, the scale does not
readily distinguish between depth and breadth; students who need
to work 30 hours a week certainly demonstrate energy in a sustained
activity, but it is an activity very different from academic competitions or athletic pursuits, and the rating scale was not designed to
allow for paid work. In other volunteer activities, such as some
forms of public service, or playing a musical instrument, there is

little or no opportunity to be recognized in the same way as, say, for participation in athletics.

A "1,1" (as we called them for short) was truly a rare, and very impressive, bird. In a typical year, there were no more than fifteen or twenty of them, and something would have to be seriously amiss elsewhere in the file for such an applicant to be denied admission. The most common rating set in a typical applicant pool at Stanford was a "2,4"; these were very fine students who had been involved in some kind of extracurricular activity in high school. The reason for the point I made earlier about not making admissions decisions by ratings now becomes immediately apparent: would you choose a "2,4" over a "3,3"? The academic differences are small; the extracurricular contributions of one may be more significant. Or would you, on principle, admit every "1,5"? Would you ever admit a "5,5"? After seven years of trying my hand at this scientific art, my answers to these last two questions would be "no" and "yes." For fellow readers to accept my point, though, they would need to read the whole file and decide for themselves—perhaps after preparing for the task by reading a few thousand other files first. The important conclusion, then, is that ratings are useful but limited in their application. It is fair to generalize that the higher the academic rating, the higher the probability of admission, but ultimately the selection of a freshman class at a highly selective institution involves considerable subjectivity, good judgment, and a sensitive understanding of the criteria for selection and the context of the individual applicant's circumstances, along with a healthy dose of experience to see beyond the quantitative measures.

The selection of international students involves some completely different considerations. At a time when Stanford, like all American colleges and universities, was experiencing the effects of a decline in the number of high school seniors, we were seeing an increase in the number of applications from international students. In the mid- and late 1980's, for example, we received applications from almost 1,200 international students each year, approximately 10 percent of the total applicant pool. In the freshman class, though, the representation was closer to 4 percent. This is in marked contrast to the total graduate student population of 6,500 students, in which the international representation is almost 30 percent. One of the major reasons for this difference in international student enrollment has to do with the awarding of financial aid. In Ph.D. programs, aid is merit-based, and four years of support accompanies virtually all offers of admission to Ph.D. programs. At the undergraduate level, the admissions decisions are need-blind, and we guarantee to meet the computed need of every admitted student. This policy has serious financial implications, and in 1986 the Committee on Undergraduate Admissions and Financial Aid recommended that, in a time of increasing financial constraints, a cap should be placed on the amount of financial aid that would be made available to international students. (These students, who are not permanent residents of the United States, are ineligible for federal and state loans.) The cap was initially set at $350,000 annually. In 1988 it was indexed to the annual increase in tuition and room and board costs. For a few years the capped amount was sufficient to meet the needs of every international student we wished to admit, but later, the financial limitation meant we could not accept some international students we would have liked to admit.

Understandably, some international students are unhappy about this state of affairs, but Stanford is, in fact, more generous with undergraduate financial aid to international students than the many U.S. colleges that offer no financial support. Only one private college that I know of, Harvard, has no limit on financial aid to international students. In fairness to all prospective international applicants, our application materials state our policy unambiguously: "Stanford does not practice need-blind admissions for international students, and financial aid is a consideration in the admission process." In practice, the way this works is that on the first round of reading, we admit a small number of outstanding international students; before we begin the "swim" round of reading, we estimate how much financial aid we will spend on the international students already admitted, and then we calculate how much more is available to spend. The international students remaining in the swim round are then ranked and admitted until the associated financial aid commitments are close to the financial aid cap. In most years, we set aside some of the money to use in the transfer student admissions process, which takes place in May, after the freshman class is virtually settled for the following fall quarter.

Being wait-listed is the most frustrating decision for the applicants, and every April the admissions office receives a large number of questions about it. The wait-list letter neither offers nor denies admission to the applicant; as the name suggests, it keeps the applicant waiting. One summer, when I was an invited guest at Stanford's popular camp in the Sierra Nevada run by the Alumni Association, I had an amusing conversation with a Stanford graduate who was working there. He told me of an experience guaranteed to strike terror in the heart of any admissions officer (fortunately, it occurred before my time). The year he applied to Stanford, the alumnus reported, he received three letters: one offered admission, one denied admission, and the third offered him a place on the waiting list. When I asked what he had done, he laughed and replied, "I tore two of them up!"

The questions pertaining to the waiting list range from "Why do you have such a thing?" to "Does it really mean anything?" and "Now that I'm on it, what can I do to increase my chances of admission?" I'll answer these questions in order. As I explained earlier, to guarantee a freshman class of 1,550–1,600, Stanford needs to admit 2,600–2,700 students. The yield from the admitted set of students varies from year to year, and it ranged between 58 and 64 percent during the 1980's and early 1990's. A variation in the yield of, say, 4 percent results in a difference of roughly 100 students in the set admitted. Since the university aims to maintain a stable total enrollment of 6,550 undergraduates, we clearly need to be able to compensate for variations in yield. At the same time, we cannot run the risk of overenrolling 100 students; doing so would make it difficult to guarantee freshman housing and would have serious repercussions for faculty who teach, to take one example, freshman English, in which a typical class has fifteen students. Even one year of overenrollment would produce a rat-in-the-python problem. In recent years, prospective students have applied to a larger number of schools, a trend that in turn affects every institution's yield. The increased competition for the dwindling number of high school seniors has exacerbated the problem of uncertainty about the yield. Stanford has been fortunate to have fared better in its yield rates than the majority of U.S. colleges and universities, but the unpredictable variation remains a problem.

One way to protect against such uncertainties is to offer a limited number of students a place on the waiting list. In the event that the freshman enrollment target is not reached, the admissions staff can then review (yet again) the applications of the wait-listed students and decide which ones to admit. It is important in making such offers to adhere to the principles of good practice in admissions. (These principles are spelled out in guidelines published under the auspices of the National Association of College Admissions Counselors.) For example, the notification letter should provide a history of the number of students placed on the waiting list and also the number of wait-listed students who were subsequently offered admission. Here is an excerpt from the wait-list letter that was sent to the 1990 applicants to Stanford:

From past experience, we believe the offers of admission already made will be sufficient to fill the available places in next year's freshman class. Stanford, however, will not be everyone's first choice, and the number of admitted students who choose to enroll elsewhere varies slightly from year to year. We have asked those admitted to give us their decisions by May 1. In case the number of acceptances falls below our estimate, we have established a wait list from which to make additional offers. Between 1985 and 1989, we admitted 80, 0, 90, 0, and 90 students, respectively, from the wait list (which each year has numbered between 400 and 500 candidates). Please let us know if you wish to be included on that list, or not, by returning the enclosed card before May 1.

We realize that candidates on our wait list may have to accept an offer of admission (and perhaps even make a deposit) at another college by May 1. Unfortunately, it is highly unlikely that we will be able to notify these students of our final decision before May 15. Candidates on the wait list are not ranked, so we cannot tell you your relative position in the group. If it *is* possible to make additional offers of admission, all students on the wait list will be reviewed again. Candidates from the wait list who have applied for financial aid will be considered for aid in the same way as all previously admitted candidates.

I hope that this description is both persuasive and informative in answering the first two questions given above: a wait list *is* necessary, and it *is* meaningful. Of course, this does not mean to say that such a process is without its abuses on the sides of both the college and the high school. Abuses contribute to the unfortunate generation of myths—some of which are frequently cited in influential and plausible places. Here are some of the most common myths and abuses; many of them violate the rules of good practice and are definitely myths as far as the Stanford admissions process is concerned. If any of them reflect realities elsewhere, it is unfortunate for all those in the profession of college admissions:

I suspect that there isn't a real wait list for public school students.
   High school guidance counselor (quoted in Durham and Syverson, "Wait Lists," p. 6)

We admit the first 14 who reply to us indicating that they wish to remain on the wait list.   College admissions officer (ibid.)

Fifteen percent of private school counselors believe that otherwise admissible candidates are put on the wait list due to high financial need.
   High school guidance counselor (ibid.)

They almost always give preference to students who make it clear they really want to attend.   Robinson and Katzman, eds., *Cracking the System*, p. 24

Institutional pride also impels colleges toward rather long waiting lists.
   Hayden, *Handbook for College Admissions*, p. 171

Very often colleges will admit in batches taking the most critical (read "vociferous") cases first. At this point, it becomes perfectly permissible to use alumni influence to bring pressure on the college. Risk overkill.
   Ibid., pp. 173–74

In concrete terms, again with emphasis, "Do not accept a place on anybody's waiting list."   Neusner, *How to Grade Your Professors*, p. 87

Counselors say that colleges often slip in a late applicant ahead of less well qualified students on the wait list. One guidance counselor at a high school in the East, who asked not to be identified, said he received calls every year from one or two top colleges to which his high school regularly sends its best students. The colleges offer to place one or two of his student-applicants on the waiting list, if it would make his job easier.

"Top Colleges Turn to Waiting Lists," *New York Times*, June 8, 1988

In addition to honoring the principles of good practice, there is another important guiding principle in establishing waiting lists: Do not put an applicant on a wait list if you would not admit him or her. A wait list, I think, is an appropriate place to acknowledge any "legacy" preference (such as parental ties to the school), or a student who is distinguished by virtue of unusually hard work and achievement but is not among the most compelling of the prospective students. A wait list is also an appropriate place to acknowledge an applicant for whom the high school's support is extraordinary but who is not among the very best applicants. The wait-list status is often helpful if the wait-listed candidate subsequently applies for admission as a transfer student. In such cases, the Stanford applicant's freshman and transfer applications are merged.

Finally, it is important for the college to specify the timeline for wait-listed students and to agree to close the freshman class by a specified date, such as July 1; this is the date agreed upon by the institutional members (Stanford among them) of the Consortium on Financing Higher Education. Unfortunately, although timelines can be clearly spelled out to the students admitted from the wait list, it is ultimately their responsibility to handle any commitments they may have made to other colleges. A failure to do so explains the understandably angry note I received from my counterpart at another college pointing out a withdrawal on September 4 of a student who had previously accepted an offer there but subsequently decided to enroll at Stanford. It is very difficult for individual colleges to cross-check their information and safeguard against such occurrences at a time in the admissions season when decisions are in constant flux.

So what are high school seniors to do when they receive a wait-list letter? At the very least, they should notify the college whether they are or are not interested in remaining on the list. This procedure is usually as simple as returning a postcard provided by the college before the specified deadline. (One year, I received a memorable and good-humored telegram from a wait-listed applicant that read, "Help, I'm a prisoner on wait list. Send admit letter. Will accept immediately. Explanation will follow.") Nothing is to be lost by staying on the wait list, although there is clearly no point in doing so if the applicant has already been offered a place at a preferred college. That is unfair to both institutions involved, not to mention the other wait-listed applicants. If the applicant chooses to remain on the wait list, there is something to be gained by writing a concise letter to the dean updating the applicant's file with information that postdates the original application deadline. This information might include new academic or extracurricular honors, scholarship awards, or anything else applicants consider important and relevant information to a re-examination of their candidacy. I do not recommend the bring-out-all-the-big-guns approach or any letter-writing campaign intended to pressure the admissions staff. Such techniques lack relevant substance and are also transparently manipulative and generally counterproductive.

Among my most memorable wait-list updates was one that I reluctantly admit violates the recommended guiding principles outlined above—although the end result was in keeping with the advice I have given. The update came from a talented young man from Massachusetts whom I'll call Dan, who sent us a hilarious videotape involving mother, father, and the family dog (named Stanford), all of whom were attired in Stanford T-shirts and baseball caps and who discussed (the dog excluded) the virtues of attending Stanford and the significance of the wait list. Unfortunately, this was in a year that we did not admit anyone from the wait list, so Dan was not admitted. A graphic emblem of wait-list frustration was the torn and toothmarked mailcarrier's shirt that an applicant enclosed with the report that it was a result of his dog's attack on an unsuspecting and unfortunate bearer of unwelcome news; please would we spare the local mailcarrier from more such wrath? Ah, the ingenuity and enthusiasm, if slightly misguided, of youth! Such devices may be unsuccessful in gaining admission, but they are wonderful reminders of the essential human element in an anxiety-provoking process.

THE PERSONAL TOLL OF SELECTION

Our director of freshman admissions, John Bunnell, always remarked (not entirely in jest) that the reading process was easier after the first 1,000 folders. While it is true that, to the experienced eye and mind, the "deny" decisions were more quickly identifiable each year, every January I was painfully reminded how difficult the selection process was. Most sensitive readers can make a convincing case for admitting many more applicants than we could possibly enroll in a freshman class; the final decisions must be the consequence of a combination of pragmatism, experience, good judgment, sensitivity to a range of circumstances, independence of thought, and an absolutely essential willingness to make tough choices. This comment can never be better confirmed than by an experiment I tried my first year as dean. In an effort to involve more faculty in the selection of the freshman class, I invited ten highly respected emeriti (reasoning that they would have more time available than faculty who had not retired) to join us in the reading of freshman applications. The seven who accepted my invitation were each asked to read 100 files and were given the usual assignment of designating 20–25 percent as admits, 45–50 percent as denies, and the remaining 35 percent or so as swims. With the best intentions in the world, they put closer to 80 percent in the swim category; even for faculty with significant experience in teaching Stanford students, it was enormously difficult to make distinctions within a random set of 100 applicants, most of whom seemed eminently qualified to be Stanford students. Multiply this assignment by 150 to produce a typical freshman applicant pool, and you have some measure of the dilemmas encountered by a new member of the admissions staff.

The challenges of selection have other dimensions that are not so readily apparent. First, it is a formidable practical task to organize and distribute thousands of completed applications among the readers. The first readings must be completed in a timely fashion so that the files can be redistributed among the second readers. The decisions must be marked on the file and returned to the support staff in Undergraduate Admissions to enter in the computer. The coordination of this large effort falls to the director of freshman admissions, but the results depend on the effective working of the team of readers. If one person falls behind in a week's reading, the repercussions affect everyone else on the team. Falling behind in the reading is a common experience for new readers, who are both unaccustomed to the pressures and inexperienced in the process. But these are not the only two factors that contribute to one's inability to complete the assigned folders: illness is not tolerated; personal problems are forbidden; family relationships are put on hold; spontaneous outings with friends must be postponed. None of life's emergencies can be accommodated by the reading process, and the uncertainties associated with the human life cycle (such as birth and death) cannot be allowed to disrupt the reading schedule. The whole day, for eleven or twelve weeks straight, revolves around reading those files. (One director once laughingly told me that, in the reading period, she found it simpler to buy new underwear than to wash the old; another director took to making most meals from the old standby of peanut-butter-and-jelly sandwiches.) The discipline demanded by such an assignment has to be experienced to be believed, and the demands make for an intellectual and physical marathon.

At the end of my first reading period, feeling greatly relieved to have survived, I was waiting at the dining room entrance of the Stanford Faculty Club to meet a friend for lunch. One of the academic deans at Stanford came up to me, took one look at my face, and said, "I was planning to ask you to take on an assignment, but you look so awful, I'll forget it!" This was not exactly the greatest encouragement to keep up the good work, but I know what he meant—and why. Yet while the professional and personal challenges of the selection process are great, the rewards are certainly commensurate. First, there is the tremendous satisfaction of having selected the next class of Stanford freshmen. The readers of the freshman applications are the first on campus to meet these talented young men and women, and their achievements are undeniably humbling. The students don't all come in the more obvious forms of prize-winning mathematicians, musicians, or Olympic gold medalists—although there seem to be plenty in all those categories. Many students make their contributions in less conspicuous ways through public service, or by exemplary leadership in their high school or community, or just by tackling challenging and unusual circumstances in ways that reach beyond what is listed on the transcript. (One of the things that I have found most interesting about Stanford undergraduates is that such high achievers are so insecure about their abilities. Why were they accepted? Could we possibly have made a mistake? And would they now be found out?) As admissions professionals, we not only have the pleasure of the first encounter with new undergraduates, but we can also then follow their progress through four years at Stanford and beyond. Among my greatest professional pleasures is seeing my former Stanford advisees join the faculty ranks, or earn some distinguished award, or take delight in high school teaching.

The second reward is the collegiality of the office. The bonding that takes place between admissions directors who have toiled together to create a freshman class is quite extraordinary. I made a point of selecting directors who were very different from one another. They included Stanford alumni from three decades as well as alumni of other public and private universities; some had attended public high schools, others private secondary schools. Some were admissions professionals with extensive experience at other institutions, some were recent college graduates, and still others had taught at Stanford. Each one brought different strengths and experiences to the process, and I felt that as a team we had a far-ranging level of expertise that accurately reflected the tremendous breadth of experience of our applicants. While such diversity produced spirited discussions, it did not always lead to the easiest of working relationships. But all differences were forgotten in the exhilaration of completing our important assignment together. The teamwork begins early, in a low-key way, in a fall retreat and the planning of the fall travel season; it builds through the reading training period in December and early January; and it reaches its peak in the reading period. Even after staff have left the office to pursue other careers or to enter graduate school, when they return to visit former colleagues the old closeness is quickly renewed. There are not many jobs in life that can make similar claims, and I think it is fair to say that working in the Stanford Office of Undergraduate Admissions was the best collegial experience I have had in 30 years of professional life in universities.

One literary dean of admissions once described the college admissions process as akin to Dante's *Divine Comedy* —part paradise, part purgatory, and part inferno. The way this description applies to admissions staff should by now be fairly clear. The description is also true, however, for the other participants in college admissions: the high school students, the parents, and the guidance counselors. As the annual cycle unfolds, each player experiences a different stage of the "comedy." It is clear that students and parents go through an inferno of sorts as those college applications are completed (assuming some prior agreement has been reached on which colleges). There is a purgatorial waiting period for students and parents as the admissions directors go through their own inferno in the reading process. Once the decisions are mailed, there is some paradise, accompanied by some more purgatory, for applicants and families. Meanwhile the admissions staff are subject to some more purgatory while admitted students decide which college they will select from those that have accepted them. Guidance counselors share in the paradise of their most successful students and the purgatory of those not so fortunate. Many parents, particularly in private high schools, place the blame for adverse results wholly on the shoulders of the guidance counselor.

A great deal of the emotional toll on college applicants and their parents can be alleviated by preparing for the process. There are a few good, comprehensive paperback guides on the college application process, written by experienced professionals, that are full of helpful advice about timelines, narrowing the choices, completing the applications, visiting the campuses, etc. Both applicants and their parents (particularly those with no experience in the college admissions process) can benefit from a timely reading of these guides. Ultimately, and ideally, all the important decisions should be made by the prospective applicant with the parents as supportive advisers, not opinionated authorities.

AFTER THE DECISIONS ARE MAILED

Most selective colleges aim to mail freshman decision letters around the first week in April; most colleges have also agreed to a candidates' common reply date of May 1. This schedule allows three to four weeks for the admitted students to make their decisions, an interesting period of role reversal for admissions officers, and a more difficult time for high school seniors than they would believe possible. Choosing between three or four excellent colleges reduces some seniors to the desperation of a coin toss. In recent years, the month of April has become more chaotic, primarily as a result of increased competition between the most selective colleges for the very best students.

At this time of year, the press is full of stories of college recruitment efforts. Some colleges provide airfare to bring their most highly prized recruits to campus; others involve alumni in their efforts; all encourage campus visits so prospective students can attend classes and meet with faculty. Most colleges mail supplementary publications to provide information they hope will tip the balance in the decision process; some provide videotapes about the campus. Others are rumored to offer free computers to all confirmed matriculants. The competition has some undesirable side effects as colleges escalate their efforts to enroll the best and the brightest, and the efforts tend to be particularly questionable when the college depends on a guaranteed level of enrollment for its financial survival. In one example of competitiveness for admitted students, a young woman was ready to send in her acceptance card to Stanford when an alumnus of another selective school called to ask about her impending decision. When he heard that she was heading to California, he immediately offered a free trip to visit his alma mater, urging that she not rush into a decision without seeing his college. She accepted the offer and changed her mind about enrolling at Stanford. A variation on this theme came from another college's alumnus who offered a student a well-paid summer job if he enrolled. Such attention is flattering to an inexperienced seventeen-year-old. At the same time, it adds confusion and an unjustified moral obligation on the part of the student to the already bewildering decision-making process.

Our policy at Stanford is to focus on helping high school seniors make the best-informed choice that they possibly can. (Once when I said this to a curious newspaper reporter, she clearly could not believe that I meant it.) We do encourage a campus visit during April, a time affectionately known as Pro Fro (short for Prospective Freshman) Week. The events of this week are generally coordinated by three enthusiastic undergraduates, who receive a small, well-earned payment for their services. The responsibility involves a massive feat of organization when close to 600 "pro fros" say they want to visit. The pro fros are assigned to a host in a specific dorm, where they and their sleeping bags are welcomed, generally for a two-night stay. This allows them to experience dorm life for themselves, to ask questions, to see the campus, and to attend classes and campus events: the spring musical, special information sessions on overseas studies, tennis team matches, lectures by visiting speakers, and the like. Since many students would be unable to make such a visit without some assistance with their travel expenses, in recent years we have provided a limited number of travel grants to students with a certain level of financial need. Groups of minority students have been particularly energetic during Pro Fro Week, and they have helped to organize special programs for admitted black, Mexican-American, Asian-American, and Native American Indian students. International students at Stanford telephone prospective students from their home countries. Indeed, we arranged to have *every single* admitted student called by a Stanford undergraduate. The general principle is that admitted high school seniors are much more at ease asking questions of current undergraduates than they are of admissions officers, besides which, they trust them to tell nothing but the truth! Finally, events in April include receptions for admitted students in selected cities, such as Los Angeles, Dallas, New York, and Boston. These receptions, hosted by alumni and the admissions office, bring some of "the Stanford experience" to students who may not make it to campus and need additional information to make an informed choice.

Simultaneously, another much less pleasant activity is taking place right in the Office of Undergraduate Admissions, an activity that was among the biggest surprises of my first year. After all the hard work of making the decisions and mailing the associated letters, I was unprepared for the resultant onslaught of angry mail and personal visits from disappointed applicants and their parents. One memorable April morning brought a furious mother and tearful daughter to the admissions office. The mother loudly announced to the receptionist that they were going to sit in the waiting room until I agreed to meet with them personally. I decided that it was better to deal with this intrusion directly and in my office, although the subsequent 30-minute conversation proved a thoroughly unpleasant experience for all participants. It began with the mother's hostile verbal assault on me for not having the good sense to recognize her daughter's talents. While I was prepared to accept this, not only as going with the territory but as an example of understandable and protective maternal instinct, it was obviously a very embarrassing time for the daughter, who spent most of the time quietly weeping into her handkerchief. The assault concluded with the demand that I provide specific reasons why "Jill" was not admitted to Stanford. When all gentle generalizations fail to satisfy, the more brutal truths must be acknowledged. Since I had the applicant's file in my office, I was in a position to say that while Jill was clearly a fine student, she unfortunately did not stand out among the top 3,000 applicants in the pool. In addition, she had been involved in very little activity outside of class. (There were other reasons, more confidential in nature, that I could not divulge, but the ones I gave seemed sufficient painful evidence.)

Although the mother asked for this information, it seems to me that neither she nor her humiliated daughter gained much from hearing the details spelled out. Instead, the exercise poured salt in an already rather painful wound. I wonder whether the mother, with the benefit of calmer hindsight, agreed with me; the daughter clearly was not consulted. In any case, I attempted in such encounters to explain, as sensitively as possible, the context in which hard decisions had to be made. Unfortunately, for parents who are deeply involved with their children, reason is sometimes an unreasonable expectation, and I was not always successful in concluding such meetings with an amicable understanding. If I had agreed to meet with all angry parents of denied applicants, I would have been able to do nothing else for months. Fortunately, the skillful and experienced staff in Undergraduate Admissions were there to help out in such cases, and in most instances their personal attention was a sufficient response.

The volume of angry correspondence, however, outweighed the volume of angry visits, and answering such letters kept us all busy for about eight weeks. Occasionally, we would even hear complaints a year or more after the decisions had been mailed. Something would reignite the unhappiness and prompt a letter to admissions. (During another visit I made to the Stanford alumni camp in the Sierras, a mother asked if she could meet with me after lunch on a personal matter; this turned out to be her dismay that her younger son had been denied admission *six years* earlier, at a time when I wasn't even dean. Parental disappointments die hard.) The general themes of such letters ranged from the mild ("Could you please read my application again and make sure you didn't make a mistake?") to the much stronger ("I am outraged at Stanford's admissions policies and decisions!") to the strongest ("I am immediately ceasing to offer any further support to Stanford," or the rare "I am consulting with my attorney about a charge of discrimination against my son"). Less frequently, alas, we received expressions of understanding, such as the following letter from the father of a denied applicant:

Unfortunately, F was not accepted. Although very disappointed, he announced this to his sister by saying "I have something you and Dad don't have, a rejection slip from Stanford." With my continuing parental bias I think Stanford may have made an error. Nevertheless, I must acknowledge admission processes are probably a more objective assessment than a father's opinion. In spite of his and our disappointments you should know I feel Stanford handles rejections well also. F's handling of his disappointment of not having been admitted to Stanford pleases me almost as much as his admission would.

Can Selectivity Be Justified?

> I am willing to bet, based on current evidence, that for young
> men and women test scores and grades forecast later success in
> business, law, medicine, and academia better than existing
> measures of personality, character, leadership, or diligence.
>
> —Robert Klitgaard, *Choosing Elites*

THE USE AND ABUSE OF STANDARDIZED TESTS

The application materials we send prospective applicants include
the following statement about required examinations. (For simplicity, I have omitted the discussion of the requirement of the TOEFL
[Test of English as a Foreign Language] for applicants whose first
language is not English.)

All applicants are required to submit official results of either the SAT (College Board Scholastic Aptitude Test) or the ACT (American College Test).
Your results should be sent to us directly from the appropriate testing
agency, but we will accept the official report sent to you by the testing
agency. In addition we *strongly recommend* that you take three of the College Board Achievement Tests. Statistics show that students who have taken
Achievement Tests are admitted to Stanford at a higher rate than those who
have not done so. We prefer that one of these tests be English Composition.

If test fees would constitute a financial hardship for you or your family, we suggest that you contact your high school counselor about a possible fee waiver.[1]

These examination requirements raise a number of legitimate questions, among them: How are test scores used in the selection process? Are the scores used appropriately? Should we require (rather than strongly recommend) Achievement Tests? I have limited the discussion that follows to the SATs alone, although similar arguments have been made for the ACTs.

Information included with the Stanford application information addresses the first question as follows: "While we are interested in the general pattern of scores, we pay particular attention to the highest score you have obtained on any of the exams. We believe that test scores, properly used in conjunction with other measures of performance, provide a valuable perspective on an applicant's abilities." It is true that SATs do not predict such human qualities as leadership, creativity, motivation, energy, persistence, compassion, and sensitivity; and in fairness, the testing agencies do not claim they do. The general information section of the Stanford application goes on to state that the single most important credential is the high school transcript. Quantitative measures have their limitations; as the writer Walker Percy has reminded us, "It's possible to get all A's and flunk life." We do not have any cutoff points for test scores, although the rate of admission is higher for applicants with higher test scores (see Table 1). Of the students offered admission in 1991, 78 percent had a verbal SAT score of 600 or above (compared with 7 percent of the national test takers), and 93 percent had a math score of 600 or above (compared with 18 percent of the national test takers).

When a prospective applicant asks for the mean SAT scores for students admitted to Stanford, we point to our entering class profile and explain that we do not keep mean scores. This is not the answer they expect or want. We are aware of these numbers, but we choose not to state them publicly. The reasoning behind this policy is simple: stating an average score immediately attaches too much value to a single number. Applicants with scores above the average tend to assume they will be admitted, and applicants with scores below it may be too discouraged to apply. Moreover, calculating the mean would not give students the information they are trying to elicit, since half of our admitted students must be, by definition, below our mean. Consequently, we provide *ranges* of scores for applicants, admitted students, and enrolling students. Very high scores alone do not guarantee admission to Stanford. Indeed, test scores are only one of the quantitative measures used to assess an applicant's academic achievement and potential; many unquantifiable qualitative elements come into play as well.

I once tried to make all these points to the very anxious mother of a prospective Stanford applicant at an information meeting I attended on the East Coast. She approached me worriedly to ask if her son should retake the SATs; his first-attempt test scores were 720 on the verbal exam and 780 on the math. When I complimented her son, explained that these scores placed him in the top 1 percent among the 1.5 million students who take the test each year, and outlined the Stanford process as described above, she replied "But isn't 800 the maximum score on both tests?" I felt a bit sorry for this talented sixteen-year-old. Unfortunately, his mother is not alone in her thinking or in misunderstanding how test scores are used in the admissions process. One year, we read in the national press of another high school senior whose father promised him a car if he scored 800 on both the verbal and math sections of the SAT. The student won his car for placing among the two or three dozen high school students who achieve such a feat each year, but I can promise that this was not what subsequently earned him admission at Stanford (he chose to enroll elsewhere).

I heard one wonderfully illustrative though no doubt apocryphal story about SATs from an Ivy League psychologist. The tale involves two high school students, one with high SAT scores, H, and the other with much more modest scores, M. H and M were hiking in a mountainous region near the Canadian border when they were startled by a grizzly bear running toward them. H immediately pulled out his calculator and estimated the bear's distance, speed, and how long it would take him to reach the frightened hikers.

Meanwhile, M was pulling off his hiking boots and pulling on his sneakers. H looked at M and said, "There's no point in running; he can outrun us." To which M replied, "All I have to do is outrun you!" The moral here is a useful one: there are many ways to measure different kinds of intelligences; SATs are only one of them.

Howard Gardner's work on multiple intelligences emphasizes the limitations of scores on intelligence tests in predicting success in later life and focuses, instead, on the range of intelligences: linguistic, musical, logical-mathematical, spatial, bodily-kinesthetic, and personal.[2] In applying this theory of multiple intelligences to selective college admissions, Professor Gardner has suggested that the SAT be made, at best, an optional examination, and that some form of student portfolio be required, thereby making the admissions process more sensitive to the range of human intelligences. "Most colleges," Gardner argues, "are not selective enough to warrant such an instrument (the SAT), and those that are have sufficient additional information about their candidates."[3] Robert Sternberg has argued that Gardner's portfolio approach would be more susceptible to socialization differences than test scores.[4] Sternberg has advocated working to improve existing intelligence tests and has emphasized the value, in the college admissions process, of combining as many sources of information as possible about a student.

Another leading opponent of the SAT, James Crouse, has said that the test "is poorly constructed, highly coachable, unfair to underprivileged and minority students, and of very little use because it doesn't measure what it is supposed to measure."[5] It is certainly true, though hardly surprising, that there is a strong correlation between SAT scores and parental income. It is also true that both the mean verbal and mean math scores of white students are higher than the corresponding scores for black, Mexican-American, and Puerto Rican students, and many critics cite the sizable differences as prima facie evidence of test bias. There are, of course, other explanations, such as disparities in educational opportunities. Furthermore, for more than two decades, the average scores for men on the SAT math exam have remained 40–50 points higher than the average scores for women; in spite of this difference, women tend to receive higher grades in both high school and college. Studies that correlate test scores and freshman grades generally *underpredict* the grades earned by women. In short, extensive research has confirmed that there are many unanswered questions associated with standardized test score differences.[6]

Any admissions officer must be aware of all these factors in incorporating SAT scores into the overall assessment of an application. As long as standardized scores are: (1) considered in the appropriate context by well-informed admissions directors; (2) included as one of a range of measures of "intelligence"; and (3) not subjected to hard-and-fast cutoffs, I believe that they can assist in the selective admissions process. Interestingly, Gardner has claimed to have fewer reservations about the College Board's Achievement Tests than about the Scholastic Aptitude Test. After considerable thought by the directors in Undergraduate Admissions at Stanford, we decided to *strongly recommend* rather than to *require* Achievement Tests. (In fact, more than 90 percent of our admitted students have taken three or more Achievement Tests.) Although it has been argued that emphasizing the Achievement Tests in admissions, rather than SATs, would improve the quality of American secondary school education and consequently better prepare students for college, it is also true that requiring such tests could unfairly penalize disadvantaged students in the college admissions process. These students, through no fault of their own, often find themselves in high schools that provide inadequate preparation for the Achievement Tests. In particular, we were concerned about the effect that such a requirement might have on minority applicants; the potential loss, for example, of just a few promising Native American Indian applicants from schools on reservations, where Achievement Tests are rarely taken, persuaded us to lean in the direction of "strongly recommending" rather than requiring the tests.

DIFFERENCES IN APPROACH

Most selective colleges share the same fundamental principles in selecting a freshman class: all focus on academic achievement and potential, energy and achievement outside the classroom, and the applicant's personal qualities. There are, however, some notable variations on these themes. Some colleges and universities require a specified number of Achievement Tests. There was a rumor a few years ago that at least one of the most selective colleges was planning to drop the SAT requirement and replace it with a requirement that applicants take five Achievement Tests. One of the arguments considered was that Achievement Tests appeared to be slightly better predictors of college grade-point averages. In 1984, the faculty at Bates College in Maine voted to make SAT scores optional for admission. The dean of admissions and financial aid at Bates, William Hiss, has written about this experience for the benefit of interested readers.[7]

Another kind of difference is seen in the use of the interview in college admissions. At Stanford, we welcome visits by prospective applicants and their parents, and we offer information sessions once or twice a day throughout the year (except during the application reading period). These sessions, however, involve no evaluation of the prospective applicant, and we do not require an interview as part of the admissions process. Many colleges ask that their applicants be interviewed, either in the admissions office or by an alumni representative in the student's hometown. Some of these interviews are purely informational, but others involve a written report from the interviewer that is then included in the application file. Many applicants are unaware of these circumstances, and they are either too inexperienced or too shy to ask about the role of the interview. I would encourage applicants and parents not to hesitate on this front; you have a right to know the purpose and role of any interview. While some kind of information session is inevitably helpful for prospective applicants, the use of an evaluative interview in the admissions process seems to me to be dubious at best. Apart from the obvious concerns about quality control—including organization, costs, training, experience, consistency, and effectiveness (the process does demand nontrivial skills)—there are questions both of the best match between interviewers and applicants and of the interviewers' conscious or unconscious biases. Even optimistically assuming that all the above concerns could be satisfactorily addressed, there remains the fundamental question of whether 30 minutes of questions and answers in the life of a nervous seventeen-year-old is an appropriate measure to include in any admissions process. Alumni are always asking, "Why doesn't Stanford interview? It would make the process so much more personal." Whenever I visited Stanford dorms, the question of interviews inevitably came up, and undergraduates who favored interviews could usually be counted in a 2 percent minority. The majority of students could tell of some unpleasant personal experience. In the Stanford admissions process, then, we agreed that evaluative interviews would not be a part of our deliberations.

The question of the use of alumni in the admissions process usually generates lively debate. It is, of course, wonderful to benefit from the energy, experience, and enthusiasm of alumni. Many of the selective colleges and universities involve alumni extensively to identify, interview, and subsequently recruit the freshman class, and their participation is considered critical to the success of the admissions office.

I do remember feeling envious, one difficult November morning, as I made my way alone to a high school visit. After a tense ride through Manhattan rush-hour traffic, I stepped out of my taxi into the pouring rain, only to pass the representative from another college who was being driven, in splendid style, from school to school by a local alumnus. But such privileges have their associated costs, both personal and professional. To begin with, the organization of a national network of alumni volunteers usually calls for the time of one full-time staff member. Even if the office can afford such an expense, almost unavoidable conflicts of interest predictably arise. What do you do, for example, when a loyal and hardworking alum has a less-than-competitive son or daughter in the applicant pool? Avoiding all alumni with high school–age children does not solve the problem: everyone has a grandchild, niece, or next-door neighbor in whom he or she takes a special interest. I know from painful personal experience that it is not easy to deny admission to a student who has the enthusiastic backing of a helpful and supportive alum.

The use of alumni in any interview process, of course, presents further complications. Despite the best intentions in the world, volunteer alumni have neither the experience nor the perspective of professional staff. At Stanford, we dealt with this dilemma in the following way: we welcomed, and greatly benefited from, alumni assistance in every part of the admissions process that did not involve evaluation of candidates. We encouraged alumni to participate in both the organization and programs of regional meetings, usually held in the fall, and in spring receptions for admitted students. Ultimately, the organization and operation of any admissions office must be determined by, and under the authority of, the dean. Defining the appropriate role of alumni in an effective and sensitive way is a prime example of the many delicate balancing acts a dean must perform.

A few years ago, a one-hour television special took viewers inside the admissions office of a selective private college during the application-reading period. Leaving aside the question of whether this was a good thing to do (and some of us had our doubts), what the camera recorded was different, in one substantive way, from the Stanford process: the final decisions on admission were made by a committee. Some colleges go even further and assign subcommittees by geographical region or set of high schools. A senior staff member chairs each subcommittee and is often assigned a specific number of admits for the assigned region. The subcommittee then serves as an advocate to the full committee for recommended admits. The analysis of such a process is of significant interest to sociologists, and some have developed their own theories of "gatekeeping."[8]

In contrast, the vast majority of Stanford decisions are made through written communication. In the final week of the freshman-selection process, however, we usually met in subcommittees, or in a committee of the senior staff, to discuss the most difficult cases. These sometimes involved heartrending cases of life-threatening illness. Late one March, I received a letter from a high school guidance counselor with an update on a Stanford applicant; he had suffered a cerebral hemorrhage and was not expected to live. Fortunately, this story had a happy ending; we decided to admit the student, and after a year's deferral, he entered Stanford and did well. Another case was more poignant. A counselor alerted us that a senior was suffering from a brain tumor and was not expected to live until April; could we send an early decision letter? This call did not require a committee discussion. The young man was an outstanding applicant, and we were pleased to send the early admit letter; he died a few days later. A more complex decision involved a request from an alumnus who was the relative of an applicant; the young woman had been killed returning from a ski trip, and the relative wanted to know if we would admit her posthumously. Unfortunately, the young woman was not a strong candidate, and I denied the request, although with some pangs of conscience.

The more complex cases certainly benefit from discussion with experienced colleagues, and I can see the considerable merits of the committee process. For the most part, however, in spite of the challenges and complexities of selection, the readings are relatively straightforward; ethical and moral dilemmas are not at issue and the written analysis allows the final reader to come to a conclusion without the complications or time-consuming meeting a committee decision would entail.

Beyond the cases of serious illness, committee discussion helps in deciding on cases of recovering alcoholics or drug abusers, or cases involving honor-code violations. While these examples may seem immediate candidates for denial to the uninitiated, there is always more to them than meets the eye. Chapter 7 provides some specific examples of dilemmas for admissions directors.

A final, and significant, difference between Stanford's admissions process and that of most other selective colleges and universities has been the absence of an Early Action or Early Decision process.[9] I immediately admit to my bias against such programs, and I have given my reasons publicly at national meetings of college admissions professionals. While a fully documented discussion of the pros and cons of "early" programs would take too much space here, a few points might help prospective applicants and parents unfamiliar with the college admissions process. First, we must understand the definitions, which can confuse even the experienced admissions officer: *Early Decision* is the process in which an applicant requests early consideration at one college. Usually, the dates are in early November for the application and early December for the notification. The applicant pledges to attend the college if admitted, usually paying a nonrefundable deposit by mid-December. Students entering under such plans also need early notification of financial aid offers. The distinguishing feature of these plans is their requirement that the applicant commit to one college early in the process and abstain from pursuing applications at other colleges.

With *Early Action*, an applicant requests consideration at a college by early November. Decisions are mailed in mid-December, just as with Early Decision. In this case, however, students need not decide to enroll until May 1, the common reply date, when they learn the outcomes of their other applications. Students admitted under such a plan often do not learn of financial aid offers until April. Many colleges limit the number of Early Action applications a student can make. Brown, Harvard, MIT, Princeton, and Yale have formed a coalition that allows students to apply for Early Action at only one of the five.

An essential piece of advice for would-be applicants is that they make sure they understand the meaning of all the options available (and some colleges offer more than one variation), as well as the conditions attendant on them. I have spoken with many unhappy students who applied to a college through an Early Decision or Early Action program without fully understanding the consequences.

Let me briefly explain why, after a thorough review in 1986, Stanford concluded that the advantages of having no Early Action or Early Decision process outweighed the disadvantages. I embarked on this review with an open mind, and after lively debate with our staff, I emerged convinced that we should, for the time being, stay with the regular decision process. Colleges that have early programs cite three main reasons for them: they eliminate the applicants' long waits for notification; they establish a base of well-qualified students for the freshman class; and they reward students who are prepared to make an early commitment. College guidance counselors who are negative about early programs complain that such programs lead to premature and uninformed decisions by applicants; make the senior year seem unimportant; increase student anxiety; encourage gamesmanship; are too confusing and too complicated, and require too much paperwork too early; discriminate against the disadvantaged; and do not give adequate financial aid information soon enough.

Of course, most of these arguments have good counterarguments. The most compelling arguments against early programs involve their effects on the high school seniors. One of the great assets of this country is the wealth of postsecondary opportunities it offers, with close to 2,000 four-year colleges from which the high school senior may select. There is no unique, predestined, perfect match of student and college; any individual student could be happy and well educated at several different institutions, and college guidance counselors and parents have a responsibility to dispel such thoughts as, "I'll die if I don't get into X University." What we should emphasize to high school seniors is the importance of making an informed choice, based on such considerations as the colleges' educational resources, financial aid, and residential life. But choice implies a selection from more than one, and choice before an offer of admission is not the same as choice after an offer of admission. In short, the time needed to make those comparisons in the month of April is important.

One could argue that Early Action allows for such choices, but unfortunately a good many guidance counselors require, as a condition for writing recommendations, that their successful Early Action candidates commit to the schools that accept them. In other words, counselors erase the distinction between Early Action and Early Decision, a distinction that, at least in principle, is significant; practice appears to be another matter. Presumably, the counselors have their reasons for imposing this limitation. The most laudable is that they want to ensure that their students have carefully thought through the reasons for early applications and are willing to commit to their chosen college; this seriousness of purpose is then appropriately rewarded by the counselors' willingness to produce all the necessary paperwork at an early date. A more questionable reason is that the counselors want to establish, or maintain, special understandings with the college admissions officers at the early colleges.

There are also sound educational arguments for the regular process from the point of view of the college admissions office. Decisions made in the context of a regular process are made with more information, with full knowledge of a student's grades in the first semester of the senior year and of the student's program of courses in the final semester. The senior year is an important one in preparing for the challenges of college, and early admission only induces an earlier senior-year slump. Furthermore, a regular decision procedure does not introduce an academic hierarchy of admits, a highly questionable practice in which applicants are labeled alphas, betas, or gammas. Finally, in the most selective colleges, for a large number of early applicants an early decision cannot be made, and they are deferred to the regular round. This scarcely fulfills any promise that early programs alleviate the stress of applicants.

Another equally compelling consideration for me is that the early program primarily benefits those students who are already advantaged. I have not done any scientific analysis, but I would be willing to wager that an overwhelming percentage of Early Action and Early Decision candidates are white students who come either from select private high schools or from established public high schools in higher-income neighborhoods with well-informed college guidance counselors. They are mostly the children of college graduates who are also well informed. They are mostly students who have been identified by enthusiastic and well-trained alumni as fine prospects. These characteristics surely violate equal opportunity, a principle that I believe needs no defense. Finally, there are many practical disadvantages to Early Action and Early Decision programs from the perspective of an admissions office, including limits on the fall visits to high schools and additional reading pressures on admissions staff. But these seem secondary to the educational and equity arguments above.

I have gone so far as to recommend publicly that all colleges, without exception, agree to the same basic procedure for selecting the freshman class: the regular program. All my arguments have education as the cornerstone: the education of the student in making an informed choice in selecting a college; the educational principles and well-being of the college in emphasizing the importance of the senior year in high school; the promotion of equal opportunity. In general, early programs work more to the advantage of the colleges than to that of the admitted students. There have even been tales of colleges discouraging early applications from students who need financial aid. And some counselors have questioned the implied message, from colleges with early programs, that the whole admissions process is so unpleasant and pointless that anything we can do to get it over with fast is justified.

The other kind of argument for regular action programs for all is the slippery-slope argument: Where will it all end? Thirty years ago, there were no Early Action or Early Decision programs. Today, we have an increasingly confusing proliferation of variations on a theme, with a sliding scale of notification dates (not to mention merit awards). What is to stop such programs from moving back, heaven forbid, to the eleventh grade? To junior high school? I won't weaken the argument by suggesting kindergarten, but with the current advance tuition payment plans, who knows? My view could understandably be criticized as that of a high-handed representative in the protective shelter of a very selective college: "It's all very well for Stanford, you don't have to worry about attracting enough strong applicants." But neither, surely, does Harvard, Yale, or MIT! In fact, I think Stanford might increase its yield of admitted students by moving to an Early Decision program—but is that the fundamental consideration? For too many colleges, it is.

Unsurprisingly, my recommendation that early programs be eliminated got nowhere. The colleges with such programs fear they have too much to lose, particularly in a time of shrinking applicant pools. It is small consolation to know that some thoughtful admissions officers are trying to buck the long-established system; it is not easy. Perhaps some form of national directory of college admission plans can be produced to alleviate the confusion. To my knowledge, this has not happened either.

MYTHS

One of the most frustrating aspects of working in undergraduate admissions is the perennial need to stanch the proliferation of myths. Maddeningly, for every myth there seems to be an equally frustrating countermyth, a classic catch-22 for the admissions officer. The Stanford alumni magazine tried to help us out on this front in 1989 by publishing a brief article listing the top ten myths.[10] I hope that careful readers of this book (and this chapter in particular) will be able to provide their own answers. For whatever help they may be, here are the most frequently heard myths, together with my responses in abbreviated form. In their specifics they apply only to Stanford, but any selective private college suffers from similar misrepresentations, and *no* college is spared its place in the mythical realm.

In pursuit of a geographically diverse student body, Stanford has quotas for specific parts of the country and specific schools. This one gets an unequivocal response: Not true! Stanford considers each applicant individually, regardless of high school or region of the country. We have no quotas of any kind, which is just as well since the number of high schools represented by applicants is typically twice the number of offers of admission. Many Californians believe that it is easier to get into Stanford if one is *not* from California; conversely, those who live elsewhere often believe it is easier to get in if one *is* from California. It is true that there has been a decline in the percentage of Californians in the freshman class (from 44 percent in 1980 to 33 percent in 1988), but rather than reflecting a change in policy this change reflects Stanford's increasingly national and international pool of applicants.

It is a disadvantage to apply to Stanford from a private high school. / It is a disadvantage to apply to Stanford from a public school. In another I-hope-not-vain attempt to dispel myths with facts, I will acknowledge that in recent years, approximately 30 percent of Stanford's applicants have come from private schools and 70 percent from public schools. Among the accepted students, the ratio is almost identical; this is a consequence of coincidence rather than statistical engineering. Again, the focus is on the individual applicant rather than on the high school. With more than 4,000 different high schools represented in any year's applicant pool, however, it is not surprising that impressions of the process can be distorted from the limited perspective of a particular neighborhood. Students, parents, counselors, and principals tend to use a few years' data to draw their conclusions, such as "Stanford never takes more than one from this high school," or "You have to be the valedictorian to be accepted to Stanford from here."

Students with grade-point averages and test scores below a minimum cutoff need not apply.   This is one that the readers of this book can now refute themselves. As emphasized in Chapter 2 and in this chapter, there are many ways to measure intelligence, and we take pains throughout the admissions process not to define excellence too narrowly.

Stanford denies admission to better-qualified students to include less-qualified minorities.   The subject of affirmative action is significant and complex enough to merit a chapter of its own. This myth is dealt with at length in Chapter 5. There is no simple answer to the charge.

Stanford is only for children of the wealthy.   Despite media reports about the material wealth of college freshmen, more than half the entering freshmen at Stanford need and receive financial aid. As mentioned earlier, Stanford is one of the few universities in the country that still maintains a need-blind admissions policy—a policy made possible by the continued generosity of our alumni and other friends of the university. Each year, approximately 100 entering freshmen have parents who are unable to make any contribution at all toward the cost of a Stanford education, which is roughly $25,000 for room, board, and tuition. This does not mean, of course, that there are no wealthy students at Stanford, or that the socioeconomic differences between Stanford students do not present problems, or that some students do not reluctantly conclude that they cannot afford to attend. Stanford's essential guiding principle, however, is that every undergraduate should have the chance to select a college on the basis of academic rather than financial considerations.

Stanford doesn't care about alumni children. / Alumni children get all the breaks.   The short answer to the question "Is there any special preference given to alumni children?" is yes, as the criteria for admission set forth in Chapter 1 confirm. No college admissions officer, at least at a private college or university, would answer otherwise. The longer answer is more complicated and merits lengthier discussion, which is provided in Chapter 4.

Spending $500 on an SAT coaching course will increase your chances of admission.   From annual surveys of Stanford's freshmen, we know that 75 percent took the SAT without taking any such course, and we suspect that those who did take a course would have done well anyway. The most recent studies suggest that coaching results in a negligible change in verbal scores and only a small improvement in math scores. The soundest preparation for taking standardized tests is a challenging secondary school curriculum that develops critical powers of reading along with mathematical knowledge and skills. My best advice, to those who have the luxury to do so, would be to spend the $500 on buying good books to read. Those without the $500 are advised to use school and public libraries and read, read, read.

In the application process, gimmicks make a difference.   Admissions officers receive an unusual array of packages during the application season, but it is definitely a myth that a gimmick can make a difference in the final decision. At Stanford, we have seen life preservers emblazoned with the words U.S.S. Sanford [*sic*], popcorn, homemade candies and cookies, stuffed animals, custom-made drinking glasses engraved with the dean's signature, books, poems, oil portraits of the staff, and personal tapes and videos. One year, someone sent a shoe with a note attached to it that read, "I hope this gets my foot in the door." One applicant, in answer to the essay question "What single adjective best describes you?" chose "reflective" and proceeded to write his essay backward so that it could only be read with a mirror (one was thoughtfully taped to the essay, but the ploy was destined to irritate the readers of his file). Although they may produce some laughs, gimmicks are not relevant to the criteria for admission and make no difference in the final decision. (We feel very guilty eating the cookies and candy.) It is true, though, that some supplementary materials are appropriate; Chapter 4 deals with the special procedures for considering talent in art, music, drama, and dance, the only areas in which supporting materials are encouraged.

The Stanford admissions process is impersonal because it does not offer interviews. At one time, Stanford did interview applicants on campus, but stopped in the mid-1970's because of concerns that students who were unable to visit Stanford were put at an unfair disadvantage. Questions were also raised about the value and fairness of such interviews, for reasons I explained earlier in this chapter. The intent in abandoning individual evaluative interviews was not to depersonalize the process, and prospective applicants are encouraged to visit campus and join the daily information sessions held between June and December.

If you don't get admitted as a freshman, apply as a transfer—it's easier to get in. Although the number of students who apply to transfer from other colleges is less than one-tenth the number of those who apply as freshmen, both admissions processes are highly selective. In recent years, the admit rate of freshmen has averaged about 20 percent, while that of transfers is closer to 10 percent. Transfer applicants present a much wider range of life experiences than do high school seniors. It is not unusual, for example, to see 40-year-old transfer applicants, and the age range during my tenure was 11 to 65.

The foregoing is by no means an exhaustive list of the myths that plague the admissions office. The imagination of the myth generators is endlessly amazing to experienced admissions officers, and we wonder where on earth some of their ideas come from. Checking the sources of confusion is both time-consuming and frustrating.

The moral, I hope, is clear: Always check your facts with the source; even the most well-meaning, and apparently reliable but second-hand, sources can be misleadingly uninformed. Any admissions officer would prefer to be called to confirm procedures than to see a myth propagated.

IS THIS THE BEST WAY TO SELECT?

In his lively and provocative book about undergraduate and graduate admissions at Harvard, *Choosing Elites*, Robert Klitgaard poses a series of "unresolved questions" about how admissions works.[11] What qualities should be sought in choosing an elite? Which criteria and measures should be used, and how? How should diversity and representativeness be considered? What admissions process should be followed? Each of these fundamental questions generates a subset of equally important questions, few of which are considered by members of the public at large.

Klitgaard further says, "We might even ponder a couple of radical questions. Given the problems of predicting success and the expense of the admissions system, why not admit more students and flunk them out more readily? Or why not select randomly among applicants who are above a certain threshold of admissibility?"[12] The first suggestion (even assuming it would be desirable, and there are many arguments against it) would be impractical at an institution such as Stanford (or most selective colleges), where a valuable part of the freshman experience is living in a campus residence with other students. The second suggestion, random selection, is not original with Klitgaard and was proposed to me by more than one faculty member at Stanford. Although such a process would undoubtedly be efficient, and definitely nonsubjective, I believe it is easier to justify the admissions decision to a denied applicant by explaining the process described in Chapter 2 than it would be to say impersonally, "You were eliminated in a random draw." Even qualified students are distinguishable from one another, and they differ not only in the ways in which they can benefit from attending a particular institution but also in the ways they can contribute to it.

Though subject to human frailties, the process of admission at Stanford has been given careful thought, receives periodic review, is explicable to all interested parties, and is arguably justified by the success of the results. Given that the admissions process is, by definition, selective, and that the associated choices present an almost impossible assignment, I believe that the way we have chosen to select Stanford undergraduates works as well as could reasonably be expected; it aims to be fair and honest and to select students who would benefit from attending Stanford and contribute to the life of the university. I do not have suggestions to improve on the principles beyond the notes of warning contained in the subsequent chapters, particularly those on affirmative action and athletics. Of course my assessment can be considered self-interested, but I hope the temptation to such criticism is deflected by the way I have written this book.

In his book, Klitgaard uses "an economist's fable" for the Harvard College admissions process and describes a revolutionary new policy of auctioning off places in the freshman class. All academically qualified applicants are asked to submit sealed bids, backed by bank guarantees, stating how much they are willing to pay to attend Harvard for four years. The plan is modified over the years until 2004, when "the philosophical foundations of the College's admissions system" is "a shambles." The system is further modified to become a political process in which each senior faculty member, for example, is given 300 points with which to vote for applicants of his or her choice. The outgoing dean of admissions concludes in 2010 that "designing an admissions system is a many-headed beast of a problem." [13]

Klitgaard's final analysis is too economically rational in its modeling to square with my practical experience, but it raises a seemingly inexhaustible set of relevant questions that focus on the objectives of selection: What is the social value added by the education to students' later lives? What is the value of various students' contributions to the university? What positive and negative incentives will an admissions policy create? To what attributes of students do you assign "intrinsic value" and how much? As one reviewer of *Choosing*

Elites somewhat caustically observed, however, "The conclusions reached . . . are so few, or tentative, or unsurprising, as to tempt a good public policy scientist to throw up his hands and turn in his card." [14] Klitgaard's summary and his critical reviewer's conclusion simply confirm what experienced admissions directors conclude on the job. In the words of one such stalwart, a former dean of admissions at Amherst, Bill Wilson, "I had hoped that there would be some common denominator in the chosen students, something that would enable us to penetrate more accurately in the future the growers from the standstillers. The factor that kept me excited during my twenty-five years in admissions was the mystery in human growth and development. . . . I had hoped to master the art of human assessment. I didn't." [15]

4

Special Talents, Special Considerations

At . . . three selective colleges, the most important determinants
of admission besides academic criteria were membership in a
minority group, having an alumni parent, living in the local
community, and having an "outstanding" interview.

—Robert Klitgaard, *Choosing Elites*

I LIKE TO THINK that *all* applicants to Stanford receive special consideration, but this chapter examines several factors that the university specifies explicitly as receiving "special consideration" in the
admissions process. These include special talents in art, music,
drama, dance, and mathematics, as well as applicants' family members' connections to the university as alumni, faculty, or staff. This
chapter also considers the issue of evaluating applications from students whose families have donated money to Stanford.

SPECIAL TALENTS

The community near a college or university has come to expect
the institutional offerings of cultural richness, and Stanford is no

exception in providing a wealth of drama, dance, music, and art. The opportunities for undergraduates with talent and interest in the creative and performing arts are notable. How do we go about identifying and admitting students who would both contribute to the arts and benefit from such opportunities?

The psychologist Howard Gardner suggests that everyone possesses at least seven intelligences, and that each person's blend of competencies produces a unique cognitive profile.[1] Among these "multiple intelligences" are musical, spatial, and bodily-kinesthetic intelligence; the Stanford admissions staff evaluates these intelligences of applicants with the valuable advice and assistance of faculty members in the departments of music, art, drama, and dance. Applicants who have exceptional talent in the fine arts are encouraged, for example, to submit cassette tapes of their musical performances, résumés of their dance training, and videocassettes of their choreography or performance; we welcome portfolios of slides and prints to demonstrate their talent in painting, photography, and sculpture. In addition, the music department conducts live auditions, which are usually held on campus in December and January. The drama department also holds on-campus auditions and interview sessions around the same time for actors, designers, and directors, and the department sends a faculty member to Chicago, New York, and Los Angeles during the fall to offer auditions to applicants. In 1991, of the approximately 13,500 freshman applicants, almost 200 submitted tapes or participated in auditions in music; nearly 100 submitted portfolios in art; 30 provided supplementary materials in drama; and 20 did so in dance.

Once the faculty in these departments have listened to the tapes, reviewed the portfolios, and assessed the auditions, they write a brief evaluative summary for each individual, which is inserted in the applicant's file. When the readers of the applications in Undergraduate Admissions review the evidence of achievements outside the classroom, they can benefit from first-hand evaluations of faculty members in specific disciplines. This procedure is similar to that used by the athletics coaches, except that the coaches first actively seek out talents in the high schools and encourage those students to apply for admission. A common misunderstanding of prospective applicants who have interests in the creative and performing arts is that they must be planning to major in music, art, or drama in order to be able to supplement their applications. But because Stanford undergraduates are not selected with an eye to prospective majors, it is helpful to *all* applicants to provide evidence of talents in the creative and performing arts. A biology major is just as likely to be found playing first-violin in the orchestra as a music major, and English and engineering majors can be seen performing in winter quarter plays as often as drama majors. The extraordinary range and strength of extracurricular activities on campus is clearly dependent on the wealth of talent that arrives with each freshman class, and the identification of such talent plays an important role in the admissions process. Although the primary criterion for admission is distinguished academic achievement and potential, this alone is insufficient to allow us to distinguish between applicants. Evidence of talents in extracurricular activities can help determine the final decision on admission. Applicants who submit material to be reviewed by a fine arts department and are rated average are not penalized in the application process; rating forms below the exceptional level are not placed in the file, so the reader has no indication that an applicant has submitted audition materials and been found wanting. When the decision is to admit, faculty and undergraduates in the departments of art, music, drama, and dance are asked to contact the talented prospective freshmen and women and encourage them to enroll at Stanford.

One of my favorite, if slightly exaggerated, tales in the recruitment of talented undergraduates came from a somewhat surprising source, the *Princeton Alumni Weekly.* I can do no better than to repeat the amusing (at least from the Stanford vantage) account of a frustrated Princeton alum:

It was my first taste of battle. Although I have been a devoted alumnus for 38 years, not until the winter of 1985 did I fly my maiden mission on behalf of the Schools Committee of the Princeton Club of Northern California.

I thought I was ready for action. But believe me, nothing you can read or be told prepares you for the real thing.

My county captain, Bob "Howling Mad" Tellander '60, had found a rose (one Kathryn L. Pearson) in no-man's land (Santa Rosa, California), and he called me in for tactical support. A typical greenhorn, I felt pretty cocky. With my orange beret at a rakish angle, I charged into the fray, innocent of the booby traps that unscrupulous adversaries might set.

We fired away with everything we had. But, alas, we lost Miss Pearson to Stanford's Class of '89. I'll just give you the facts, and you can plot them on your own learning curve.

During her high school career, Pearson had never received a grade below A. She was, at age 15, president of the California Scholastic Federation. Her leadership qualities were evident: she was a member of Students for Social Responsibility, president of the Sonoma County Junior Etude Club, student representative to the Santa Rosa Symphony Association, and she had held student-body offices from eighth grade on.

Pearson has traveled extensively in Europe, has facility in French and is fluent in Spanish, especially since attending the University of Valencia last year. Athletically, she set junior high school and all-league records in the 800 meters, 400 meters, and high jump, and participated in the AAU State Championships. A soccer player for eight years, she was on the Santa Rosa A-Team. Certainly she has a hobby—scuba diving.

If all that sounds positive, I'm just warming to this narrative. Her trump suit is music. Guitar and piano, of course, but we're talking violin virtuosity: (1) At age 12, concert mistress of the Santa Rosa Junior Symphony; (2) At 13, winner of a four-county violin competition; (3) At 16,—just last year—concert mistress of the San Francisco Youth Symphony, finalist in the Young Musicians Competition for Northern California, which is cosponsored by the San Francisco Symphony and Pepsi Cola, plus seventh chair in the World Youth Symphony at Interlochen, Michigan. Not a bad year!

I recite such detail to persuade you of my anguish. To frost the cake, this young lady, who turned 17 only this month, is exceptionally poised, gracious, articulate, and comely. We had a real prize in our sights, and the Admission Office duly extended her an invitation. Out here in the bunker, we foot soldiers were delighted and hopeful, little suspecting what those guerrillas down on the Leland Stanford Junior Farm were up to.

The advice to know your enemies is as imperative as ever. Old Nassau, of course, long ago identified some and has strategically withdrawn from competing for athletes with Oklahoma, USC, and Georgetown. We properly disdain the provision of Cadillacs, apartments, and degrees in pumping iron. But in vying for candidates who are academically, artistically, and temperamentally suited, we have felt confident, perhaps, smug. And there's the rub.

Who would have imagined that "reputable" Stanford would outflank us by zinging in a perk that tipped the scales? The knockout blow was struck when those blighters, with music professor Andor Toth as point man, captured the heart and mind of violinist Pearson by offering her personal use of a Stradivarius for four years. I ask you, is that sporting? A flippin' stroke of genius! In our league, the game may appear refined, the dialogue civil. But this is hardball, baby.

One matures quickly out here on the firing line; the pink has left my cheek. I would never, of course, suggest that Princeton compromise its principles. But maybe, to avoid being blindsided, we should at least stay *au courant* on the latest weapons and field tactics. Losing is bad enough. But to be outsmarted, that smarts!

I was momentarily consoled by Pearson's telling me that she does not expect to pursue a career in music, but rather to study biochemistry, with an eye to becoming a physician, like both of her parents. Perhaps we have not lost a future Menuhin or Stern after all. However, Stanford still wins big. As I see it, she leads them to victory in the Symphony Bowl and becomes a doctor with two Mercedes and three tax shelters, annually adding to that school's endowment. On top of that, Stanford recycles the Strad.[2]

I think most of the facts about the talented Santa Rosa student are correct, not to mention impressive. The "knockout blow," however, perhaps has an element of exaggeration; while Stanford's music department *does* own a Stradivarius or two, these prize possessions are not reserved solely for recruited musicians but are available to all serious students of the violin. Second, I doubt whether "zinging in" such a "perk" would tip the balance; high school seniors usually give much more substantive thought to making a choice between attractive alternatives. No one with Stanford Cardinal blood, however, would question the humor of the tale.

On a more serious note, an immediate question for prospective applicants is, Do we encourage supplementary materials from applicants who have talents in disciplines beyond the creative and performing arts? At present, the only other field in which faculty are involved in the evaluation of applicants during the admissions process is mathematics. The inclusion of mathematics has an interesting history that began in 1984 during my first year in office. It illuminates yet again the delicate position the admissions office maintains within the university and in managing a "zero-sum" exercise. Is it part of our task to actually mold a class, slanting it in one direction or another—for example, by admitting more prospective engineers or fewer musicians? How much can we, or should we, take into account the requests from various departments? How much pressure should we take on to produce outstanding award winners in every academic discipline? And if we elect not to have advocates for each discipline, how do we decide what will be represented and what will not?

In 1984, a distinguished faculty member in the statistics department wrote to the provost (to whom I then reported) with a revealing analysis about Stanford students in the mathematical sciences. He was able to show, quite persuasively I thought, that while the *graduate* programs at Stanford attracted and enrolled an impressive number of holders of National Science Foundation fellowships, Stanford *undergraduates* were not well represented among such fellowship holders. In other words, Stanford was a recipient of mathematical and scientific talent for graduate programs, but it was not among the most notable producers of such talent. There is, not surprisingly, some serious national competition among colleges for the very best mathematics students; Caltech, MIT, Harvard, Princeton, the University of Chicago, UC Berkeley, and some of the other most selective state universities have strong math, science, and engineering departments. In addition, they produce formidable teams of students to compete in the prestigious Putnam math examination (an annual national mathematics competition for university students). At the time this analysis was produced, the faculty in the mathematical sciences had nothing to do with the evaluation of Stanford applicants for undergraduate admission.

I initiated some discussions with key faculty in mathematics and related departments, which revealed that the faculty lacked confidence in the admissions office to select those undergraduates whom the faculty were most interested in teaching: those with unusual talents in mathematics. Consequently, I agreed that my staff and I would annually identify a set of applications for the faculty in the math department to review and evaluate; their comments would then be included in the applicants' files for consideration by the readers in undergraduate admissions, just as the evaluations of the arts faculty were. The "set of applications" was identified, as a first pass, by SAT math scores above 750, comparable achievement scores in mathematics, and the applicants' professed preliminary interest in majoring in mathematics or a math-related science. Some of these applicants were found to have already published a paper in mathematics or been recognized in national or state math competitions; many of them would write their application essays on math-related topics or be acknowledged by math teachers as having extraordinary talents. (Mathematical talent is unusual in that, like musical genius, it becomes apparent at an early age.)[3]

The most effective procedures for this faculty review took a couple of years to put into practice, but it is now well established, and five or six math faculty annually review about 400 applications to assist in the assessment of what Howard Gardner calls logical-mathematical intelligence. We also supplemented the process by actively seeking out the best math talents among high school students with the help of the Mathematical Society of America, which conducts annual math competitions for high school students. High school seniors who have been successful in these competitions receive a letter from faculty in the math department encouraging them to consider applying to Stanford. (We have some further assistance in identifying math and science talent from a different source: the annual announcement of the Westinghouse Science competition winners. Because these awards are announced each year around March, though, they are difficult to factor into the selection of a freshman class.) It is fair to say, I think, that the math faculty are pleased with their role in the admissions process, and they are also satisfied that their involvement has produced some good results. These results are confirmed in Stanford's improved records in the Putnam competitions and an increased number of national awards in math and science fields.

As news of this procedure to identify talented math students spread through the Stanford community, I was interested to see some anxiety develop among current undergraduates. The unfortunate stereotyping of "math nerds" was sufficient to convince the current undergraduates that these whizzes were not the kind of classmates they wanted to see at Stanford. I was amazed at the number of times I found myself, in visits to the dorms, defending the identification of students with "extreme talents" (to use the phrase introduced in an annual report of our oversight Committee on Undergraduate Admissions and Financial Aids). Why, I would ask, should intelligent undergraduates feel so threatened by the search for such students? There was certainly plenty of such talent already present. And why is "extreme talent" immediately associated with "nerd" or "uninteresting classmate?" Surely "extreme talent" and "well-roundedness" are not mutually exclusive characteristics. Why would I be made to feel defensive in talking to some undergraduates about identifying and admitting such students? Perhaps it is the fear suggested by Alfred North Whitehead's observation that "so long as you are dealing with pure mathematics, you are in the realm of complete and absolute abstraction."[4] It is also perhaps a consequence of the fundamental human fear of change, although I do not think that the changes brought about by involving the math faculty are anything other than good for the university. The undergraduates at Stanford seemed to like things as they were and did not want to alter the characteristics of their undergraduate classmates. One senior majoring in political science pursued these thoughts in an article in the *Stanford Review*.[5] His line went as follows:

When I first visited Stanford as a Pro Fro in the spring of 1987, I was very impressed. The weather was beautiful, the campus was magnificent, and the people I met were quite interesting. They were outgoing, well-rounded, sociable, and seemed to party pretty hard.

Overall, I thought I had pretty much found heaven. Unlike certain other schools in its class, I thought Stanford would be a fun place to go to school while developing my intelligence. It was a unique place—quality academics, superb athletics, and cool people.

Unfortunately, what I did not realize in my naivete as a Pro Fro was the dramatic shift that was just then taking root. With the change of the dean of admissions two years earlier, the Faculty Senate put pressure on the department to recruit more one-track intellectual wonders.

In other words, since Dean Fetter took over, there has been a noticeable decline in the prevalence of well-rounded students in favor of those intellectually gifted in one way or another.

In more direct parlance, there is an increase in the number of dorks-nerds-geeks-tools or whatever word you choose. . . . Since Stanford achieved its impressive reputation by catering to a certain type of student, this will ultimately be the downfall of our university.

Apart from some obvious personal disagreements with this vocal Stanford senior, I would add that he manages to overlook the paradox between his claims and those of other Stanford undergraduates that the university is anti-intellectual; both camps can't be right. (The allegation of anti-intellectualism has been around Stanford for at least the past twenty years and under three different deans of undergraduate admissions. It is not uncommon for some students to complain that life in the dorms is anti-intellectual and that, considering the selectivity of the undergraduate population, they are disappointed with the level of discourse over dinner and in the lounges. I have heard similar criticisms at other selective colleges, and I remember the same kind of debate at my alma mater, Oxford University. One explanation could be that highly selective institutions admit students with high expectations. It is certainly true that any residential college or university faces a challenge in meeting, at all times, the expectations of a diverse and talented set of individuals. In any case, each undergraduate carries some responsibility for the quality of intellectual life on a campus.) I suppose it is not altogether surprising that the faculty and undergraduates might disagree about which student characteristics are desirable ones. From the perspective of those of us who worked in Undergraduate Admissions, the discussion provides yet another example of the delicate balance in creating a freshman class in the face of multiple competing interests.

On the popular subject of extreme talents, a related question of principle is, Why stop this further identification of talent with the field of mathematics? In fact, I initially thought that it would be beneficial to extend the process to creative writing, but this suggestion was not enthusiastically received by the faculty in the English department to whom my staff and I talked. Their general view was that the identification of writing talent in seventeen-year-olds is no easy assignment; in addition, the task could be overwhelming in an applicant pool of 15,000 or so high school seniors, many of whom would submit supplementary materials with the hope of boosting their chances of admission. In any case, we never embarked on this experiment at Stanford. Some colleges do encourage the submission of writing samples, but they are not used to measure creative writing talent.

The possibility of broadening the identification process to include other talents actually made some of my staff nervous. There was some consideration given to the question of access—an applicant who was fluent in four or five languages would bring a vibrancy to the academic community at the university, but such a student would either have grown up abroad or have been in a school system that consistently offered multiple foreign language courses from elementary school on. These options were not available to most applicants, and it seemed misguided to begin to attach value in the admissions process to opportunities that relatively few applicants could consistently attain. Not only were the staff concerned about adding complications in what is already a very complex process, but I believe there was also the concern of control. We were the admissions professionals; the responsibility of selecting the freshman class had been delegated to the dean (and, in practice, to the dean's staff). The role of faculty in the decision process, many staff felt, should have some well-defined boundaries. Fortunately, these concerns were moot since the Stanford faculty seemed content with their more limited role in evaluating talents in the creative and performing arts and in mathematics. Furthermore, there are natural limitations; talents in fields like history or engineering are not readily identified in seventeen-year-olds. Certainly, one of the rewards of working in a university is seeing academic interests blossom—watching the potential of an art history major develop out of an introductory course or observing the senior applying to materials science graduate programs when she may not have known the subject existed in her freshman year! In spite of the associated concerns and a few minor rumblings of discontent, the collaboration between Undergraduate Admissions and the faculty has been both useful and mutually beneficial, and a wealth of talent has been added to the university as a consequence.

ALUMNI CONSIDERATIONS

A publication of the Stanford Alumni Association in 1958 included an article by the chairman of the Admissions Committee of the Alumni Association, an organization that has long since disappeared from existence. The passage of time, however, has not changed the wisdom of the opening line: "No matter how you put it, there just isn't any diplomatic way of telling me my kid is stupid— even if he is," said a member of the association's Executive Board. The remark was prompted by a meeting "to consider ways to approach alumni whose children are denied admission—especially those who have been loyal workers for Stanford over the years and who could hardly help feeling temporarily that their efforts had not been appreciated." The article goes on to note that alumni enthusiasm for Stanford is dampened, among other things, by the fact that so many applicants who meet the stated minimum standards must be turned away.[6] *Plus ça change, plus c'est la même chose*. . . . Thirty-five years later, while the laments remain the same, the competition for admission to Stanford is even more intense, as Table 2 confirms.

TABLE 2
Admissions to the Freshman Class at Stanford University, 1960–90

Year	Number of applicants	Percentage admitted	Year	Number of applicants	Percentage admitted
1960	6,546	31%	1980	12,731	19
1965	7,689	25	1985	17,652	14
1970	9,880	23	1990	12,953	22
1975	9,730	25			

The Stanford numbers from the early 1950's provide an even more dramatic contrast; for example, 77 percent of the 2,014 freshman applicants in 1950 were offered admission, as were 85 percent of the 2,016 applicants in 1951. Since, roughly speaking, the Stanford classes between 1950 and 1965 are the parents of today's applicants, it is not surprising that alumni find it difficult to understand why their children-who-are-smarter-than-their-parents are denied admission to Stanford.

I was interested to learn, in the same Alumni Association magazine article of 1958, that the members of the Alumni Association Admissions Committee saw their function as "one only of satisfying ourselves that the criteria of selection are fair and flexible—and that they are consistently applied." Today, alumni play no such role, and the Faculty Senate's Committee on Undergraduate Admissions and Financial Aid has responsibility for the associated policies and procedures. This is, I think, the correct delegation of responsibility; in 1958 there was no Faculty Senate. Then, just as today, children of alumni were given special consideration in the admissions process. An obvious question to ask is, *Why?* The current criteria for admission simply state, without justification, "Children of Stanford graduates receive preference in choices among applicants of approximately equal qualifications." In 1958, the justification offered was that "strong family ties with Stanford are valuable in themselves." There is merit in examining more closely the reasons for special consideration afforded to these "legacies."

In another 1958 article about the consideration given to the children of alumni in the admissions process, the director of admissions, Rixford Snyder, began with the story of a disgruntled Princeton alumnus who wrote to the Princeton alumni magazine after his son had been denied admission. The alumnus admitted that while he knew his son couldn't make the grade academically, "why couldn't Princeton let him in for one term and then flunk him out so he'll at least qualify for membership in the Princeton Club of New York?"[7] (I doubt that anyone would find such an argument persuasive, but I also wouldn't be surprised that the alumnus was serious in his question.)

Dr. Snyder continued with the Stanford description:

Each year a substantial percentage of our applicants are legacies—sons and daughters of former Stanford students. Many have parents who met while undergraduates and thus are "double legacies." For many years, legacies have been given preference in the selection of successful candidates.

Those who clearly meet the competition for places are, of course, automatically admitted. All the rest are reviewed *individually* by the Admissions Committee. If they appear to have the academic and personal potential to succeed at Stanford, they may be accepted in preference to non-legacies whose qualifications are a little higher.

The Committee must always weigh carefully, however, the element of justice involved in this policy. It cannot, for example, assign places to legacies when doing so would exclude other candidates who have markedly superior qualifications. Likewise, if legacies do not meet the entrance requirements, or if they appear likely to flounder and become subject to academic dismissal, the Committee deems it no favor to admit them. . . .

With increasing competition for admission developing everywhere, it is becoming steadily more difficult for students academically disqualified at Stanford to gain admission to any other institution of higher learning. What favor has the Committee done for a student if it admits him to satisfy the parents, when by doing so it jeopardizes not only the education of these young people, but in many instances their entire future lives?"[8]

The same article describes the "minimum requirements" in 1958 for an applicant to be "eligible" for the competitive selection process at Stanford, including "a minimum of 11 college recommending or certificate units earned during the 10th, 11th, and 12th grades ('A' or 'B' in most high schools)." In addition, "he must make a satisfactory score on the Scholastic Aptitude test given by the College Entrance Examination Board." What a "satisfactory score" actually meant was not specified, but the statement clearly implies some range or cutoff on the SAT. Today, of course, no minimum requirements are specified. (Ironically, the competition for admission is much tougher than it was in the 1950's and 1960's.) And today eleven B grades would not make an applicant competitive at Stanford. Admission requirements aside, however, the question still unanswered is, *Why* do legacies merit special preference?

I tried to answer this question directly in a special letter that was sent in early February each year, beginning in 1985, to the Stanford applicants who identified themselves as legacies in their applications. This letter was an attempt to be responsive to complaints we had heard from alumni that the Stanford admissions process was not as sensitive to the children of alumni as those of some other colleges and universities were. Writing such a letter, however, creates a catch-22 situation, as you will see. The 1991 letter, after some preliminary greetings, continued straightforwardly enough:

We noted on one of your forms that you are the son/daughter [as appropriate—the letters were personally addressed and tailored] of a Stanford graduate, and I thought this would be a good time to tell you and your family what this means to us in the Office of Undergraduate Admissions. The ties of the Stanford family have been important right from the signing of the University's founding grant by Senator Leland and Jane Stanford. We value the loyalty and devotion of the Stanford community, particularly as seen in the commitment of alumni to the values of the University. This commitment is never more apparent than in the applications we receive from their children, such as you. It is reassuring to see that the University experiences of many Stanford parents are so valuable that their sons and daughters also are interested in what the University has to offer.

It is, of course, reasonable for you to ask in what way being a Stanford "legacy" might help your application. You may have read already in one of our publications the answer to this question. When an applicant is in the top part of the applicant group, and where all other things are equal, the fact that one or both of the applicant's parents graduated from Stanford will be weighed in our decision.

In practice, over the past few years, this has contributed to a higher admission rate for alumni children. Last year, for example, 2,874 students (22.2 percent) were offered admission from a total of 12,953 applicants. In this class, and over the past decade, alumni children were admitted to the freshman class at almost twice this rate. Even with this higher acceptance rate, however, applications for undergraduate admission to Stanford are part of an increasingly competitive program.

I provide this information not to send any implicit message about your own chance for admission, but to reassure you on a number of points that may well concern you about your application. We *will* take note of your Stanford legacy. We *will not* admit you simply because you are the son/daughter of a Stanford graduate. The latter point is important not only because it would be unfair to you if we were to offer admission on this consideration alone, but also because it would be unfair to those who are not the children of Stanford alumni.

This letter raises a number of immediate issues for the recipient. First, some egalitarian applicants feel strongly that they want to be admitted solely on their own merits, and they believe that the alumni status of their parents should play no part in the process; I had some letters to support this view. Second, the description is (necessarily) vague about how the practice actually works for legacy applicants; what does "weighed in our decision" mean? The reader of Chapter 2 is now in a position to understand the details (which would be too cumbersome to include in a letter such as that quoted above). When the first or second reader of an application is debating between a recommendation of "admit" and "swim," or "swim" and "deny," the fact that the applicant is a legacy should tip the balance to the more favorable recommendation. It is this tipping of the balance that results in a much more favorable admit rate for legacies. Of course, just as some would argue that any such tip is unfair, there are some alumni who have argued that the tip should be much more generous. The latter view presents a dangerously slippery slope for an admissions officer: at one extreme is the position of admitting all legacies; less extreme, but still very generous, is to admit all legacies who we think could graduate from Stanford, irrespective of the quality of the pool; a variation on the latter case is to add the further alumni-parent condition of demonstrated loyalty to the university. All of these are difficult judgments for the conscientious admissions officer who is well aware of the overall competition for admission.

Although Stanford has been criticized for being less generous in its "legacy tip" than some other selective universities, the university is in fact more generous than some in its definition of "alumnus." At Stanford, an alumnus is defined as any holder of a Stanford degree, graduate or undergraduate; in a typical year, about 5 percent of the applicants, and about 10–12 percent of the enrolling freshman class, would be legacies. Most private universities define an alumnus as the holder of an undergraduate degree only (I suppose this stance follows the reasoning that such degrees engender the most loyalty). I specify private universities because few public universities even consider legacy status in the undergraduate admissions process. This point was brought home to me in a rather public way when I was invited to appear on a morning television talk show with my counterpart from UC Berkeley. A member of the audience asked us both what influence a parent's degree had on the application of a child for freshman admission. I answered first, with an abbreviated form of the explanation above. Members of the audience hissed to demonstrate their disapproval of the perceived inequities in the Stanford admissions process. My counterpart from the public sector was able to answer unequivocally, "None," and his reply was much more favorably received.

The same view was presented by a University of California faculty member, together with a colleague from Bryn Mawr College, in a somewhat scathing article that appeared in the *New York Times*. The authors reported on a two-year investigation by the Office for Civil Rights at Harvard of charges of discrimination against Asian-Americans in admission to its freshman class. The investigation concluded:

Asian American applicants to Harvard were admitted at significantly lower rates than white applicants despite statistics suggesting that the two groups were similarly qualified. The higher admission rate for whites, said the Federal report, is largely explained by the preference given to "legacies"—the children of alumni—and to recruited athletes, two groups at Harvard that are predominantly white.

Such preferences were deemed "legally permissible" and "legitimate." Secretary of Education Lauro F. Cavazos described them as consonant with our nation's "principles of justice and equity."

Yet giving preference to the children of alumni—long a standard practice in the leading private colleges—may properly be described as affirmative action for the privileged. In 1988, the last year investigated, 280 of 1,602 Harvard freshmen, more than one in six, had fathers who had attended Harvard. Roughly 40 percent of alumni children are admitted each year as against 14 percent of non-alumni children, with alumni children who do not apply for aid enjoying a significantly greater advantage still. Yet these offspring of alumni possess qualifications that are, at best, slightly above the mean. If 'legacies' had been admitted in 1988 at the same rate as other applicants, their numbers in the freshman class would have dropped by close to 200—a figure that exceeds the total number of blacks, Mexican Americans, Puerto Ricans and Native Americans enrolled in the entire freshman class.

The professors go on to note that the preferential treatment for underrepresented minorities in college admissions is "the one type of affirmative action singled out for the most intense legal, political and moral scrutiny," yet it is also

the single policy designed to benefit groups historically denied the opportunity to attend elite colleges and universities. . . . Attention has focused selectively on those programs that benefit the historically excluded, while the often larger programs that favor the already privileged have been ignored. . . . The real question, therefore, is: which qualities of applicants will receive preferential treatment and whose interests will be served by such programs? [9]

I must admit that the authors, professors Jerome Karabel and David Karen, make a good point. For the most part, the special consideration afforded legacies in the admissions process is indeed "affirmative action for the privileged." Alumni parents of children who are denied admission often see the denials as a consequence of the places' being offered to minority students. (These critics forget a relevant fact: a few legacy applicants today are themselves minorities.) Of course the admissions selection process doesn't operate in such a quid-pro-quo fashion, but it is true that the exercise has zero-sum limitations. Harvard is also not alone in explaining the lower admit rates of Asian-Americans by the preference given to legacies and athletes. A comparable study at Stanford (presented in more detail in the next chapter) found results similar to Harvard's. In fact, I would be willing to wager that the analysis of Asian-American admissions, and the associated explanation of the differential admit rates, would be similar at most private colleges and universities.

Clearly, in the special consideration given to legacies, alumni children benefit from the connections of their parents; and colleges and universities benefit from the continued loyalty of the associated alumni, usually through financial contributions. Is such a mutual benefit wrong? Not, I think, if all other things are equal. As one who has made the decisions, however, I will admit that it does not always seem fair or right, particularly in times of increased competition, for some applicants to be disadvantaged only because they lack an institutional connection.

In her book *Democratic Education*, Professor Amy Gutmann cites Justice Felix Frankfurter's "four essential freedoms" of universities, including that of deciding who is admitted to study. She comments:

Nobody doubts that the freedom to decide "who may be admitted to study" is essential to a university's ability to maintain its own academic and associational standards, but many doubt how absolute this "essential freedom" should be. This doubt raises some of the hardest and most controversial questions concerning the distribution of higher education. . . .

An admissions committee is free to set nonacademic qualifications within three principled bounds. Each nonacademic qualification must be (1) publicly defensible, (2) related to the purposes to which the university is publicly dedicated, and (3) related to associational purposes that are themselves consistent with the academic purposes that define a university as such. These three criteria leave ample room for different universities to count different characteristics as qualifications (and to weigh the same characteristics differently), depending on their particular associational purposes.[10]

Whether the preferential treatment of legacies meets these three criteria, all of which seem eminently reasonable on the surface, is debatable. The question is not one considered by Professor Gutmann, who focuses instead on racial considerations. The U.S. Department of Education has been asked to consider whether the preferential treatment of legacies is actually discriminatory; in the 1990 investigation at Harvard, the Department of Education said it was legitimate for colleges to give preference to children of alumni. According to the most recent reports, the U.S. Commission on Civil Rights has said the issue "deserves to be debated and articulated by the larger community of legal scholars and civil-rights advocates against the broader context of civil-rights enforcement."[11] The outcome of such debate could alter the makeup of freshman classes at selective private institutions.

OTHER FAMILY CONNECTIONS: SIBLINGS, TWINS, AND TRIPLETS

When the question of special consideration for legacies arises in any public discussion of freshman admissions, an inevitable follow-up question relates to that of siblings. What influence does the fact that a brother or sister is enrolled at, or graduated from, Stanford have in the admissions decision of a sibling applicant? Although we do ask applicants a question about relatives ("If any of your relatives have attended Stanford, check the box to the right and list their names, relationship to you, and year of graduation"), we do this more out of general interest, and with an eye to sensitivity of relationships, than for any reason of process. The truth is that each applicant is considered on his or her merits, and the decisions on siblings are made independently.

I received a number of letters, over the years, from parents who would make pleas of a different persuasion. They would proudly cite the achievements and record of first-child-enrolled-at-Stanford and then go on to argue that second-child-and-current-applicant was as good as, if not better than, the first; therefore, we should be sure to admit child number two. When I acknowledged such letters, I explained the principle of independent decisions, but I also pointed out a flaw in the parental argument: if first-child-enrolled had *not* had a good record, would they make the counterargument for second-child-and-current-applicant? In both cases, I think the principle of making independent decisions is a sound one. There are, however, a number of associated pitfalls. In any given year, the competition among applicants varies somewhat. This means that first-child might have applied in a year when the competition was less fierce than that in the year when second-child (who actually has a stronger record) applies; if we admitted first-child and deny second-child, the decisions undoubtedly appear inconsistent to both the siblings and their parents. A variation on this theme appears when the references of one sibling are much more compelling than those of the academically stronger sibling, or the self-presentation of one sibling is much more effective than that of the sibling with the stronger academic record. Again, the outcomes could be decisions that not only appear inconsistent, but also are not easily defended when the parents challenge and compare.

We received about twenty sets of applications from twins in any given year and perhaps one set from triplets every other year. These family relationships make for particularly sensitive decisions, especially if the siblings are personally close but academically far apart. Consequently, we had the custom of keeping the two (or three) applications bound together with a rubber band so that in the random distribution of files to readers, we guaranteed that the twins and triplets were all read together. This procedure did not alter the guiding principle of making a decision based on the individual, but it did help to ensure consistency in the case of close calls as well as a general sensitivity to the circumstances. The decisions on twins covered the range of combinations: both were admitted; one was admitted and the other denied; and both were denied—with a few other combinations when we throw in the wait-list decisions. When I described this procedure to Stanford undergraduates, I think they were reassured to learn that they were admitted as individuals on the basis of their own merits and not simply offered a place on the coattails of a sibling.

Twice in my seven years in undergraduate admissions we admitted identical triplets, one set male and the other female. Alas, we lost all six of them to other universities. The male triplets were an interesting admissions case study because one selective college accepted two of them but not the third—a decision that struck me as very odd; the three of them finished up in different institutions. The female triplets stayed together, but not at Stanford. Another year, the *Stanford Daily* ran a joke article about the admission of triplets, actually nonexistent, complete with photograph and an invented and amusing interview. The day the article was published, I got a slightly panicked call from the staff member in the housing office responsible for freshmen to ask why we hadn't alerted them to admitting triplets. It took a few phone calls to set the record straight.

UNIVERSITY DONORS

At any meeting on freshman admissions, a question from the audience that was guaranteed to capture the attention of prospective applicants and their parents went as follows: "What role does a large gift to Stanford play in an admissions decision on a family member?" The short and deceptively simple answer to such a question is that places in the freshman class are earned, not bought; but the careful reader of this book will appreciate that few issues in admissions can be adequately explained with such brevity and simplicity.

Frequently, misunderstandings arose about the role of financial contributions to Stanford. More than one alumnus was under the false impression that large gifts to the university could, and indeed should, guarantee a place in the freshman class to associated family members. One alum went so far as to ask me when the policy had changed about donations to the university guaranteeing a place!

While it is absolutely true that student places are earned and not bought, it would be disingenuous of any dean of admissions to claim that donors to the university are ignored. In any university, all of the key offices are interdependent: what happens in the admissions office has inevitable repercussions in the president's office and the development office; the kind of students admitted has consequences for each of the academic departments, the office of the dean of students, and the alumni association—to mention a few of the most obvious interdependencies. In particular, it is important for the dean of undergraduate admissions to be fully informed and aware of the repercussions that admissions decisions might have with major donors; to think otherwise would be both professionally naive and injudicious. After all, no major university in the United States is without an office of development; in times of increased concern about financial resources and stability, institutions depend on the loyalty, commitment, and generosity of alumni and other friends. It is no news to anyone, but rather a fact of life in higher education, that university presidents spend a large fraction of their time raising money.

But for a dean of undergraduate admissions to be aware of, and sensitive to, fund-raising implications is far from saying that the development office or the university president has any control over admissions decisions. As the criteria for admissions explicitly state, "The Dean of Undergraduate Admissions retains final authority over all admissions." In the long haul, such a policy has distinct advantages for varsity athletics coaches and the director of athletics (although some of them may not see it that way some of the time!), just as it does for vice presidents of development and even the university president. I am glad to say that in my seven-year tenure as dean, I never once felt pressure from the president or vice presidents to admit specific applicants. Unfortunately, I do not think that all of my counterparts could make the same claim; for me, it would have been difficult to remain in the job if the circumstances had been otherwise. When the president of Stanford received appeals from alumni or donors to pay particular attention to an admissions case, he always responded that he played no role in admissions decisions and that he was passing the request on to the dean of admissions. Of course, this did not mean that he was spared the associated complaints, and they came like clockwork in April of every year.

Among my most difficult and painful admissions decisions were those to deny applications from the children and grandchildren of university trustees and generous friends of Stanford. I am indebted to at least one honest and understanding trustee who readily admitted that it was much easier to talk to disappointed alumni and others about admissions decisions because, after all, his own child had not been admitted. Obviously, adherence to the principle that places must be earned and not bought (or owed for service) implies that not all applications from the relatives of donors will be admitted. The difficult part is in deciding where to draw the line when all considerations are taken into account. Certainly some alumni believed that my calls were too tough and consequently a disservice to the university. On balance, I would prefer to err in that direction than the other and to maintain the essential integrity of the process. This path was not always an easy one to live with, and even talk of "integrity of the process" seems to smack of self-righteousness. Nevertheless, parents who decided to withhold further contributions to the university because of their disappointment with an admissions decision seemed to me fair-weather friends.

The admissions process involving university donors needs to be conducted with full integrity, knowledge, sensitivity, and fairness. The qualities of honesty and good judgment are never more tested; good communication is essential. When I have moments of regret at having left such a rewarding responsibility in undergraduate admissions, it helps to remind myself that these tough calls are behind me.

FACULTY AND STAFF

As I have mentioned, some of the most painful admissions decisions that I was called on to make involved extraordinarily loyal and generous friends of the university. In many such cases, however, I was not personally acquainted with the individuals, a fact that mercifully allowed for some personal and emotional detachment. After having lived on the Stanford campus for almost 25 years, I could not say the same about Stanford faculty and staff and their children, many of whom had become good friends and were long-standing colleagues and neighbors.

According to the criteria for undergraduate admission, "children of eligible faculty and staff receive favorable consideration . . . provided they meet the basic requirements." As in the case of the special consideration of alumni children, it is useful to question the legitimacy of such a proviso.

Like all universities, Stanford has a faculty and staff benefits program; at many universities, this includes a supplemental compensation plan for faculty and staff with children in college. The purpose of the plan is to assist with the cost of providing undergraduate college education for eligible children (those who are natural or adopted, and foster and stepchildren within specific time limitations). The plan provides salary supplements for eligible faculty and staff whose children attend accredited institutions. After July 1, 1985, the plan specified that "the University will increase the participant's gross salary by an amount equal to the tuition or required fees charged by the eligible institution in which a participating child is enrolled, up to a maximum for each school year of one half the then-current Stanford tuition, PLUS 33 percent." The plan then makes payments based on four years of work toward a bachelor's degree at the educational institution attended by the student.

When my husband and I came to Stanford in 1965, then the parents of one child, the tuition grant program was different in a significant way. Faculty and staff could choose between an option that offered full tuition at Stanford or up to half of Stanford's tuition payable to cover the costs of attending another university or college. As many parents did, we decided that it was unreasonable to expect that our daughter would want to attend Stanford (or even that she would be admitted), so we opted for the alternative elsewhere. At that time I was not working in undergraduate admissions, so I was unaware of the pressures that such a tuition benefit plan imposed on the dean of admissions. To quote from the annual report of 1978–79 from the oversight Committee on Undergraduate Admissions and Financial Aids:

The natural result [of the tuition benefit] was intense pressure on the Admissions Office to give special consideration to faculty and staff children. Although not formally articulated, the practice was generally to accept all sons and daughters of faculty and staff members so long as they could be expected to graduate.

Subsequently, the tuition fringe benefit has been changed generally to provide one-half tuition at any institution, thus alleviating the need to enroll at Stanford. At the same time, however, admission to topflight colleges and universities has become much more difficult as more and more applications have been received. As a result, the pressures on the Admissions Office to admit children of faculty and staff members have shifted but not altered substantially. And those pressures are now most intense with respect to children who have academic records so poor that they are clearly precluded from admission to other topflight schools. Moreover, as a result of rumors arising from ambiguities that necessarily flow from an admissions policy not subjected to quantification, plus fond hopes for the future of their children, some faculty and staff members have formed an unrealistic expectation that admission of their children to Stanford will be virtually automatic.

All of this has put a strain on the Admissions Office. It has asked the Committee to determine the extent, if any, of the special consideration to be given to faculty children and to publicize the policy so as to avoid painful confrontations that sometimes have resulted when a child has been denied admission. The Committee unanimously supports the position that poorly qualified students should not be admitted merely because their parents receive Stanford paychecks. Therefore it should be made clear that faculty and staff children have not been and will not be automatically admitted and that admission will be denied to those who do not meet basic requirements of intellectual capacity and personal achievement. Faculty and staff children who do meet these criteria will receive favorable consideration.[12]

The current statement uses the same phrase in describing successful applicants who are children of Stanford faculty and staff: "They meet the basic requirements." "Basic requirements" are not precisely defined, but the implication is that successful applicants meet the general criteria of academic achievement and potential, achievement outside the classroom, and personal qualities, all as described in the full statement of the criteria for admission.

This implication is, of course, more than a little vague; the achievements of faculty and staff children must also be considered in the context of the overall applicant pool, another reason why we publish annually an academic profile of applicants, admitted students, and enrolling students. In a typical year, we received about 75 applications from students whose parents were employed at Stanford, a small proportion of the total applicant pool. The Stanford faculty and staff parents of unsuccessful applicants are, alas, often unaware of the competition, and their disappointment on hearing of the admissions decision is often intense. I made every effort to notify personally such faculty and staff, expressing regret that the decision was not one of admission, but every year without fail I had some very difficult conversations with these parents. The easiest discussions were those that simply followed up on my offer to review alternative college plans; some parents asked pointed questions about the caliber of the applicant pool or wanted to verify that we had not overlooked specific qualifications of their son or daughter; others were less understanding and very critical of the decision, inevitably with some reference to the prospect of diminished commitment to the university; at least two faculty and staff members now ignore me on campus—not a pleasant circumstance, but such consequences seem to be an unfortunate accompaniment to the job.

The discomfort is not limited to the admissions office. Successful applicants to Stanford who are seniors in local high schools, and whose parents work at Stanford, often face cynical comments from their peers, or behind-the-back-whispers. The typical description bandied about on local high school campuses in recent years is "faculty brats." Along the same lines, there were also my regular visits, after admissions decisions were mailed, from one or more of these seniors. Understandably, they sought reassurance that they had not been admitted to Stanford simply because their parents worked at the university. Some successful applicants chose not to attend Stanford because they wanted to establish an independent identity at a school with which their parents were not associated. I am sure that this phenomenon is common to faculty families at colleges and universities across the country; fortunately, there are plenty of excellent colleges to absorb the children of faculty as far from home territory as they might wish.

One of the more unfortunate circumstances associated with applications from children of faculty and staff is mistaken identification. Fortunately, such occurrences are rare, but the magnitude of the repercussions tends to compensate for the quantity. When students complete their freshman applications, they are asked to list the occupation and employer of both parents. If "Stanford University" is listed as the employer, the admissions office checks with the university benefits office to confirm that the employee is eligible for the tuition grant program. During my seven years, a couple of employees were, through innocent but unfortunate human error, mistakenly confirmed as ineligible when in fact both were eligible. The associated decisions were denials, and both were subsequently challenged, one by a parent and one by the applicant. When we double-checked on the eligibility, I was dismayed to discover the mistakes. Since it seemed grossly unfair to penalize the applicants for mistakes that were not of their making, I decided to change the decision and deal with the delicate consequences. In one case, I actually called the applicant's high school guidance counselor to explain the circumstances; this was a small private school and the well-informed counselor would have been disconcerted by the reversed decision if there had been no explanation. I outlined the circumstances, apologized for the error and the consequences, and was surprised by the counselor's disbelief at the special consideration afforded to faculty and staff children—and that is at least one good reason why the program merits an explanation here.

The guiding principles in making these faculty and staff decisions are similar to those for alumni and donors. All need to be handled with the sensitivity deserved by loyal and hardworking Stanford employees who have made valuable contributions to the university. At the same time, all places in the freshman class must be earned. The consideration is special because of the ties to the Stanford family, but there are inevitable limits on how far such consideration can extend. The crux of the matter, as in all considerations in selective admissions, is where the lines should be drawn. Unfortunately, the limits are not always easily defined.

5

Affirmative Action

As the twentieth century spins towards its close . . . it is hard to
hold an honest conversation about affirmative action.
—Stephen L. Carter, *Reflections of an Affirmative Action Baby*, 1991

A TYPICAL COMPLAINT

In any given year, three or four topics dominate the letters-written-
in-fury to deans of undergraduate admissions. Always at or near the
top of the list is the issue of affirmative action. Alumni were the
most frequent writers, and typically the complainants would send
copies of their letters to the president of the university and every
member of the Board of Trustees.

After a few years of receiving such letters, I found that their content was quite predictable. In 1991, for example, one alumnus noted
that the accepted freshman class was 52 percent white, 3 percent
international, and 45 percent ethnic minorities. His concerns were
threefold: that there had been significant increases in the percentages of Asian-Americans, African-Americans, Mexican-Americans,
and Native American Indians in the freshman class; that there was
no correlation between the representations of these ethnic groups
at Stanford and in the national population; and that white students

who would have been admitted if the ethnic breakdown had been more representative had consequently been denied admission. He argued that such a situation amounted to reverse discrimination against white students, and concluded with the assertion that the admissions policies at Stanford had been developed in response to pressure from minorities.

A debate class could have a field day with the unsupported arguments and assumptions in this particular letter. Even after seven years in the job, I never ceased to be amazed at the unabashed confidence of the complaining correspondents, none of whom had ever read a single application for admission or even informed themselves on the policies and procedures of the office, not to mention other relevant facts. In responding to an angry surgeon who had written with a similar complaint, I asked how he would feel if I came into his operating room and told him how to conduct the operation. For some reason, the profession of admissions is considered one in which a critical layperson, whose solitary qualification is having had a son or daughter go through the application process, becomes an instant expert. As was my usual approach, I began my response to the letter summarized above with some facts, enclosing a current application with the detailed description of the criteria for admission. I continued:

The section immediately relevant to your letter concerns the University's commitment to minority students. "A few categories of applicants receive special consideration provided they meet basic requirements of academic excellence and personal achievement. Stanford University is committed to a substantial representation of Blacks, Mexican Americans, and Native American Indians in the undergraduate student body. . . ." As part of this commitment, we seek out the most talented African American, Mexican American, and Native American Indian students nationwide. I have also enclosed some minority newspapers that are part of this outreach effort.

I then gave him an ethnic breakdown of the admitted freshman class for 1991 and for comparison added the same data for 1986, along with percentages of the national population of minority students. These figures are shown here in Table 3. Although Stanford admits students from every state, approximately 42 percent of

TABLE 3

Ethnic Breakdown of Freshmen Admitted to Stanford,
1986 and 1991

Ethnic group	1986 Stanford admittees	1991 Stanford admittees	National population of 15–17-year-olds (1987)
African-American	7.7%	8.9%	13.5%
Mexican-American	7.3	9.5	5.3
Native American Indian	1.6	1.3	0.7
Asian-American	15.4	23.7	2.5
International	2.9	4.3	—
White	64.3	50.7	75.0
Declined to state	.8	1.6	3.0

SOURCE: For Stanford statistics, Office of Undergraduate Admissions, Stanford; for national population statistics, U.S. Bureau of the Census, *Current Population Reports* (Washington, D.C.: GPO, 1988).

TABLE 4

Breakdown by Race of California's Population of 15–19-Year-Olds,
1985 and 1990

Race	1985 No.	1985 Pct.	1990 No.	1990 Pct.	Percentage change, 1985–90
White	1,102,004	56.0%	884,857	47.5%	−8.5
Black	189,442	9.5	164,080	8.5	−1.0
Hispanic	508,048	25.5	625,823	33.5	+8.0
Asian-American	180,760	9.0	200,615	10.5	+1.5

SOURCE: California Department of Finance, Population Research Unit, "Projected Total Population for California by Race/Ethnicity" (Sacramento, Calif.: February 1988).

our applicants come from California, so I also gave him the ethnic breakdown for California's youth (see Table 4).

The information I provided showed that, contrary to the assertions in his letter, the only significant increase in admission rates in recent years has been among Asian-American students, who are not targeted for special consideration. Indeed, African-Americans are underrepresented when we compare Stanford admittees with the national population, and Mexican-Americans are underrepresented when compared with the California population.

The question of Asian-American representation prompts an important, related comment. In recent years, some selective universities—including Harvard, UCLA, UC Berkeley, Brown, and Stanford—have been charged with discrimination against Asian-Americans in the admissions process. An internal review at Stanford in 1985–86 found that Asian-Americans were, in fact, *underadmitted* when their admission rate was compared with that for white students. Consequently, I was asked to report to the Committee on Undergraduate Admissions and Financial Aids (C-UAFA) annually on comparative admission rates for Asian-Americans and whites. The differential in admission rates, though small, persists, and it can be accounted for by the admission preferences given both to children of alumni and to recruited athletes, two groups in which Asian-Americans are rare. My correspondent was probably surprised to learn that some people consider the preference for alumni children in itself discriminatory. I pointed out to him that Senator Bob Dole had written to the secretary of education, Lamar Alexander, requesting a review of the practice of alumni preference.

As is often the case, I had no response from this complainant. I hope he was convinced of my case and not simply dismissive of it. Perhaps it is expecting too much to want to know, but these are important matters of principle to those of us in admissions, and having the truth, rather than wild rumors, circulating among alumni is important to the university's relations with the community. Some correspondents send a gracious acknowledgment of our reply, but further correspondence is the exception rather than the rule.

Although the subject of affirmative action in undergraduate admissions at Stanford continues to be highly current, its history begins about twenty years ago. I should inform the reader that at Stanford, unlike some other institutions, affirmative action applies only to minority students and not to women. Stanford has been a coeducational university since its founding in 1885. The criteria for undergraduate admission make no mention of special consideration for women. In fact, we do not read files by applicant's gender at any point during the selection process. By contrast, some colleges, usually those that were all male in earlier years, have special goals for the admission of women. It is our good fortune that the female applicant pool is exceptionally strong, as the admit rates confirm. The admit rate for men in 1991 was 19 percent, for women 21 percent. The entering class of 1991 was 47 percent female, a reflection primarily of the lower number of women applicants. With these facts in mind, this discussion of affirmative action is limited to ethnic minorities.

THE BEGINNING OF AFFIRMATIVE ACTION AT STANFORD

The moral problem of American racism was tackled head-on by Gunnar Myrdal 50 years ago, in his book *An American Dilemma*, at a time when people of color were unquestionably not treated as the equals of whites.[1] Two decades passed before the first published mention of special consideration for minorities in college admissions was to appear. In 1966, the director of admissions emeritus at MIT, B. Alden Thresher, wrote a short book analyzing the practice of admissions.[2] Today the text sounds, in places, jarringly sexist in its language, but at the time the book was hailed as an exemplary guide to the practice of admissions. It is a telling commentary that even in the mid-1960's the subject of minorities merited no more than a dozen lines in some 90 pages of text.

The subject first received serious consideration at Stanford in 1968, in a comprehensive university review entitled *The Study of Education at Stanford*.[3] One of the ten reports that the study comprised focused on undergraduate admissions and financial aid. This 80-page report made 28 recommendations, eight of which related to minority admissions and a ninth to financial aid for these students. The Black Student Union at Stanford was also making its voice heard at this time, with the assassination of Martin Luther King, Jr., providing a catalyst for change. The key recommendation in the admissions section was, "Admissions and procedures should favor applicants from minority groups." The text of the report explained, "Stanford has long been a white, middle- and upper-middle-class university. This fact does not distinguish it from any other leading American private college or university or from most public ones" (p. 59). The report goes on to provide some "history since 1960 of Negro freshman applications and admissions." No data on other ethnic groups were cited for Stanford; and "minority" seemed to be used synonymously with black. In 1960, there were six "Negro" applicants, three of whom were admitted. By 1967, the number of black applicants had increased to 114, of whom 52 were admitted and 37 enrolled. The report also cited Stanford's dean of admissions as saying, "Minority group students are judged essentially 'outside the competition.' That is to say they, like athletes and children of faculty members, must meet the University's basic entrance requirements, but they need not be more qualified than all rejected applicants" (p. 62). The faculty and student authors of this report conclude by regretting the absence of minority undergraduates: "We may be getting the best [students], but they are only the best of a partial universe. . . . We believe that each institution must find its own unique strengths and put them to the service of social justice" (p. 67).

About a year after the publication of this report, C-UAFA proposed special financial aid packages, first for black and a little later for Chicano and Native American Indian students. By the end of the 1960's, then, Stanford University was targeting black, Mexican-American, and Native American Indian students for undergraduate admission. It appears, however, that no policy was formulated to guide decisions concerning the future targeting of additional groups, and no time limitation was placed on the newly approved practices. In 1969, Undergraduate Admissions hired its first full-time black and Chicano directors—and the first steps were taken on a significant road to change at Stanford.

PROGRESS AT STANFORD, 1970–90

The changes in the enrollment of targeted minorities at Stanford are immediately apparent from Table 5. While there have clearly been some fluctuations in the enrollment of targeted minorities since 1970—which at least confirms my claim that Stanford has no

TABLE 5
Freshman Admission Data for Targeted Minorities at Stanford, 1970–90

	1970	1975	1980	1985	1990
Total					
All applicants	9,880	9,730	12,731	17,652	12,953
Admitted	2,243	2,442	2,415	2,507	2,874
Enrolled	1,401	1,501	1,558	1,530	1,600
Yield rate	62%	61%	65%	61%	56%
Black					
Admitted	134	148	193	205	213
Enrolled	78	92	109	122	101
Yield rate	58%	62%	56%	60%	47%
Percentage of enrolled freshmen	6%	6%	7%	8%	6%
Chicano					
Admitted	92	120	170	225	266
Enrolled	71	86	109	152	159
Yield rate	77%	72%	64%	68%	60%
Percentage of enrolled freshmen	5%	6%	7%	10%	10%
American Indian					
Admitted	31	11	12	17	29
Enrolled	22	7	8	13	16
Yield rate	71%	64%	67%	76%	55%
Percentage of enrolled freshmen	1%	1%	1%	1%	1%

quotas—there has been a general, if modest, upward trend. During my tenure Mexican-Americans reached a high of 10 percent of the entering class in 1985, and blacks made up 10.1 percent of the entering class in 1988; the change in the percentage of Native American Indians is not apparent because of the small number enrolling, but again the trend is generally upward. It is interesting to note that the yield rate for blacks has been slightly lower than the overall yield rate for freshmen, whereas the yield rate for Mexican-Americans has been higher than the overall rate. Again, the small absolute number of Native Americans distorts the significance of the yield rate for this group.

Another helpful way of viewing Stanford's progress in the enrollment of targeted minority undergraduates is to compare the Stanford data with those from the universities with which we have the greatest overlap in admitted students. Table 6 shows a three-year comparison with Harvard, Yale, Princeton, MIT, and Dartmouth, the last college being included because of its long-standing commitment to Native American Indian students.

The data in Table 6 confirm that Stanford has a good comparative national record in the admission of targeted minorities. In some years it has enrolled the largest number of students from a particular

TABLE 6

Minority Freshmen at Six Universities, 1986–88

	Total in class	Black		Hispanic (includes Mexican-American)		Native American Indian	
		No.	Pct.	No.	Pct.	No.	Pct.
Class entering 1988							
Stanford	1,602	162	10%	162	10%	17	1%
Harvard	1,602	136	8	89	6	n.a.	n.a.[a]
Yale	1,275	98	8	61	5	n.a.	n.a.
Princeton	1,130	70	6	54	5	n.a.	n.a.
MIT	999	86	9	99	10	n.a.	n.a.
Dartmouth	1,090	91	8	38	3	n.a.	n.a.
Class entering 1987							
Stanford	1,529	129	8	140	9	13	1
Harvard	1,602	135	8	86	5	9	1
Yale	1,312	103	8	70	5	3	<1
Princeton	1,141	75	7	47	4	8	1
MIT	1,001	68	7	79	8	2	<1
Dartmouth	1,070	79	7	27	3	30	3
Class entering 1986							
Stanford	1,575	108	7	134	9	13	1
Harvard	1,600	104	7	84	5	4	<1
Yale	1,291	84	7	51	4	4	<1
Princeton	1,128	72	6	50	4	2	<1
MIT	991	59	6	58	6	4	<1
Dartmouth	1,035	49	5	15	1	17	2

SOURCE: Personal communications with the admissions offices of the institutions listed.

[a]N.a. means "not available."

TABLE 7
Asian-American Freshmen at Stanford, 1982–90

Year	Number admitted	Number enrolled	Yield	Percentage of total enrolled
1982	205	116	57%	7%
1984	221	132	60	8
1986	388	245	63	16
1988	439	256	58	16
1990	699	385	55	24

ethnic group, Hispanics being the most consistent example. Although Asian-Americans have never been a targeted minority group for undergraduate admissions at Stanford, it is important to set forth the recent history of their enrollment, too. No such statistics were kept before 1982, and from 1982 to 1986 there were some inconsistencies in record keeping; in particular, from 1982 to 1986 Asian-Americans who were permanent residents of the United States were counted among international students. Nevertheless, the trend in the enrollment of freshman Asian-Americans at Stanford is striking. Because the counting of Asian-Americans was modified in 1986, we estimate that 2 percent of the increase in the Asian-American enrolling class is attributable to the inclusion of students who were permanent residents. Nonetheless, as Table 7 illustrates, the Asian-American enrollment at Stanford has clearly shown a significant increase in recent years even though Asian-Americans have not been a targeted minority.

In the mid-1970's, a proposal was made to C-UAFA that Asian-American applicants, or at least low-income Asian-American applicants, be given the same special consideration as black, Mexican-American, and Native American Indian applicants. C-UAFA did not accept this proposal, but the dean of admissions supported the development of a recruitment brochure addressed to Asian-Americans. In 1985, C-UAFA appointed a subcommittee to investigate charges (brought by an Asian-American undergraduate) of discrimination against Asian-Americans in the admissions process. In its 1985–86 annual report to the Faculty Senate, C-UAFA detailed its findings.

The central fact was that while Asian Americans were being admitted to Stanford in numbers proportionally much larger than their representation in the California and U.S. populations, the rate at which they had been admitted had been consistently lower than that for white students. Generally similar conditions have prevailed at other universities. Between 1982 and 1985 . . . Asian American applicants to Stanford had admission rates ranging between 66 percent and 70 percent of the admission rates for whites. . . . The subcommittee found no factor that they analyzed could completely explain the differential. . . . They found that it did not arise from an implicit quota, nor from lesser academic/non-academic ratings for Asian Americans; nor from the interaction of ethnicity with other factors such as gender or geographic origin.

The subcommittee concluded that there was no evidence of conscious bias on the part of the admissions staff, but it did make a series of recommendations that were subsequently approved for action by the Faculty Senate:

I. C-UAFA affirms that it is the policy of Stanford University not to discriminate against applicants of Asian American or any other ethnic extraction in determining undergraduate admissions.
II. C-UAFA recommends that the Dean of Admissions:

1. Request all applicants to self-identify, voluntarily, by ethnicity.
2. Review, annually, the admissions data on Asian American applicants, compare them with white applicants, and report the results to C-UAFA. The Dean then should determine whether any differential in the rate of admission of Asian Americans is unaccounted for by articulated criteria and, if differentials exist, to consider whether they arise from internal practices or external sources.
3. Communicate to high school teachers and college guidance counselors Stanford's concern about the possibility in letters of recommendation of stereotyping regarding ethnicity and gender.

A particular concern is with stereotyping Asian Americans.

4. Include in the training period of new admissions officers a session to address the possibility of unconscious stereotyping of individual applicant groups, including Asian Americans.[4]

Beginning in 1986, in addition to carrying out all the above recommendations, my staff and I made the recommended annual report to C-UAFA on the comparative admit rates. In each of the groups afforded special consideration (sons and daughters of alumni, of faculty, and of staff), there was a very small representation of Asian-Americans, although the alumni representation will clearly increase in the next 25 years. C-UAFA has carefully monitored the results and has been satisfied with them. This was a valuable if time-consuming exercise from which my staff and I benefited, and one from which I personally learned a great deal. There is much to be said for tackling controversy head-on, in an honest and open way, although it is not always easy on the nerves.

In 1987, C-UAFA took on another challenging topic, the possible targeting of other minority groups. The two groups that were brought to the attention of the committee, under slightly differing circumstances, were Puerto Ricans and native Hawaiians. Since the 1968 recommendations for targeting black, Mexican-American, and Native American Indian students contained a very basic rationale (that is, a general regret that students of these ethnicities were not adequately represented in the undergraduate population at Stanford), C-UAFA wanted to see if fair and defensible guidelines could be formulated retroactively and then used to determine future action on other minority groups. The exercise may sound easy, but it proved to be difficult. The final statement, which was approved by the committee in the summer of 1989, comes to almost four pages. The proposed guidelines have yet to be adopted, but I quote some excerpts here. They give some sense of the complexity of both the deliberations and the application of affirmative action in undergraduate admissions.

A. The two special circumstances that, in combination, should trigger concern of C-UAFA, and which should prompt serious consideration of the creation of a new affirmative action group at Stanford, are as follows:

   1. A group should be under-represented in Stanford's student body by both national and State standards. As a "rule of thumb" (but not as a hard and fast rule), the targeting mechanism should not be used if: (a) the Stanford student body in that group is within 75 percent of the national or State percentage of the population; or (b) the number of new admittees in the special category would be less than 10.

2. The under-representation should result from clear historical inequities in this country, rather than result from problems of poverty, recent immigration, or discrimination in some foreign country, or similar conditions. The inequities should be apparent in our national history; it is not sufficient to merely argue from some shortfalls in Stanford's admissions record.

B. As well as giving due weight to the points above when discussing a proposal to target a new group, C-UAFA should also consult with the Provost, the Dean of Students, the Dean of Undergraduate Studies, the Dean of Undergraduate Admissions, the Director of Financial Aid, and the Registrar, to ascertain the practicality of making a positive decision about targeting, given the substantial institutional costs that might be incurred.[5]

The reasons why no action has yet been taken on these guidelines include the subsequent and significant reorganization of the administrative structure at Stanford, along with considerable budgetary pressures. Moreover, C-UAFA had authority to discuss undergraduate admissions only, and it was generally agreed that the guidelines should also be considered with respect to graduate admissions, a step considerably complicated by the decentralized process by which the various schools and departments admit graduate students. Since these discussions were inconclusive, the subject will inevitably resurface.

Beyond the work of the oversight committee for undergraduate admissions, in 1989 Stanford undertook a significant and exceptionally thorough self-study of the university as a multiracial, multicultural community. This study was conducted by the University Committee on Minority Issues (UCMI) and its 240-page report covers the undergraduate curriculum, the faculty, undergraduate and graduate students, student life, and staff.[6] Most of the items related to undergraduate admissions discussed above are, not surprisingly, covered in the UCMI final report, together with a detailed set of recommendations. In April 1990, the university published a report responding to these recommendations, and in August 1990 an external review panel presented a progress report.[7] Stanford cannot be criticized for lack of thoroughness on this subject!

TABLE 8

Matriculated Undergraduates at Stanford, 1991

	Number of undergraduates	Percentage of undergraduates
Men	3,638	55.5%
Women	2,917	44.5
Asian-American	1,205	18.4
Black	543	8.3
Hispanic	640	9.8
Native American Indian	65	1.0
Total minority students	2,453	37.4

Table 8 provides a snapshot of the undergraduate population at Stanford in 1991 by sex and ethnicity. By contrast, in 1968 there were 100 black and 175 "other minorities" enrolled as undergraduates at Stanford. In just over twenty years there has been an almost nine-fold increase in minority representation at the university.

HOW DOES IT WORK IN PRACTICE?

Within the statement of criteria for admission is a section that pertains to the discussion of affirmative action at Stanford:

A few categories of applicants receive special consideration provided they meet basic requirements of academic excellence and personal achievement. Stanford University is committed to a substantial representation of Blacks, Mexican Americans, and Native American Indians in the undergraduate student body. . . . While all applicants receive careful consideration, in reviewing applications we take note both of extenuating circumstances and a variety of cultural and economic situations, including ethnic backgrounds, recent immigration to the United States, and students who are the first in their families to attend college or are from economically disadvantaged backgrounds.[8]

Before examining how this statement is put into practice in the selection of the freshman and transfer classes at Stanford, we must address a number of immediate and associated questions. First, some reasons for implementing affirmative action. Ira Glasser suggests three helpful concepts: affirmative action as a legal remedy "to redress effects of past or present discrimination"; affirmative action as "a form of temporary compensatory opportunity"; and affirmative action as "an effort to achieve fair and visible representation for minorities."[9]

Although they are not often stated so explicitly, these are the reasons why we think it is important to act affirmatively in college admissions. As the UCMI report noted: "The University also has a responsibility to seek out and develop talent wherever it is found, to produce role models for our society's youth, to prepare future leaders, to compensate for past discrimination, and to serve as an example for other public and private institutions."[10]

It is important to emphasize that affirmative action programs for college and university students are voluntary actions on the part of the institutions. Why are the three particular ethnic groups chosen at Stanford, and not others? Are there any specific goals and timetables for the application of the affirmative action policy? What are the consequences of such a policy? I return to each of these questions, and related ones, later in this chapter and in Chapter 8.

The practical applications of Stanford's affirmative action policy are, not surprisingly, easier to describe than the underlying philosophical issues, although even the applications prompt a number of pointed questions. First, we make considerable effort to encourage the applications of potential minority undergraduates. In a typical year, for example, I would sign personally addressed letters to approximately 13,000 black, Mexican-American, and Native American Indian high school seniors whose names and addresses we purchased through the College Board's minority search service. In recent years, we extended this effort to the American College Testing program as well. These students were selected on the basis of their excellent high school records and strong performance on standardized tests. The personal letters encouraged students to consider applying to Stanford; there is some anecdotal evidence to show that the process worked, although the returns (that is, requests for applications) were never more than about 30 percent. Each letter contained a response card and was followed up with one of three informative newspapers especially designed for this outreach effort. Each version of the newspaper focused on the relevant minority community at Stanford.

This recruitment correspondence was supplemented by high school visits, college nights, and regional meetings conducted by one of the admissions directors, together with special phone calls, correspondence, and daily interaction through visits of both groups and individuals to campus. Although three directors were assigned specific responsibility for the recruitment of black, Mexican-American, and Native American Indian students, all the professional staff in the Office of Undergraduate Admissions made efforts to reach out to these prospective applicants. In most years, a staff member traveled with representatives of other selective universities and colleges so that prospective applicants could learn about an array of institutions at the same meeting. Mailings to guidance counselors alerted high schools to opportunities at Stanford for minority students. Beginning in 1987, we also made considerable strides in developing an undergraduate ambassador program, coordinated to arrange the visits of minority undergraduates at Stanford to high schools in their home region. Some groups of students, notably the Mexican-American students, conducted their own minority outreach programs, encouraging high school students to prepare themselves for college while highlighting Stanford in particular. Many of these undergraduates spoke Spanish as their first language and helped immeasurably by talking to Spanish-speaking parents of prospective applicants. In the summer of 1992, Native American Indian students, with support from Undergraduate Admissions, planned outreach visits to some reservations and schools with high Native American Indian enrollment. Black alumni have also joined in recruitment efforts in their hometowns.

Starting in 1985, we asked all students voluntarily to state their ethnicity on their applications; until then, ethnic identification was established on a best-guess basis, a less than satisfactory process. Even with voluntary self-identification, about 4 percent of applicants chose not to mark their ethnicity. In such cases, we were often able to determine the applicant's ethnicity from other information, such as ethnicity classification on standardized test records. This always posed an interesting, and complicated, question: If a minority applicant chooses not to self-identify as a member of a minority group to which we give special consideration, should he or she receive that consideration? My opinion is that if we are reasonably sure of the ethnicity, the answer is yes. Stephen Carter recounts a painful story about one of his own applications to law school. He was originally assumed to be white and received a denial letter; when an admissions officer discovered that he was black, the school changed its decision and offered Carter admission.[11] I am not surprised that he was insulted, or that he did not accept the belated offer. I would not have approved such a call at Stanford, although I would have been sympathetic to a reconsideration of the decision if the circumstances had become apparent before the decision letters were mailed. This latter course of action is, after all, faithful to what we say we do, and it does not violate the sensitivities just described.

Every application to Stanford from a targeted minority received at least one of its readings from the appropriate minority director in undergraduate admissions: all applications from black students were reviewed by the director with primary responsibility for the recruitment of black undergraduates; similarly, all applications from Mexican-Americans had as their first or second reader a Mexican-American director. During my tenure we did not have a Native American Indian director, but we did benefit from the significant knowledge and sensitivity of an experienced director well acquainted with Native American students. We also consulted on many applications with a Native American assistant dean in the Office of Student Affairs. The purpose of this same-ethnicity reading of the minority files was both to ensure maximum sensitivity in the review and to benefit from the perspectives and expertise of our minority directors. Another way of putting this is that we wanted to allow for the fullest understanding of these applicants' circumstances. The vexed question of whether this exercise can best be conducted, or perhaps can *only* be conducted, by a same-ethnicity minority is one to which I return in the final section of this chapter. The write-ups from the minority directors were very influential and helpful to the dean with the authority for the final decision on the applications. However, they were not always decisive. As with all applications, there were those on which the various readers disagreed, and in such cases it was the sign-off dean who necessarily made the final decision. Collegial trust, judgment, and mutual respect were never tested more than in these decisions, and moments of tension were compounded by the significant pressure all the directors felt to make responsible decisions on all the applications. In addition, I worried about the political and moral pressures this exercise placed on individual directors—pressures caused by divided loyalty, guilty conscience, and the need to act as advocates while at the same time maintaining balanced judgment, to mention a few.

The leading question of disgruntled critics is to be anticipated: Do we have different (meaning lower) standards for minority students? We surely must have or the applicants wouldn't need "special consideration" in the first place, right? Such critics are always anxious for an unambiguous, monosyllabic answer to confirm their suspicions, and I risk the further criticism of evasiveness by not answering "Yes" or "No," although I will do so after some essential preamble. It just is *not* that simple a process, as I hope the following illustrations will confirm. First, a glance at Table 1 will show the outstanding academic profiles of the overall admitted and enrolling class of Stanford freshmen. As noted earlier, such measures are but one of many considerations in this subjective selection process. I can confirm unambiguously, however, that the students falling in the lower ranges of these objective measures (*someone* has to be in the bottom half even in a very talented group) are not, as some cynics suspect, all minority students. Just as white students are distributed among the tables of grade distributions and scores, so are minority students—and women and athletes, for that matter. No minority student is admitted unless we are confident on three counts: the student (1) shows a high probability of completing a degree course at Stanford; (2) has *earned* a place (as opposed simply to showing good test scores and little else as evidence of academic achievement); and (3)comes well supported by high school references.

When questioned by skeptical alumni on the appearance of, say, verbal test scores below 550 among admitted students (a score that places a student close to the top 20 percent of national test takers), I like to cite as one example the quadrilingual seventeen-year-old, living in the Netherlands, whose first language is Chinese. How would you score on the verbal SAT, I ask, if you tackled the test under these circumstances? Students for whom English is not the first language are generally required (unless, they have received all their education in English, for example) to take the additional Test of English as a Foreign Language (TOEFL), and these scores for admitted Stanford students are exceptionally high.

Or consider another example: A nationally ranked athlete with a grade-point average of 3.5, when we could admit all 4.0 applicants, is not "unqualified" in our admitted class. These numerical examples are simplistic, as I pointed out in Chapter 2. Quality is assessed in ways beyond the quantitative measures, and grade-point averages in particular vary with the high school, the difficulty of the student's program, and even the state. In short, the overall records of all members of the admitted class are distinguished, and those toward the lower ends of the quantitative distributions offer compelling characteristics and experiences that make them desirable members of the entering class. So the short answer to the hypothetical critic of differing standards for different students must be: Sometimes yes, sometimes no.

Even with these caveats, quantitative measures are just a starting point. The examples that follow give some inkling of the complex realities to which we apply the criteria for admission. Applicant A, Sarah, was born and raised in Manhattan, and both parents are white college graduates; her father is a successful lawyer with a Wall Street firm, her mother a distinguished musician. Sarah was sent to an established New England preparatory school, as was her brother and only sibling, and has spent most summers in Europe; she is fluent in Spanish and an experienced sailor (the family has a house in the Caribbean). Sarah has a good but not spectacular transcript; her SAT and Achievement Test scores are in the mid-600's; and she earns warm references from her teachers. Her self-presentation shows admirable evidence of public service and persistence in out-of-class activities. Applicant B, Anna, was born and raised in the Bronx, the eldest of four children. Her mother is from Puerto Rico, finished grade school, and works as a maid in a Manhattan hotel. Anna's father is black and was born in Harlem; he now attends night school and drives a cab by day. Anna is fluent in Spanish because her family speaks Spanish at home. Anna's high school record is very good apart from a period in eleventh grade when there were some serious family problems and Anna had primary responsibility for her younger siblings' welfare. Her math score is close to 700, but her verbal score is in the low 400's; she scored in the 700's in her Spanish Achievement Test, the only one she took. Anna's teachers say she has much potential but acknowledge the risks of family instability. Anna's self-presentation reveals her significant financial contributions to her family through a part-time job she has maintained throughout high school. She is also the track star at her local public high school. You are the first director to read both files. What action do you recommend?

You have nothing to lose, in this hypothetical exercise, by saying you'd like to admit both; but imagine the same exercise extended over 15,000 applicants, roughly 11,000 of whom have to be denied admission. They surely can't all be this difficult to decide between, you respond. No, not all, but you could make a very good case for admitting a great many more than the 2,600 we accept in a given year.

I may be guilty of some racial stereotyping in the examples above, but I think all would agree that in the United States of the 1990's, a student like Sarah is more likely to be white than black. To offset the stereotyping, here is another actual, though slightly disguised, set of cases. Charles is the only child of professional parents who both attended Ivy League colleges; his father is a doctor, a general practitioner, and his mother teaches in the local community college. The family is black. Charles attends the excellent local public high school in a large Midwestern city; he is in the top 10 percent of his graduating class, with standardized test scores in the high 500's. Charles plays soccer and occasionally writes for the school newspaper, but he lacks any notable leadership roles. References from his teachers are good but not memorable. His self-presentation does not show much energy or imagination, but he clearly has potential. David was born in southern California; his parents were born and raised in Taiwan. Both his mother and father have bachelor's degrees in the sciences and work in computer companies in a large city. David attends the excellent local public high school; he is in the top 10 percent of his graduating class, with standardized test scores in the mid-600's. David plays tennis and occasionally acts in school productions, but with no notable leadership roles. His teachers' references are good but not memorable. David's self-presentation is very earnest, and the essay shows evidence of thoughtfulness and critical thinking. Your third application of the morning is Edgar, whose profile is almost identical to those of Charles and David—that is, none of them stands out in any significant way from the applicant pool. Edgar is white. What action will you recommend on each of these applicants?

The unreasonableness in the way I have presented these cases is twofold. In the actual reading process, a director is never called upon to choose between two applicants such as Sarah and Anna, or to choose among three others, such as Charles, David, and Edgar. Interestingly, however, many of the critics of affirmative action who write to complain see the selection process in just those terms. Disappointed parents believe that an underqualified minority student took their child's rightful place in the freshman class. I often wished I could introduce these parents to the equally outraged parents of minority students who were denied admission, who wrote to ask what more a minority student needed to do to be admitted to Stanford. In reading 100 folders over the course of a few days, a director must recommend admission for no more than 20 or 25 applicants. The selection of the freshman class is an ongoing process of winnowing down the pool of applicants.

The second unreasonable element of my exercise is that the reader here is unfamiliar with the context of the total applicant pool, the very point I made to the unhappy alumnus at the beginning of this chapter. When our director of freshman admissions, John Bunnell, told new readers that the decisions would get easier after the first thousand files, he did not make this statement in jest. New directors receive significant training and analyze previous years' applicants; but still they are disconcerted by their reading of that initial thousand (or more). Even after reading tens of thousands of applications, I found that each new reading marathon, with its brand-new and unknown set of applicants, brought a fresh wave of anxiety, especially after the comparative intellectual and physical lull of the intervening months when we were not reading. (I often thought, privately, that the process was in many ways analogous to childbirth; if a mother focused on the difficulties of past experiences in the labor room, she would be reluctant to repeat the exercise.) The point of introducing you to the responsibility of deciding on actual cases here, though, is to impress upon you the importance of our focus on the *individual* applicant in the context of available opportunities, as well as to provide some insight into the challenges of selection between very different and for the most part very well qualified young men and women.

When the eleven weeks of concentrated reading are over and the decision letters have been mailed, the selection process takes on a different focus. For many minority students in particular, this is often a time of concern about finances. Following a policy approved by the Faculty Senate in 1969, financial aid offers to targeted minority students required a lesser self-help component than for other undergraduates. This university policy illustrates the disingenuousness of Shelby Steele's observation that "preferences are inexpensive and carry the glamour of good intentions—change the numbers and the good deed is done." [12] Once Stanford made the commitment to target a minority group, it took considerable work to put that commitment into action through staff, publications, travel, special reviews, and the like, in the admissions process; providing special packages of financial aid; and arranging staff and programs through the dean of students once the students were enrolled.

It is our mandate to do everything possible within Stanford's budgetary limitations to minimize a student's financial concerns. Unfortunately, this does not mean that no undergraduate has financial concerns, or that all families agree with the financial aid analysis in their individual case. There were many individual cases of hardship that I found very moving. Such was the circumstance of the young Mexican-American freshman who was, by the "luck" of the housing draw, assigned to room with two wealthy white freshmen. When the Mexican-American arrived in the fall with all of twenty dollars in his pocket, he found his roommates blithely planning the decoration of their rooms, and it was assumed he would contribute equally. Understandably, he was both embarrassed and dismayed by the prospect. This situation is not unique to minority students, of course, but it is a clear example of the challenges we faced in aiming to assemble a socioeconomically diverse class of undergraduates. It also serves to remind us of the very real consequences that accompany our admissions decisions, and the personal discomfort some students experienced at the hands of their unwitting peers. I don't think, however, that poignancy or discomfort are sufficient arguments to return to the more homogeneous classes of bygone years.

One reasonable measure of success in admitting minority students is their graduation rate. The 1989 Stanford self-study concluded, as detailed in the UCMI final report, that although there had been some fluctuations for particular groups in the previous decade, overall there was no significant difference in graduation rates between minority and white students.[13] Minority students from Stanford have distinguished accomplishments. Of the first four black Rhodes scholars from the United States, two were from Stanford; two of the black women astronauts are Stanford graduates. It is also clear, however, that the success of graduation is not achieved without personal cost, and that there are more unseen pressures, such as lack of self-confidence in academic preparation, on minority students than on their white peers.

ADVOCATES AND ADVERSARIES

As difficult as it is to explain how affirmative action affects the process of selecting Stanford's undergraduates, more difficult still is presenting a balanced argument for and against affirmative action in college admissions. It seems best to begin with my personal view:

I believe that many minority students, the institutions in which they have enrolled, and society at large have all benefited from the practice of affirmative action in college admissions. Stanford is among the universities that have maintained their commitment to increasing the enrollment of underrepresented minorities; I am glad to have participated in these efforts, and I am proud of the results. They have not been without hard work, patience, and persistence, as well as some moments of doubt and crises of confidence; and the efforts are far from complete. Our affirmative action programs have made it possible for a good number of minority students to graduate from Stanford who would not otherwise have had that opportunity. I hope they will contribute to, among other things, another generation of minority graduates, although that responsibility cannot and should not rest entirely on their shoulders. The redress of past and present injustices, of lack of opportunity, and of the negligible representation of minorities in positions of authority and responsibility had to begin somewhere, and affirmative action in college admissions had an essential part to play.

Behind these simple statements, however, lie many complex, controversial, highly emotional, and divisive issues; an attempt to summarize them in six lines, six chapters, or even six books cannot do them justice. Unfortunately, thoughtful discussions of the issues rarely take place at all. Even in the supposedly enlightened environments of college campuses, where lively and passionate debates on every conceivable topic are the norm, an honest and open discussion of affirmative action is rare. As an illustration, a Stanford undergraduate came to me in frustration a couple of years ago. He was trying to arrange a debate on affirmative action but couldn't find anyone to speak *against* it. Plainly, an honest discussion of the core elements of affirmative action can be too personal and too painful to deliver or to receive, is sometimes counterproductive, is often highly emotional and fraught with misunderstanding, and has the potential to be destructively divisive. This characterization may seem exaggerated, but any reader who has engaged in such discussions will confirm its validity. The instinct of self-preservation deters even the bravest and most principled. Instead of open debate, then, "discussions" are reduced to private mutterings at the back of meeting rooms, immoderate pronouncements over drinks at dinner parties among close friends (usually of the same ethnicity), or even thoughts that are never uttered. Interestingly, the contemporary spokespersons on affirmative action most frequently quoted are black males: Derrick Bell, Stephen Carter, Thomas Sowell, Shelby Steele, and Clarence Thomas.[14] They are more often adversaries than advocates.

Perhaps the easiest way to proceed through this tough territory is to pose a series of critical statements, each followed by a comment. The order of presentation does not reflect any personal judgment of the relative importance of the issues; all are included because they are important dimensions of the discussion. The comments that follow focus primarily on my experience in undergraduate admissions at Stanford because this is where I am best informed, but some of our experiences undoubtedly apply at other universities. My observations are not intended as an official Stanford institutional response, for there is no such thing. I have never seen *any* university attempt much more than a basic statement on affirmative action, an omission that may contribute to existing misunderstandings but that is intended to avoid conflict: if it isn't written down, the reasoning goes, no one can object to it (a technique I have seen practiced with considerable effect by some college administrators). As a white woman, I am not a member of any minority group in this country (except perhaps the female physicists and agnostics, neither of whom I will bring into the discussions here), and some will be quick to charge that I therefore have no authority or credibility on these questions. In a paradoxical way, *not* being a member of an ethnic minority allows one more freedom to be critical, given the avoidance it permits of any issue of divided loyalties and representation. I am answerable only to my own conscience (which extends, of course, to my work), a circumstance that is not without its anguish and isolation. And so to the critical comments of the adversaries, accompanied by the advocates' response:

Affirmative action in college admissions means admitting minority students who are less qualified than white students. This is probably the most frequent criticism by parents, and sometimes by faculty and others who should have a better understanding of the issues. I quote from a 1991 letter from the parent of a denied white applicant. It was written in response to my letter answering his complaint about our decision on his son's application; the complaint compared his son's record with that of an admitted minority applicant from the same high school.

The [local newspaper] article gives the lie to all the sanctimonious statements contained in your letter. . . . Whatever the semantics, "goals," "groups targeted," etc., Stanford has a racist policy of ethnic, class and gender quotas in its admissions policy. I confess to being one of those alumni who find this hard to accept . . . it does not require a great deal of elaboration to see that compromising admissions standards will lead to a student body which is less qualified intellectually, spiritually and from the standpoint of leadership to deal with the world of the 21st century.

This father wrote again one month later with the hope that I "would reflect upon the ethical problems that Stanford has in pursuing the politically correct admissions policy which you have carried out," and expounding on "the immorality of the whole diversity syndrome." Those are strong words and painful reading from someone I suspect is so firmly placed in the anti–affirmative action camp that no amount of reasoned debate will bring him to the center, much less to the other side. Unfortunately, this parent is far from alone in his views.

Many such critics, not surprisingly and with *some* justification, focus their argument on quantitative measures and the differences in achievement levels by ethnicity. Here is one such example from Thomas Sowell, a black scholar at Stanford's Hoover Institution:

There are dozens of American colleges and universities where the median combined verbal SAT score and mathematics SAT score total 1200 or above. As of 1983, there were less than 600 black students in the entire United States with combined SAT scores of 1200. This meant that, despite widespread attempts to get a black student "representation" comparable to the black percentage of the population (about 11 percent), there were not enough black students in the entire country for the Ivy League alone to have such a "representation" *without going beyond this pool*—even if the entire pool went to the eight Ivy League colleges.

Clearly, with dozens of top tier institutions across the country competing for these and other black students, there was no realistic hope of approaching a proportionate representation of black students in these institutions without a widespread lowering of admissions standards for them.

Sowell goes on to say that "the actual consequences of admitting blacks to institutions where they do not meet the usual admissions standards have been educationally disastrous for these students." [15]

I will not dispute Sowell's numbers, but readers of this book will not be surprised that his application of quantitative measures to the selection process at Stanford is ill-founded. We do *not* admit by SAT scores (although the selection process would be much simpler if we did, entailing no more than a few hours of computer time, depending on how sophisticated we wanted to make the numerical cutoffs). It is inevitably a surprise to the parents of students with SAT scores of 1400 when their children are not offered admission, but high scores cannot compensate for a mediocre or poor high school record and an undeveloped extracurricular profile. We do *not* admit by SAT scores and grade-point averages. It is not difficult for high school students to maintain a 4.0 grade-point average when they take the least difficult courses or attend a high school with a less-than-rigorous grading system. We do *not* admit by SAT scores, grade-point averages, and Achievement Test scores. We do *not* admit by SAT scores, grade-point averages, Achievement Test scores, and the number of courses taken in high school.

All these quantitative measures (and I haven't quite exhausted the list) do come into play in the review process, and it is true that the higher the numbers, the higher the probability of admission. The reading of the applications, however, focuses very carefully on the quality of the academic program tackled, within the context of available opportunities, as the details provided in Chapter 2 explain. The comprehensive selection process is subjective and allows for extenuating circumstances extending far beyond quantitative measures.

An argument similar to Sowell's was found in a 1989 review, written by Andrew Hacker, of some recent books on affirmative action.

In talking about "separate standards," Hacker says, "advocates of affirmative action know that they are claiming that Blacks or Hispanics should have places that could go to others who are better qualified." [16] Here again, "qualified" appears to be defined as a certain level of standardized test scores and high school grades. These factors are indisputably correlated with graduation rates, but they do not measure personal qualities such as persistence, resilience, and determination, all of which can play a critical role in whether a student graduates or not. Neither do test scores and high school grades provide any measure of hardships or disadvantaged circumstances overcome or exemplary personal qualities. In an ideal world where all high school seniors apply for selective college admission with a history of equal opportunities (similar preparation and socioeconomic parity, for starters), the selection process might well be determined on the level qualifying field of scores and grades. Yet we live in a country where we cannot agree on a national set of education measures or a standard set of academic coursework, and as a consequence the selection process calls for some complex and compensatory corrections. In some eyes, this means admitting less-qualified students. No responsible admissions officer would, in good conscience, recommend admitting a student who showed evidence of a low probability of graduating. Setting a student up to fail does no good to the student or to the institution. Unfortunately, there is no infallible method of predetermining who will graduate. Senior officers in colleges with low graduation rates for any or all students—let's be generous and say less than 60 percent in five years—should be seriously concerned about what is wrong in their system.

We never made any claims to have mastered a perfect admissions process at Stanford; the human beings responsible for college selection do the very best they can in a difficult process, and they do make mistakes in judgment. Similarly, the human beings who are selected are not altogether predictable. And their future personal circumstances are not immune to factors beyond their control or guaranteed to meet the expectations of college admissions officers. Surprises come in all packages; some very well qualified entering students do not graduate. And those students we turn away are no slouches either.

The criteria for admission are, in the most fundamental sense, threefold; however, those who cry "unqualified" rarely extend their analysis beyond the academic criterion. These critics lack the broader context—they do not have other privileged information (a student's references, for example) and are unaware of the larger considerations, such as socioeconomic diversity, that are among the ingredients in the selection of any freshman class.

Affirmative action policies are unfair to white students and amount to reverse discrimination. The arguments behind this claim usually follow a number of predictable lines. I have already tried to answer the most common criticism, that of the unfairness of admitting "unqualified" or less-qualified minority students. The second kind of argument is that of personal responsibility. Critics may agree that the United States has a shameful history of discrimination against minorities, but when it comes to the college applications of their sons and daughters, they argue that their children are not responsible for that history. Yet their children, they say, may be denied admission to the college of their choice to make room for minority applicants. Carter uses an effective analogy in responding to this point: "the provision of tax dollars for emergency disaster assistance after a hurricane devastates a coastal community. The people who bear the costs of these programs are not the people who caused the damage, but they still have to pay." [17] The analogy is not perfect because most hurricane damage is not the result of human actions; racism and discrimination are all too unfortunately the direct effect of human actions.

Individual examples bring the force of the arguments and counterarguments into painful focus. Richard Rodriguez's anguished (and anguishing) autobiography provides several such examples, one of which illustrates the unfairness charge. When Rodriguez, a Stanford graduate, was completing his graduate studies at the University of California, Berkeley, he was discussing his future plans with a fellow graduate student. The student asked if it was true that

Rodriguez had been offered a position at Yale, a fact that Rodriguez confirmed, adding that he had not yet made up his mind about accepting. Rodriguez's own account continues the tale:

He asked me if I knew that he too had written to Yale. In his case, however, no one had bothered to acknowledge his letter with even a postcard. What did I think of that? He gave me no chance to reply. . . . Suddenly it was to me that he was complaining. "It's just not right, Richard. None of this is fair. You've done some good work, but so have I. I'll bet our records are just about even. But when we go looking for jobs this year, it's a very different story. You're the one who gets all the breaks."

To evade his criticism, I wanted to side with him. I was about to admit to the injustice of affirmative action. But he continued, his voice hard with accusation. "Oh, it's all very simple this year. You're a Chicano. And I am a Jew. That's really the only difference between us." [18]

After this conversation, Rodriguez made up his mind to say no to all his offers. "I wrote a note to all the chairmen of English Departments who had offered me jobs. I left a note for the professor in my own department at Berkeley who was in charge of helping graduate students look for teaching positions. (The contradictions of affirmative action have finally caught up with me. Please remove my name from the list of teaching job applicants.)" [19]

This anecdote raises more than one fundamental issue about affirmative action programs. First, with all the best intentions, proponents of such programs affect the lives of the "beneficiaries" whether they wish to be affected or not. Once individuals are identified as members of a group targeted for affirmative action, they have no say in how considerations of ethnicity affect decisions about them; department chairpersons, deans, faculty, and hiring officers are the ones in control of the affirmative action programs. A comprehensive affirmative action policy does not allow for any disagreements in principle by affected individuals; they become pawns in the process. It is the Richard Rodriguezes, however, who must deal daily in their own lives with the consequences of affirmative action decisions. I can understand why Rodriguez would choose to withdraw from the faculty searches. Not surprisingly, no minority members of a university community feel comfortable with the thought that perhaps they are there only for reasons of ethnicity. Such thoughts contribute to lowering the self-esteem and reducing the confidence level of the affected individuals, and open discussion of the details of affirmative action programs often just exacerbates existing conservative criticisms. How can affirmative action programs be openly and honestly discussed (as they must be) without producing such unfortunate repercussions for the affected individuals?

Rodriguez's Jewish classmate raises another complex issue about affirmative action programs. Why should one group of individuals benefit and not others who have also suffered from discrimination in the past? Over the past decade, I have heard reasonable arguments for including many different groups as affirmative action targets in addition to the three that Stanford presently includes at the undergraduate level (blacks, Mexican-Americans, and Native American Indians / Alaskan natives). These groups include Puerto Ricans, native Hawaiians, Filipinos, Appalachian whites, Central Americans, recent immigrants, Vietnamese, low-income Asian-Americans, and low-income whites; this list is not exhaustive. Quite simply, though, there is a limit to what one institution of postsecondary education can do to address the significant problems of society. The primary missions of a research university, such as Stanford, are teaching, learning, and research; the individuals who engage in these activities are critically important because they determine the quality of the outcomes. No one, I believe, would argue with using the characteristic of excellence in assembling the members of a university community; a few would argue with using the characteristic of diversity in its broadest sense (discipline, gender, ethnicity, age, and place of origin). In undergraduate admissions, we focus on excellence *and* diversity.

Even when criteria are apparently well defined, however, complexities remain. For example, in focusing on three minority groups for undergraduate admissions, we have not distinguished between the socioeconomic status of individuals in these groups. Many middle-class blacks have grown up in circumstances of greater economic advantage than lower-class whites. Should all black applicants be treated equally? An additional consideration comes in the degree of cultural heritage. Should we give more weight to a first-generation Mexican-American than to a third-generation child of a mixed marriage? Should urban Native American Indians receive lesser consideration than those who have grown up on a reservation? How should we consider the daughter of mixed heritage—part black, part Asian, part white?

Other difficult questions about affirmative action are raised, often more than once, throughout this chapter. I pose the questions not to argue against affirmative action in undergraduate admissions, but to present the full range of complexities and factors in what I hope is an honest and evenhanded discussion. Despite the many questions, I have no doubt that what we were trying to achieve through affirmative action during my seven years as dean was the right thing to do. As I heard, many alumni disagreed.

Those of us who support and implement affirmative action programs have to grapple personally with these difficult individual dilemmas; there are simply no easy answers, and the associated internal philosophical debates are often unresolved and result in periodic waverings of commitment. Even critics of affirmative action sometimes appear ambivalent in their positions. The former president of the University of California, David Gardner, has wisely noted that anyone who thinks he has the solutions to such problems doesn't understand the issues; and anyone who understands the problems knows that there are no simple solutions.

Assuming support for the general fairness of affirmative action, an associated question is, For how long should the period of redress be extended? Even when critics concede a need to redress past discrimination, they presently cry, "Enough is enough." Affirmative action programs are now more than twenty years old, and some progress has been made. Some public universities in California, for example, have entering student populations that are now less than 50 percent white. In the fall of 1991, the freshman class at Stanford was more than 40 percent nonwhite, although 24 percent of the total number of freshmen were Asian-American, a group that is not a targeted minority in undergraduate admissions. It is hard to know what to say to critics of affirmative action who, on hearing such statistics, exclaim, "Well, Asian-Americans are all right," or "Well, I don't mind including *them*." The word minority is taking on an entirely new meaning in the 1990's, a subject to which I return in the next section and in Chapter 8. But we are talking of time scales of very different magnitudes. Black people were slaves in this country for more than 200 years, recently enough that former governor Douglas Wilder of Virginia had grandparents who were born into slavery. The abolition of slavery hardly ended discrimination against blacks throughout the United States, a disgraceful scar on the history of a country that proudly claims to represent "liberty and justice for all." Racism persists in various guises, not only in the United States but in most other countries as well. Twenty years of special programs, I would argue, are a long shot from redressing such a record. The number of minority men and women in positions of authority and responsibility is still dismally low, and a lot of work still remains to be done through affirmative action, education, and other social reforms.

Critics of affirmative action sometimes conveniently forget that it was not so long ago that white males, usually Protestant, were the sole recipients of offers of admission to the most prestigious colleges and universities in this country. That was plainly unfair to all other talented students; indeed, the discrimination against women and Jews was quite unabashed.[20] Stanford admitted women from the time of its founding, and its policy on nondiscrimination states that the university "admits students of either sex and any race, color, religion, sexual orientation, or national and ethnic origin to all the rights, privileges, programs and activities . . . at the University." Moreover, Title IX of the Education Amendments of 1972 specifically prohibits discrimination on the basis of sex in the administration of any university or college program. So how should a college compensate for any prior unfair treatment of women? In the zero-sum exercise of selecting a freshman class, if some colleges and universities are now going to include more women, it obviously follows that in most cases they will have to admit fewer men. Is this policy unfair to the men who are not admitted? I don't think so. When an injustice is recognized, some expectant beneficiaries of the old unjust system are going to lose out. The established old-boy networks may still benefit white males in the corporate world and other spheres of life, but they are being questioned and challenged as never before. The beneficiaries of such networks who criticize affirmative action are usually oblivious to the contradictions of their position: special consideration for white males (ironically a group who never needed it) is all right, but special consideration for women and minorities is all wrong.

Beneficiaries of affirmative action programs suffer lasting self-doubts. One of the most enjoyable, if unspecified, parts of my job as dean of undergraduate admissions was visiting the dorms to meet with the undergraduates in an informal setting. We often sat down after dinner for what was inevitably a stimulating question-and-answer session. The students kept me on my toes with the range of topics, the sharpness and sensitivity of their thinking, and their occasional youthful and good-humored irreverence, all of which were to be expected after reading their applications. Not surprisingly, they often asked about the practice and procedures of selecting a freshman class; the issue of affirmative action came up occasionally. How *did* we factor race into the selection process? Were there different standards of admission for different groups? Given, as I have noted, that there are almost no honest discussions of this subject, it took some courage for students to raise these questions in such a public setting. (Some might attribute less-than-honorable motives to those who raised such questions, but I do not.) The group of students at these dorm discussions was usually representative of the undergraduate student body, and so there were usually a number of minority students present. I often tried to imagine how my explanation would sound to them, and how they were left feeling after the discussion had finished and everyone made their way, with their own private thoughts, to the evening's work on a paper, to a dorm meeting, or to the library or a social event.

My answer generally began with a statement similar to the one in this chapter about the criteria for admission, the special considerations, and what they meant. In answering, I was always conscious of an incident described to me by one of the resident fellows (faculty members and administrators who oversee the residences) about an encounter between two white students and a minority student at a Stanford football game. Said one white student to the other, within earshot of the minority student: "Go on, ask him what his SAT scores were." It takes a lot of self-confidence for an undergraduate not to brood over the question, "Am I here only because I am black / Mexican-American / Native American Indian?" Although I tried to address this question directly with the statement, "You are not here simply because . . . ," the self-doubt may nonetheless linger. On academic grounds, self-doubting students should be reassured by the graduation rates for all Stanford undergraduates (89 percent of entering students graduate within five years, which is among the highest graduation rates in the country). Less than one-half of 1 percent of an entering class gets into serious academic difficulty in the first year. None of the freshmen who entered in 1990, for example, was suspended for academic reasons by the end of freshman year. The question of the personal cost (and I don't mean financial, although this factor does enter the scene) individual undergraduates must pay to achieve such results is often overlooked.

A recent *New York Times* article addressed this issue under the headline, "A Remedy for Old Racism Has New Kind of Shackles: Children of Affirmative Action Are Ambivalent."[21] The article provides a number of painful examples of 1990's "success" stories: A corporate counsel in Chicago said he felt he was "under constant scrutiny from his colleagues and always had to justify being there." A New York gastroenterologist complains, "You're going through the same curriculum as everybody else. But all along the way everyone is questioning you." These laments are not just the products of recent years. Again, the writer Richard Rodriguez speaks with searing frankness about his personal experiences at Stanford, Columbia University, and Berkeley:

My essays [on affirmative action] served as my "authority" to speak at the Marriott Something or the Sheraton Somewhere. To stand at a ballroom podium and hear my surprised echo sound from a microphone. I spoke. I started getting angry letters from activists. One wrote to say that I was becoming the gringos' fawning pet. What "they" want all Hispanics to be. I remembered the remark when I was introduced to an all-white audience and heard their applause so loud. I remembered the remark when I stood in a university auditorium and saw an audience of brown and black faces watching me. I publicly wondered whether a person like me should really be termed a minority. But some members of the audience thought I was denying racial pride, trying somehow to deny my racial identity. They rose to protest. One Mexican-American said I was a minority whether I wanted to be or not. And he said that the reason I was a beneficiary of affirmative action was simple: I was a Chicano. (Wasn't I?) It was only an issue of race.[22]

Rodriguez also provides a personal example of another questionable "benefit" of affirmative action. Not only has he suffered from an alienation from his culture and many of his people, he also experienced the anguishing alienation from his parents, an experience that has had many poignant echoes in the 1980's and 1990's. Students from disadvantaged backgrounds who are given the opportunity to pursue an education that is unknown territory for their parents inevitably pay the high price of familial alienation. Many feel they no longer belong at home but do not feel at home in college. It takes a rare individual to handle these conflicts successfully. The media were quick to report the recent case of the admission of a Stanford minority student whose family had been homeless. I was fortunate to have had some experience handling human-interest questions from the press ("Is this the first homeless student that Stanford has admitted?"), but my heart went out to the inexperienced student who suddenly became the focus of nationwide media attention.

Such accounts make advocates of affirmative action, of whom I am one, stop and consider. Shelby Steele adds the ills of "historic reparation" through "society's guilty gestures of repayment," and the incentive of preferences "to be reliant on others just as we are struggling for self-reliance."[23] I agree it is all very fine for supporters of affirmative action to propose and practice, but we do not have to live the lives of those who are, by default, social pawns of our good intentions. The examples cited also give reason to pause before using the word "beneficiary" of an affirmative action program, although personally I hope that, on balance, the term will prove accurate. Social progress is inevitably achieved by the actions of pioneers; one can only hope that the sacrifices they have made, and continue to make, will be for the unambiguous benefit of their successors. It is not surprising, all conflicts and questions considered, that the current generation of college graduates who "benefited" from affirmative action programs have mostly emerged stronger from the experience; they must have been highly resilient going into it. I wish I could live long enough to see the generation of minority graduates who are admitted without affirmative action, but given the unfortunate strength and length of the historical record and the current climate of racism, I doubt that is a realistic hope.

Affirmative action means quotas of admitted students. After the three difficult preceding topics, this one seems relatively straightforward. At Stanford, it is unequivocally the case that we had no quotas of any kind for minority students, or for any other subset of students for that matter. This fact is clearly borne out by the data on admitted minority students provided in the tables at the beginning of this chapter.

The percentages of all groups of admitted minority undergraduates at Stanford, which is not the same as the percentages of *enrolling* undergraduates, show fluctuations from year to year. The percentages are also different from the absolute numbers; each year, we have a slightly different target for the absolute number of enrolling first-time Stanford students (freshmen and transfer students combined). This total number is determined primarily by the number of seniors graduating in the previous year, because the goal is to maintain a stable undergraduate enrollment of 6,550 students. Understandably, there is concern among individual minority communities when the number of admitted students declines. For an entering class, however, when the number for one set of students goes up, others *must* go down. Our procedure is to admit targeted minority students using the principles described earlier in this chapter. Unfortunately, in some years there are marked declines in the number of minority applicants; for various reasons (for example, enlistment in military service) black males have been in this set in recent years. These declines are separate from the national decline in the total number of high school seniors. In other years, we see an increase in a particular minority applicant pool, but this does not guarantee an increase in quality, which is of course an essential ingredient in the selection process.

One unfortunate consequence of providing the kind of comparative data given earlier in this chapter is the temptation of minority group members, and others, to compare "track records." I am appalled, but at this stage not altogether surprised, to have heard the following myth: As a consequence of the admission of larger numbers of Asian-Americans, the other minority groups will be reduced in size in order to preserve the percentage of white students in the freshman class. A variation on this theme is: If the number of black students increases in a given year, the number of Mexican-American students decreases. Words provide a particularly inadequate form of protest here; suffice it to say that these are absolute myths. The minority group with the best statistical case for arguing a quota (although I have not heard them do so) are the Native American Indians. In my tenure, the number of Native American Indians admitted never exceeded 1 percent of the total students admitted. It is important to keep the national population representation in mind (it is about 1 percent) and to remember that, while we can always do better, as a consequence of national demographics we are not going to see large numbers of Native American Indians in the Stanford applicant pool.

Although I am focusing on the perspectives of minority groups here, the views of white parents and students cannot be overlooked. The characteristics of race and ethnicity have become paramount in any selection or appointment process in the United States: nominations for the Supreme Court; the selection of university faculty, administrators, and students; and the hiring of firefighters and secretaries. Shelby Steele thinks "the real trouble between the races in America is that the races are not just races but competing power groups—a fact that is easily minimized, perhaps because it is so obvious."[24] There will always be power struggles at all levels in this world, but the best outcomes of affirmative action in the United States can help to alleviate some of the present-day power plays between races by improving the representation of minorities in positions of authority. There is no turning back on the path that has been taken, but we are unquestionably encountering detours en route to the final destination.

Critics of affirmative action are racist. / Practitioners of affirmative action are racist. These laughable generalizations become less amusing when one realizes that such charges are made in all seriousness. It is clear that affirmative action has generated significant debate and, as in any debate, right is rarely the monopoly of one side. The most extreme participants on both sides of the debate exhibit little tolerance for ambiguity and are satisfied only with all-or-nothing answers.

Just as "affirmative action" means different things to different people, so does "racism." Irrespective of definitions, however, name-calling is a cowardly attempt to terminate a debate that could benefit from more (not less) free discussion. If our views are well-founded, they benefit from probing criticisms, and we should welcome them and encourage debate—although such philosophical stoicism is easier to write about than to put into action in the midst of an angry crowd.

Affirmative action does not benefit those for whom it was intended, the truly disadvantaged minorities; affirmative action programs should be based on class, not race. In the early days of affirmative action programs, there seem to have been very few subtleties (at least in college admissions) in trying to address the fundamental concern: in the arena of higher education, for many different reasons, there simply were very few minority students and faculty in the nation's colleges and universities. The assignment was to increase these numbers, with little regard given to socioeconomic disadvantages. Now that some progress has been made in improving representation, other underlying assumptions have been called into question.

Stephen Carter claims, "What has happened in black America in the era of affirmative action is this: middle-class black people are better off and lower-class black people are worse off." [25] This is not an isolated view. When we consider the criteria for admission, it is not surprising that middle-class minority students have a better chance of enrolling at a selective university, because they have more and better educational options available to them. Almost all colleges, for example, require the submission of standardized test scores (the SAT and/or the ACT), and the results of these tests are strongly correlated with family income. In a 1990 series of monographs on selective admissions published by the College Board, McPherson and Schapiro provide an analysis of the current distribution of educational resources and opportunities, along with the associated inequalities. The authors cite College Board data showing "that the difference in SAT scores between low-income whites (family income $10–20,000) and high-income whites (family income over $70,000) is 107 points." The comparable figures for blacks and Hispanics "are even more striking (163 and 162 points respectively)."[26]

Almost inevitably, middle-class minority students are going to attend better-quality high schools than lower-class students. Life in middle-class neighborhoods is more conducive to pursuing a college education. (Both these statements are amply confirmed in, for example, the work of Jonathan Kozol.)[27] It also is clear that the best-educated minority parents are in the strongest position to offer guidance and support in their children's college plans and preparation. They are equipped to hold the schools accountable and are often prepared to advocate for their children within the schools if they feel their needs are not being addressed adequately. Similarly, middle-class students have the most opportunities for pursuing and developing extracurricular interests and leadership abilities, while their lower-class peers may be working twenty hours a week at the local mall to contribute to family income. Stanford's admissions criteria emphasize sensitivity to individual circumstances and the effect they may have on an applicant's record and on available resources; admissions literature states explicitly that extenuating circumstances, including economically disadvantaged backgrounds, are considered and that the financial aid program "aims to promote broad socio-economic representation." As a consequence of all these commitments, each year approximately 100 entering Stanford freshmen of all races have parents who are unable to make any contribution to the total cost (tuition, room and board, and personal expenses) of a Stanford education. I would agree with Carter, however, that the lower-class minority students, as an immediate consequence of their circumstances, undoubtedly have not benefited as much as middle-class minority students.

I would also add that moving into a middle-class suburb does not eliminate prejudice, discrimination, or racism. The fact that middle-class blacks have arrived in the neighborhood does not mean they are welcomed or even treated with civility. Minority parents often have to take on skeptical guidance counselors to ensure that their children are offered access to college preparatory courses. For every middle-class black student who enrolls at Stanford, there are others of similar socioeconomic background who find their college choices limited to community colleges and less rigorous universities.

Minority undergraduates and administrators at Stanford have sometimes criticized the scope of recruitment efforts in undergraduate admissions, charging that we should spend more time in inner-city high schools seeking out talented minority students. I once felt the full fury of this criticism when I joined, by invitation, officers from five other selective universities on a brief visit to some international high schools in Europe. Although I also undertook, at the same time, other Stanford work beyond admissions, the visit did not sit well (to give it the most positive interpretation) with some Stanford undergraduates. I made the point to them that, in our efforts to increase the diversity of the student body, international students were a valuable component. (Some colleges actually have a director whose full-time assignment is international outreach.) But for the critics, the priorities revealed in this overseas travel appeared distorted, and they did not understand the extension of my responsibilities as a senior administrator beyond those of the Office of Undergraduate Admissions. I agree that we should recruit as energetically as possible in both inner-city and rural high schools, and we do make such efforts, but there are a number of associated considerations. First, the suggestion assumes that no lower-class students are to be found in private high schools; nowadays this is untrue. Many of the established private schools in this country have their own vigorous affirmative action programs—and they admit and support disadvantaged students of all ethnicities. These programs have met with limited success, although the schools are in an excellent position to provide the best academic and extracurricular preparation for an undergraduate education. Unfortunately, all the dilemmas associated with affirmative action at the college level are also present at the high school level, when the burdens of adolescence are most fierce.

Another kind of consideration is financial. In an office with a limited travel budget and staff, how do you make the optimum use of resources in choosing which of the 25,000 or so high schools across the country to visit? In a typical year, we can reach only a small fraction of individual high schools (about 700). A Stanford visit to a high school with disadvantaged students does serve the admirable educational purpose of raising the sights of many students toward a college degree and providing some personal encouragement, but it also runs the risk of raising false expectations in a highly selective admissions process. This dilemma provides yet another example of the delicate balance of good intentions and outcomes in college admissions.

The personal dilemma of the middle-class minority professional is well described by Shelby Steele, a professor of English. In a section of his book on affirmative action, Steele presents the case of his two children, who are not, he claims, disadvantaged.

> Both of them have endured racial insensitivity from whites. They have been called names, have suffered slights, and have experienced firsthand the peculiar malevolence that racism brings out in people. Yet they have never experienced racial discrimination, have never been stopped by their race on any path they have chosen to follow. Still, their society now tells them that if they will only designate themselves as black on their college applications, they will likely do better in the college lottery than if they conceal this fact. I think there is something of a Faustian bargain in this.[28]

I would present the case differently to Professor Steele in his Faustian contemplations. He admits early in his book that about 70 percent of black students at his university drop out before graduation.

This does not help the cause either of society at large or of black people, when what we need are more students who successfully graduate from college. With their background, Steele's children are well-prepared and promising candidates; they have not (as he tells us himself) escaped the experience of racism; they are in a position to appreciate the dilemmas of affirmative action beneficiaries. As Steele points out, "The white children of alumni are often grandfathered into elite universities in what can only be seen as a residual benefit of historic white privilege." At the same time, he also believes that "affirmative action has shown itself to be more bad than good and that blacks . . . now stand to lose more from it than they gain."[29]

A variation on the theme of this section is that some students, and the occasional faculty member, will challenge that universities like Stanford are admitting the "wrong kind" of minority students. This criticism takes two forms. One is the middle- vs lower-class argument just mentioned, accompanied by the claim that the latter should benefit more than it does from the affirmative action efforts in undergraduate admissions. The second argument is that the minority students of any one group should be "representatives of the people." As Stephen Carter writes:

The opportunities the civil rights movement opened up have been diluted by the imposition of a stereotype that the black people on the inside will hold a particular, and predictable, set of political positions—will be, in effect, black people of the right kind. Not only does this notion stereotype the black professionals whom it burdens; it also stereotypes the people themselves, the less fortunate, who become a faceless monolith without any of the richness or diversity that characterizes people of color. They become simply possessors of a "viewpoint" that the black people who reach positions of influence are expected to articulate. And what goes often unspoken yet clearly implied in all of this is that people of color who do not hold or represent this special viewpoint (whatever it is) are not the right people to fill these representational slots.[30]

This call for broad representation is not unique to black people. Similar examples are seen in the Mexican-American and Native American Indian communities. In the latter, not only are tribal distinctions important, but so is the difference between the rural and the urban Indian. There are further distinctions in the "degree" of Indianness: a full-blooded Navajo brings a different experience and perspective than someone who has only one grandparent with some tribal affiliation. Mexican-American people differ considerably in their degree of ethnicity and disagree, for example, on the role of bilingual education, as Richard Rodriguez confirms.[31] In short, it seems to me that neither individual ethnic groups of people nor the individual members of any particular group can be stereotyped. This simple statement seems obvious, yet unfortunately it is rarely acknowledged.

Recently, some have proposed readjusting the emphasis of affirmative action programs from race to class. News articles have suggested that economic need should replace race as the basis for affirmative action, arguing that blacks would still be disproportionate beneficiaries but that all poor people, including whites, would benefit from the change.[32] Eleanor Holmes Norton, the Democratic delegate to Congress from the District of Columbia, was quoted in response: "Don't you recognize a diversion when you see one?"

So far, no one has proposed applying this idea to college admissions. I see a number of difficulties in doing so, which I illustrate by referring to the undergraduate admissions process at Stanford. Even in times of serious budget constraints, the university remains firmly committed to the principle of need-blind admissions, whereby no consideration is given to applicants' ability to pay for a Stanford education when their applications for admission are reviewed. We are committed to meeting the demonstrated need of those students who are admitted. In principle, then, socioeconomic class should not be a disadvantage to any applicant. This is clearly not the case, as I mentioned earlier, but through no fault of the admissions process. Lower-income high school seniors are, in general, not as well prepared for a college education or as competitive in meeting the criteria for admission as their higher-income classmates. In short, however sensitive the selection process, the senior year of high school is too late for most applicants to overcome their disadvantages. Furthermore, if a college operates a need-blind admissions process, how does it simultaneously give special consideration to class? Although disadvantaged circumstances are always factored into admissions decisions at Stanford, socioeconomic status plays a larger role in the allocation of financial aid, which happens after a student is admitted.

I believe that Eleanor Holmes Norton makes a valid point. The fundamental reasons for affirmative action are independent of class (although often issues such as poverty are clearly interrelated). Norton and others have raised questions about the relative weight that race would be given if the preferences should shift from race to class; this is not a trivial issue to consider in the complex process of selecting a freshman class. At least one analyst has concluded: "Programs based on race or sex could have one big advantage—simplicity."[33] As we have seen, considerations of race are far from simple, but everything is relative. Simplicity is good, but principles are better operational guides for developing programs. I would give my vote to the development of educational and social welfare programs for poor families and, for the near future at least, the maintenance of affirmative action programs. The former would contribute to a shorter lifetime for the latter; both contribute to the causes of liberty and justice for all.

Without affirmative action programs in college admissions, there would be very few minority students enrolled today. The distinguished former president of Harvard University, Derek Bok, has contributed to a number of discussions on social issues related to universities, including affirmative action. In one article, he claims that without such programs, only 1 percent of Harvard's freshman class would be black.[34] I never attempted such a calculation at Stanford; in fact, it is difficult to know how one would go about making such an estimate. Even if we eliminated "special consideration" for selected groups of minority students, we would still pay careful attention to extenuating circumstances, socioeconomic diversity, limited opportunities, and other nonethnic characteristics specified in the criteria for admission. Specific calculations aside, it *is* undoubtedly true that without the special considerations, the number of entering minority students at Stanford would be smaller than it is today; if it were *not* true, we certainly could not claim anything "special" about our affirmative action considerations and should eliminate the item from our criteria.[35]

Since close to 90 percent of the undergraduate students who enter Stanford graduate, and since the number of black, Mexican-American, and Native American Indian students who enter is larger than it would be without our affirmative action efforts, it is tempting to conclude that these numerical facts prove that affirmative action is a good thing. Carter poses this question explicitly: "The question for advocates of affirmative action, then, remains what it has always been: Is it a good thing, is it a *safe* thing, to encourage white America to continue to think in racial terms? And people who insist on color blindness must face the analogous question: Is it a good thing, is it a *safe* thing, to deny the differences among people, and among our many subcultures, that make our nation the wonderfully heterogeneous land it is?" He concludes:

What is needed, rather, is the development of a better grammar of race, a way through which we can at once take account of it and not punish it. And a sensible way to start . . . is to say that with all the various instances in which race might be relevant, either to the government or to individuals, it will not be used as an indicator of merit—no one will be more valued than anyone else because of skin color. The corollary is that everyone's merit would therefore be judged by the same tests, and if the tests in question are unfair . . . then they will be swept away *and replaced with something else. . . .* My argument is that the standard should be explicit, and that once it is selected, everyone should be required to meet it."[36]

There is an understandable thread of ambivalence in Carter's discussion, understandable because—as I hope no one at this stage will deny—the issues are enormously complex. And for people of color, the debate is more immediately personal, ever present, and unavoidable. Carter's suggestion that we select explicit standards for all is also not without its problems. A selective undergraduate admissions process is ultimately subjective. Every applicant, and parent, would like nothing better than to be given an unambiguous, specific set of standards that would guarantee an offer of admission. In a

highly selective process, however, the characteristics of the applicant pool vary from year to year in ways beyond the control of the
admissions office, and judgment on each individual circumstance is
necessarily going to come into play. For example, admissions
officers cannot control the number of high school seniors who plan
to apply to college in a given year, let alone to their particular college. Similarly, an applicant to Stanford in a given year cannot control the number of applicants who are children of Stanford alumni
and consequently are given special consideration in the admissions
process. In short, there are many factors over which neither the admissions officer nor the applicant has control.

*The era of affirmative action in college admissions should soon come to
a close.* This issue has been on the political table in Washington,
D.C., for some time and, like many other debates, it neatly distin-
guishes Democrats from Republicans. When President Lyndon
Johnson gave the memorable commencement address at Howard
University in June 1965, he declared: "You do not wipe away the
scars of centuries by saying: Now, you are free to go where you want,
do as you desire, and choose the leaders you please. You do not take
a man who for years has been hobbled by chains, liberate him, bring
him to the starting line of a race, saying, 'you are free to compete
with all the others.'"[37] Johnson thought of affirmative action as a
transition program. It seems reasonable that any program introduced to address historical injustices must, almost by definition,
have some finite lifetime, but affirmative action is also a current
safeguard against continued racism in this country, and it helps to
alleviate the underrepresentation of minority groups. Consequently,
when I say that I hope the time will come when affirmative action
programs should be abolished, I mean it as a statement of optimism
about the future.

Affirmative action programs should cease when we reach a more
reasonable and realistic representation of people of color in all
professions and positions of responsibility. I am not advocating
proportional representation as a necessity, but we should certainly
aim to do better than 2 percent black lawyers and judges and 2 percent Hispanic faculty in colleges and universities. Affirmative action

programs should cease when racism is no longer tolerated and when "liberty and justice for all" is more than an admirable constitutional premise. Affirmative action programs should cease when a black nominee for the Supreme Court is no longer noteworthy or controversial among all the people of this country. Affirmative action programs should cease when the police respond to complaints from minorities in the same way that they respond to complaints from whites, and when court sentences for blacks are the same as for whites who are guilty of similar crimes. The complete list of grievances is long, and we can all add our own personal examples.

As noted before, I do not see all this happening in the near future—not before the end of this century. Indeed, there may never be a time in this diverse country when the color of someone's skin is not someone else's ready ground for discrimination. We can certainly make progress, however, by working in other essential directions.

Affirmative action in college admissions does not address the fundamental problems of society in the United States. Amen. Surely no one would disagree with Shelby Steele that "preferential treatment does not teach skills, or educate, or instill motivation."[38] Unfortunately, too many children of all colors in this country suffer the disadvantages of parents who cannot, or do not, guide them; poverty; poor schools; minimal health care; substandard housing; dangerous neighborhoods; and exposure to drugs, disease, and crime. While all children suffer, minority children suffer disproportionately.

A chilling portrait of minority children in 1990 is drawn by Jonathan Kozol. He describes his visits to the schools and neighborhoods of young children in East St. Louis; the south side of Chicago; New York City; Camden, New Jersey; Washington, D.C.; and San Antonio, Texas. In each city, he found insufficient books for any class, laboratories with no working faucets, schools without librarians, and teachers who have to provide their own equipment; he found school bathrooms without toilet seats and toilet paper, without paper towels and soap; classrooms crowded beyond their capacities, with no windows, and ceilings falling down; school nurses facing children with rotting teeth, chronic and untreated illnesses, and pregnancies. In these cities, home life is often just as grim. Houses suffer from regular backups of the local sewage system and are surrounded by abandoned buildings whose yards serve as the local garbage dump. In many of these streets, violence and crime are everyday events, crack and whore houses are neighborhood features, and the local factories spew pollution into the air and water.

In short, the depressing details Kozol provides confirm the conclusion that "because of the way our public schools are funded in this country, the rich get a richer quality of education while the children of the poor get less—less real education, less hope, less of our concern."[39] (This conclusion, of course, transcends the boundaries of ethnicity; it holds for *all* disadvantaged children in this country, and addressing a problem that affects *all* children avoids most of the criticisms and philosophical dilemmas we have seen in affirmative action programs.) In such circumstances, even with the efforts and concerns of the most devoted teachers, principals, and parents, personal survival becomes paramount. Survival to high school graduation seems a luxury, and a college education is often beyond conception. Such descriptions portray a world essentially unknown to admissions officers at selective colleges; applicants from high schools in such neighborhoods are a rarity, and when they do appear, their chances of admission are slight. These were the cases I felt the least comfortable acting "affirmatively" on because the probability of success appeared so small. This is a difficult confession; the fault lies not with the disadvantaged applicants, or necessarily with their teachers, or with the staff in undergraduate admissions. Our sympathy and regrets will make no difference on the road to change, but more successful college graduates, both minority and nonminority, who understand the underlying causes can make a difference. The guiding principle of the public service programs at Stanford, in which more than half the undergraduates participate each year, is just that: You *can* make a difference.

Steele offers a slightly different view in his argument against "preferences."

I think we need social policies that are committed to two goals: the educational and economic development of disadvantaged people, regardless of race, and the eradication from our society—through close monitoring and severe sanctions—of racial, ethnic, or gender discrimination. . . . To be against [preferences] is unkind. But I think the unkindest cut is to bestow on children like my own an undeserved advantage while neglecting the disadvantaged children on the East Side of my city who will likely never be in a position to benefit from a preference. Give my children fairness; give disadvantaged children a better shot at development—better elementary and secondary schools, job training, safe neighborhoods, better financial assistance for college, and so on. Fewer blacks go to college today than ten years ago; more black males of college age are in prison or under the control of the criminal justice system than in colleges. This despite racial preferences.[40]

I strongly agree with Steele on the necessity for the educational and economic development of all disadvantaged people in this country. I would argue, though, that the preferences for minority students do help; the changes that we have seen in colleges and universities since 1970 have made, and will continue to make, a difference. We are not yet ready to abandon affirmative action programs, but open debate on the reasons for their existence, and the value of their continued existence, is both healthy for the discussants and beneficial to the cause.

THE CHALLENGES OF THE 1990'S

The most serious and fundamental challenges in university affirmative action in the years ahead include: choosing which groups to target; addressing the issue of "representation"; avoiding the pitting of race against race; dealing with changing demographics and identities; finding alternatives to affirmative action; addressing the long-term future of affirmative action; and maintaining an equitable admissions policy and process. In summary, we need to fulfill the goals expressed in the Constitution of the United States of America: "to form a more perfect union, establish justice, . . . promote the general welfare, and secure the blessings of liberty to ourselves and our posterity."

Stanford targets three ethnic groups in undergraduate admissions: blacks, Mexican-Americans, and Native American Indians.

(At the graduate level, Puerto Ricans are also included, an inconsistency that was something of a historical accident and one that has not escaped the notice of some members of the Stanford community.) Other selective colleges and universities define their targets somewhat differently; some include Hispanics generally, others add Filipinos, and others focus efforts on low-income Asian-Americans. The general Stanford criteria for admission, I believe, are sensitive to individuals who have experienced disadvantages of any kind even if they are not members of any of these three groups. One of the reasons that Stanford focuses specifically on Mexican-Americans is the university's location in a region of high (and increasing) Mexican-American population. The representation of Mexican-Americans among Stanford undergraduates is consequently higher than at almost any other selective college in the country; the campus community flourishes through the Center for Chicano Research, Casa Zapata (one of four ethnic theme dormitories), El Centro Chicano (the student cultural center), and various publications. Not surprisingly, new students perceive the community as welcoming and supportive.

I have tried to show that affirmative action has its limitations in addressing social problems, and I also believe that there must be some reasonable limitation on the expectations imposed on any one institution in its affirmative action efforts. Specifically, it is unreasonable for any university to target every arguably underrepresented or underprivileged ethnic group. We at Stanford could not do everything we would have liked even for the three specified groups. These deficiencies became even more apparent in times of severe budget reductions, as the following anecdote illustrates.

At a meeting of the College Board a few years ago, I listened with considerable sympathy to the case made by a young native Hawaiian for more colleges and universities to give preference to native Hawaiians in the admissions process. When I tried to present the dilemma from the perspective of a dean of undergraduate admissions, his response was, "That's your problem, not ours." All very easy to say (and all very easy for the audience to agree), but these are times of extraordinarily difficult choices in institutional maintenance and survival. The solution lies in more institutional sharing of affirmative action responsibilities, and more collaborative efforts such as those we have seen through the Consortium on Financing Higher Education (a group of 32 selective private colleges and universities), the College Board (for example, through its Equity Project), and the National Association of College Admissions Counselors, among others.[41] Even in collaborative efforts there are pressing demands on staff time, there are necessary limitations in program expansion, and the priority list includes other very pressing issues such as the cost of attending college, standardized testing, and graduate student affirmative action (another enormous challenge beyond, but clearly related to, the scope of this book). Stanford can effectively target blacks, Mexican-Americans, and Native American Indians; other colleges can include Puerto Ricans, Filipinos, native Hawaiians, and other groups they have determined to be deserving. This does not mean that groups would or should be limited to attending certain institutions, but rather that the responsibilities for their well-being and development would be shared.

Previously, I mentioned my concern about the difficult role of minority admissions staff in carrying out the demanding work of the office where they are employed and in being held responsible, often unreasonably so, by their individual communities for any declines in minority enrollment. The pressures on minority staff within and outside the office are undoubtedly more severe than those on majority staff. For one thing, they have to wrestle in a very personal way with all the issues of affirmative action; others on the staff frequently turn to them for "solutions." Add to this the external political pressures, and we produce one very tough job. I always emphasized the importance to all the staff in undergraduate admissions of remaining neutral; once we were perceived to be partisan in any small way, we would lose both the trust of the community and any credibility we might have earned through the integrity of the selection process. Anyone who has worked in a large (or even medium-sized) public office can quickly imagine the effect of these tensions in action. One of my most memorable experiences relates to the question of "representation" presented earlier in this chapter.

At the beginning of fall quarter one year, just as we were preparing for high school visits and fall travel, our experienced Mexican-American director resigned. She had been offered an attractive promotion in another office on campus, and I agreed that it would be a wise career move for her to accept it. Unfortunately, the timing left us in a less than ideal position. University policy required that we announce the vacancy for this position, a process that included twenty working days of posting. After the posting, staff members needed to review all the applications, interview a set of candidates, and check references. In addition, we needed time to allow the selected candidate to arrange a departure date from his or her previous job. It is very difficult to accomplish all of this in less than six weeks, and the process often takes longer. Consequently, we would have to function without a key director for at least six weeks at one of the busiest periods of the year. The job was quickly posted, the preliminary interviews were completed, and the time came for the final round of interviews, in which I took part. After much discussion, I decided that we did not yet have a candidate who would meet the needs of the office and the community. This was a difficult decision to reach, particularly when the finalists had been interviewed by a small group of Mexican-American students and staff who had subsequently presented their evaluation and recommendations. As always, however, the buck stops at someone's desk, in this case mine. Word of this decision quickly spread, faster than I would have believed possible, and I soon received some critical letters from students and calls from concerned faculty. Their concern and disappointment were understandable; I shared these feelings. When you lose one important staff member from a group of twelve, the consequences are significant for all concerned, and in this case there were also repercussions for the community.

I offered to explain my decision to interested students, faculty, and staff, and a meeting was soon arranged. It was a hot evening, and the meeting room was soon crowded with about 70 people who wanted to hear what I had to say. I believed, and still believe, my case was a reasonable one: In the past six years, I had been responsible for hiring the two previous Mexican-American directors, both of whom had produced excellent results (and had gone on to positions of greater responsibility at Stanford); the enrollment of Mexican-Americans in my tenure had reached a record high. I understood what was needed in the position, and I was willing to look further to guarantee it. Not surprisingly, my presentation received mixed reactions. Some understood my position and supported it; others were more critical and unsympathetic and took the decision as a sign of my diminished commitment to the community. "How could *you* possibly know what is best for us?" asked one student. And how could we ensure adequate evaluation of Mexican-American applicants without a Mexican-American reader of the files? To the latter question, I answered that the recommendation of the Mexican-American director was never a final one, but rather an advisory recommendation to the deans, and I hoped our record of past years was convincing evidence of our commitment to increasing the enrollment of Mexican-American undergraduates.

I may have convinced some critics, but definitely not all of them. Although members of my staff always encouraged me not to take things personally, this experience was painful however I looked at it. Perhaps most personally disappointing was the presence of some people I had thought to be friends and supporters who now aligned themselves with the critics, not offering any support when they had plenty of information to do so. But clearly more important was continuing to focus on completing our assignment, both in that year's reading of Mexican-American files and in the hiring of a replacement director. Both were subsequently, and I believe very successfully, completed. The story is an unfortunate commentary on the status of affirmative action in 1990, in which only representatives of a specific minority group can be considered "qualified" to assess applicants of the same ethnicity. As Carter observed: "So many black people, maybe most, simply do not trust white people to be fair." [42] This point can be further refined by the "representation" arguments presented earlier; only certain kinds of Mexican-Americans qualify to review the applicants of the same ethnicity to ensure that the "right" kind of students are admitted.

Just as divisions have emerged within ethnic groups to contest the "right representative" line of thought, so have divisions between ethnic groups. In recent years, the national press has given coverage to the tension between Asians and blacks, particularly in New York City and Los Angeles, and between Hispanics and blacks in Miami and Washington, D.C. The City University of New York has been in the news with reports of black and Jewish faculty members making insensitive and disparaging comments about each other.

The importance of ethnic groups coexisting on college campuses is a critical concern for every admissions office across the country. According to analyses of the Western Interstate Commission on Higher Education and the College Board, by 1995 one-third of American public school students will be "minorities." The elementary and secondary school enrollment figures cited show dramatic changes for the period 1985 to 1994: The enrollment of Asians and Pacific Islanders is expected to increase by 70 percent; Latino enrollment is expected to increase by 54 percent; black students will remain the second largest ethnic group in public schools, behind whites, and are expected to increase by 13 percent; American Indians and Alaskan natives enrolled in school are expected to remain the smallest group but will increase by 29 percent; and white, non-Latino enrollments are expected to decrease from 71 percent to 66 percent. In this same period, the overall number of high school graduates is expected to decline by close to 4 percent, although this number varies significantly from region to region. In 1989, the article continues, Hispanic and nonwhite students already made up more than 50 percent of public high school graduates in Hawaii, New Mexico, and the District of Columbia. California and Mississippi are expected to join this group by 1995. In 1991 at a few universities, such as UC Berkeley, less than 50 percent of the freshman class was white.[43]

These numbers give new meaning to the term "minority," as used in college admissions, although in 1989 the proportion of blacks, Hispanic Americans, and Native American Indians and Alaskan natives in college was still well below their proportion of the college-age population. This continued underrepresentation of particular groups is reason enough to continue affirmative action programs; at the same time, the projections present a new kind of dilemma for college admissions officers. With the expected dramatic changes, should we continue as before with affirmative action programs? What do we make of the Asian-American representation, which is already higher in college enrollments than in the national population? It is clearly wrong, and in fact illegal, to limit the enrollment of Asian-Americans (or any other ethnic group) among freshmen. Then what gives in the equation governing the size of a freshman class?

As if the changing demographics were not sufficient challenge in the admissions profession, minority considerations are exacerbated by the issues of self-identification and racial intermarriages. The first page of the Stanford application includes an optional section on ethnicity, which is accompanied by an explanation that colleges and universities are required to submit to government agencies information regarding (among other things) ethnicity. Applicants who are citizens or permanent residents are encouraged to self-identify by checking a box marked Black / African-American; Mexican-American / Chicano; Ethnic Hawaiian; White; American Indian / Alaskan Native (indicate tribal affiliation); Asian / Pacific Islander; Other Hispanic / Latino (please identify); Decline to State; or Other (please identify). Some students will legitimately check four different boxes, leaving the admissions office in a quandary about how to classify them. If a student is one-quarter black, for example, does she benefit from our affirmative action considerations? What about one-eighth Mexican-American? Here again, the reader of the application needs to consider a wide range in the degree of ethnicity. Should the first-generation daughter of Spanish-speaking migrant workers from Mexico, now living in California's Central Valley, be considered in the same way as the self-identified, one-quarter Mexican-American son of professional parents from Colorado, who does not speak Spanish and whose Mexican heritage stems from a physician grandfather who was born in Mexico City?

Fortunately, in a subjective process all these considerations can be brought into play, and we do not have to come up with definitive answers. (I have often wondered how ethnicity is factored into the admission procedure at colleges where the selection process is far less subjective.) In the example I just gave, at Stanford the latter candidate might still be compelling on grounds other than his comparatively less significant heritage. But the complexities are not difficult to imagine, and many cases are not as clear-cut as the ones I have just described.

The self-identified Native American Indian / Alaskan native presents special complexities. Applicants who check this box are subsequently sent a letter from the admissions office at Stanford asking them to provide details of their tribal affiliation. This can prove an embarrassing question for some who respond: "Oops, sorry, I checked the wrong box" (but better for us to know up-front), or who can provide little more than a vague answer. Why should we question Native Americans and not the other ethnic groups? As the UCMI report noted:

While the tribes themselves, as sovereign nations, determine tribal membership, the Bureau of Indian Affairs has specified the requirement of one-quarter Indian blood for people receiving benefits, including higher education benefits. Thus admissions officers recruiting Indian students must consider not only the federal regulations, but also the subtleties of tribal and community recognition. With over three hundred Indian tribes, and more than half the American Indian population now residing off reservations in urban, not rural, communities, recruiters face a complex challenge indeed.[44]

To alleviate the confusion in assessing the considerable degrees of variation of any ethnicity, we resorted to trust in the applicant's self-identification. If applicants self-identified as black or Mexican-American, we believed them. The question of self-identification and its role in the college selection process will become increasingly complex as the national demographics reflect the next decade of dramatic changes, and mixed marriages expand the variety of ethnic backgrounds in college applicants.

A separate dilemma related to Native American Indians, and reflecting contemporary changes, is seen in the choice and history of Stanford's mascot. After an unsuccessful initial introduction of the American Indian symbol by the chairman of Stanford's athletic board, Dr. T. M. Williams (class of 1897), the idea was revived in the early 1930's, and the Indian served as the mascot for Stanford's athletic teams for over 40 years. The early 1930's were the proud days of the "Vow Boys," who made good on their pledge never to lose in football to USC and led Stanford to the Rose Bowl for three consecutive years. They were the days of Hank Luisetti and his astonishing running one-handed basketball shots. And this was when fans began wearing the feathered headdress, a show of support for Stanford athletes that grew into even more elaborate performances involving a mascot.[45] In a 1966 university publication, for example, we can read, "Prince Lightfoot represents in life the University's Indian mascot. A full-blooded Yurok, he dances in elaborate ceremonial dress at major athletic events."[46] These were times, of course, when almost the only nonwhite faces seen on campus were those of international students. As the university became more concerned about diversity, and the undergraduate population changed in ethnic makeup, questions began to be asked about the appropriateness of having an Indian mascot. And in 1971, over the objections of vocal alumni, the university quit using the Indian as a mascot. Today, American Indians and Alaskan natives make up 1 percent of the Stanford undergraduates, and the American Indian heritage is celebrated on campus in ways very different from earlier decades. We have the Native American Cultural Center; a theme house, Muwekma-Tah-Ruk, where students reside; and the American Indian Program office. Tribal dances are performed at the annual Stanford Pow-Wow, established twenty years ago and now the largest gathering of its kind in California—but not on the football field. A few Stanford alumni still lament the passing of their mascot (and some can still be seen insensitively and stubbornly sporting their feathers and sweaters with a caricature of an Indian at football games), but most understand why the mascot was inappropriate. This is the day of the Stanford Cardinal—the color, not the bird.

A Stanford trustee once asked me a tough question: How would I measure my success in the position of dean of undergraduate admissions? I don't remember quite how I answered this at the time, but when I discussed the question with my staff, someone suggested that my task was to keep most of the people happy most of the time. It is true that the dean necessarily produces many unhappy people; 10,000 a year (roughly the number who don't receive the thick letters) is probably an overestimate because not *all* of those who apply to Stanford really want to enroll. Besides, after seven great years in the job I don't like to think of being responsible for nearly 70,000 unhappy seventeen-year-olds. In addition to all of those unsuccessful applicants, there are disappointed parents, critical alumni, unhappy sports fans, and community members who don't think the dean is doing the best job. One elderly lady came up to me after my presentation to a group of senior citizens in Palo Alto, looked me straight in the eye and said, "You know, you admit some real losers at Stanford." Hers was one of the more disconcerting complaints I ever heard, but I admired her straightforward approach!

The trustee's question is a particularly tough one to answer with regard to affirmative action. When Stephen Carter, Richard Rodriguez, or Shelby Steele writes about the subject, he understandably focuses on his own personal perspective as a black or Mexican-American in an academic environment. In creating a freshman class, the perspective constantly changes for those who are responsible for the decisions, but the outlook is very different for the individual students who are admitted and enroll. I believe that you learn most from those who do not think as you do, from those who have had very different life experiences, who come to the university with very different talents and interests. Students in homogeneous classes do not offer each other much potential for learning; high achievers in a diverse community do. The critical question in the art of selecting the freshman class is how to produce an optimal mix of characteristics, with a student population of fixed size. I am reluctant to rank order the challenges faced by a dean of undergraduate admissions, but addressing the concerns and perspectives of every ethnic group must rank near the top. It is an exquisitely delicate exercise in balance, in which the admissions staff, led by the dean, are guaranteed to make many people unhappy most of the time.

The Role of Varsity Athletics

Mens sana in corpore sano (A sound mind in a sound body).
—Juvenal, *Satires X*, c. 125 A.D.

FIRST IMPRESSIONS

I arrived at Stanford in 1965 as the wife of a newly appointed assistant professor of physics. We had spent the previous year, our first in California, at UC Berkeley, where the intensity of the Stanford–Cal rivalry had somehow escaped my notice. In retrospect, I chalk up that omission to the arrival of our first child and to other somewhat overwhelming first impressions of the "wild" West after living on the more established Eastern seaboard. It did not take long, however, to appreciate that we had arrived in a sporting paradise—glorious weather most of the year, breathtaking physical surroundings of sea and nearby mountains, and a wealth of athletic facilities. As I sometimes told prospective applicants to Stanford many years later when I made high school visits back East as dean of undergraduate admissions, it was possible in California to swim in the Pacific in the morning and ski in the Sierras in the afternoon. (New Jersey or Massachusetts in late fall were particularly impressionable spots to pass on this information.) On a more serious note, I went on to add that one of the features that distinguished Stanford from other fine research universities was the combination of first-rate academics and Division I athletics. Maintaining these dual strengths is an exceptionally ambitious undertaking for all concerned. President Emeritus Richard Lyman once called the effort "a Hindu rope trick." [1]

My introduction to the quality of athletics at Stanford came in the early 1970's. One hot afternoon as I was walking by the varsity tennis courts, I paused to watch a fierce singles match in progress. As a longtime tennis enthusiast, I remember thinking that it was every bit as good as matches I had seen at Wimbledon. It was only later, when Roscoe Tanner and Raul Ramirez (the two I'd seen in action that day on campus) were actually playing at Wimbledon, that I appreciated the aptness of my comparison. These were world-class tennis players competing in intercollegiate athletics, Tanner for Stanford and Ramirez for the University of Southern California (USC). This first encounter was only a glimpse of the formidable range of talent in both men's and women's sports that was nurtured at the university, and I have since watched comparable talents and equally memorable events in football, basketball, baseball, swimming, track, volleyball, and soccer, to mention a notable sample of Stanford varsity teams. A typical Saturday on campus brings a seemingly endless stream of games to delight both participant and spectator.

SUCCESS AT STANFORD

Given the setting, it is not surprising that athletics play a large role in the lives of many Stanford students; activities range from participating in one of the 29 Division I varsity sports to supporting classmates at one of the many weekly events. It is quite an experience to cheer on the football team in the 86,000-seat stadium, although admittedly it is rarely filled to capacity except every other year for the so-called Big Game against UC Berkeley or for the occasional visit of a top-twenty team such as Notre Dame. (On a few occasions I was privileged to be an invited sideline guest, cautioned to stay well outside the line of action of advancing 300-pound linemen; but no one there is spared the brutal sound of clashing helmets. The sideline provides an intimate view of the intensity and pressure of competition—sweat, blood, tears, and all.) In recent years, both the men's and women's basketball teams have drawn capacity crowds to Maples Pavilion on Thursday or Saturday evenings. Sitting in the bleachers during the final minutes of a close game, with the Stanford Band blasting away in its energetic and inimitable style, is an unforgettable and unifying event for enthusiastic fans; many visiting teams don't forget it either.

In 1992, almost 400 students competed in sixteen men's varsity sports at Stanford, and more than 200 women competed at the varsity level in thirteen sports. The competition is primarily in the Pacific-10 conference (the University of Arizona, Arizona State University, UC Berkeley, the University of Oregon, Oregon State University, the University of California, Los Angeles (UCLA), USC, the University of Washington, and Washington State University), one of the strongest conferences in the country. At another level are Stanford's 20 club sports, including men's and women's cycling, lacrosse, squash, rugby, and skiing. Over 1,000 students participate each year in club sports, which are entirely student-run and also provide opportunities for Stanford students to compete against teams from other colleges and universities.

Finally, thousands of other students compete on intramural sports teams affiliated with campus residences, organizations, and departments. These popular competitions are not as public as the varsity sports, but they are nevertheless lively and intense. And almost every undergraduate elects to take at least one of the coeducational classes in physical education, perhaps because there is so much emphasis on physical fitness in California. In addition, Stanford's facilities are excellent, and the addictive California weather enhances the offerings: the campus is home to three outdoor swimming pools; 26 tennis courts; a driving range and an 18-hole golf course; a new indoor sports center for volleyball, wrestling, and gymnastics; riding stables; and 40 acres of playing fields. It is not surprising that some have referred, somewhat unkindly and perhaps a bit enviously, to the university on its 8,000 acres as a country club; in fact, the facilities would put many country clubs in the shade, but they provide a wealth of much-appreciated opportunities for all Stanford's students, faculty, and staff, not to mention the local community. In all, more than 80 percent of the student body take advantage of the athletic facilities and programs in one form or another.

It is one thing to provide the opportunities and quite another to produce the success that the varsity teams have earned. The list of modern championships and champions is impressive.[2]

Between 1980 and 1991, Stanford won 27 NCAA team championships and 28 collegiate team championships, the most in the nation.

Between 1989 and 1993, Stanford won thirteen NCAA team championships, the most in the NCAA.

The baseball team has been a regular participant in the College World Series, and the two handsome, signed bats on my office wall are reminders of their championship seasons in 1987 and 1988.

In 1990, we celebrated Stanford's first NCAA championship in women's basketball, a title that was hard-earned and well deserved. I was among the diehard Stanford fans who attended the championship game, dwarfed in that 27,000-seat stadium in Nashville, Tennessee; it was an unforgettable scene. The title was repeated in 1992, a year in which Stanford won five NCAA championships (women's basketball, men's gymnastics, women's swimming, men's swimming, and men's tennis), more than any other school.

The U.S. Olympic teams that competed in Barcelona in 1992 had 38 competitors and coaches from Stanford, and the total number of medals earned put Stanford ahead of many countries. Stanford alumni and students participated in ten different sports: baseball, basketball, crew, fencing, gymnastics, soccer, swimming, track and field, volleyball, and water polo.

In 1992–93, Stanford won four NCAA team titles: women's volleyball and swimming, and men's gymnastics and swimming.

For those of us who are perennial fans, the list of honors never seems to end, and the schedule of fierce match-ups in every sport never ceases to thrill.

Most undergraduates, of course, do not perform at the national level in a sport. For those who do, including many varsity athletes at Stanford, the hard work and commitment, day after day, year after year, usually begin at an early age. By the time high school comes around, these dedicated student-athletes usually do little other than go to school, study, and work four or five hours a day at their sport, with the remaining hours given up to the essentials of eating and sleeping. Their athletic activities often require a united family commitment, notably parents who are willing to devote hours driving to competitions, to offer financial support for training and equipment, and to provide general emotional support amidst the stress of training and competition. The most talented student-athletes are usually identified by observant college coaches at a young age, and the early pressures from the most persistent recruiters can be overwhelming for students and parents inexperienced in such courtships. The students who enroll at Stanford and who choose to continue their sport while pursuing an undergraduate degree are rare, apparently dauntless beings. In the academically competitive world of the selective university, there are pressures enough; it takes an exceptional individual to handle the physical and emotional stresses of maintaining a rigorous athletic training schedule along with an increased level of competition.

In any given year, about 8 percent of Stanford undergraduates, around 600 young men and women, belong to this distinctive set, and they have earned my admiration. All could have opted for a less challenging academic setting, and a few could even have entered the world of professional sports directly from high school. They decided instead to tackle the most difficult combination—earning a degree from a demanding university while contributing to their sport. In 1991, two varsity athletes, Cory Booker in football and Bob Sternfels in water polo, were among the 32 Rhodes scholars selected in the United States. The third Stanford Rhodes scholar named in 1991, Oomphemetse Mooki, competed at the club level in track and cross-country; all three provide fitting exemplars of *mens sana in corpore sano*.

Stanford's treatment of varsity athletes is distinctly unlike that of many big-time sports schools. Varsity athletes are treated the same as all the other incoming students. They do not receive special housing privileges but are assigned throughout the freshman and four-class dorms. It may be exciting to have an Olympic record holder as your roommate or next-door neighbor, but such celebrities receive no recognition in daily life at Stanford. A favorite anecdote that confirms this point is one I heard, second-hand, about the Olympic gold medalist swimmer Janet Evans. In her freshman year, the story goes, Janet was looking for one of the men on the swim team and knocked on his door to see if he could be found. "Is Brian here?" she asked the roommate. The answer was no. "Please tell him that Janet came by," she requested, to which the roommate innocently replied, "Oh, are you a swimmer too?"

There is the risk of omission in attempting to provide a representative sample of Stanford graduates who have gone on to careers as successful professional athletes. But even a short list of the most recent alumni and alumnae offers verification of the range of talent: John Elway and Brad Muster in football; Patty Fendick, Debbie Graham, Patrick McEnroe, and Tim Mayotte in tennis; Jennifer Azzi, Adam Keefe, and Todd Lichti in basketball; Debi Thomas in figure skating; PattiSue Plumer in track; and Jack McDowell and Mike Mussina in baseball.

Just as the student-athlete who chooses to enroll here faces substantial challenges, so do the coaches. In addition to the responsibility of preparing for the tough prospective competition within the Pac-10 and beyond, the coaches can only recruit from a very limited field of prospective freshmen when they allow, as they must, for the selective admissions process. These men and women coaches are a special breed. All good coaches want to produce winning teams, but some circumstances offer better chances of success than others. If anyone has to be able to master that "Hindu rope trick," it is the Stanford coaches. They show courage and confidence similar to those of their student-athletes in accepting a position here, perhaps the ultimate challenge in college coaching; these are positions that should not be taken on by those who are unable to accept the importance of the primary criterion in the admissions process, academic achievement and potential, or by those who cannot accept the way the admissions process works. Of course there is a constant and healthy tension between the aspirations of the coaches and the reality of the acceptances; there are also periodic disappointments and complaints from the coaches when a prize recruit is not accepted for admission. On balance, however, I think it is fair to say that a coach who chooses to work at Stanford acknowledges the advantages of a system in which the admission of student-athletes is ultimately the responsibility of the dean of undergraduate admissions. And so to a key question: How are the future Stanford varsity athletes selected for admission?

SELECTING THE STUDENT ATHLETES

First and foremost, prospective varsity athletes at Stanford are considered through fundamentally the same admissions process as every other applicant for the freshman and transfer classes. The same guidelines outlined in Chapter 2 apply to this set of candidates. *No* admissions decisions for athletes (or for any other category of student) are made by the president of the university, athletes' admissions are not discussed and decided by a special faculty committee, and perhaps most important, no decisions on the admission of any Stanford undergraduates are made by a coach or any other member of the Department of Athletics. For better or worse (not surprisingly, I believe it is for better), the criteria for admission state that while "the Department of Athletics may designate outstanding athletes for special attention, the Dean of Undergraduate Admissions retains final authority over all admissions." Along with this significant responsibility comes the potential wrath of the alumni and fans, and sometimes the press, when the season closes with a losing record. As someone once noted, when the Stanford team performs well, the coach gets a lot of credit; when the team performs badly, the dean of undergraduate admissions is held responsible. I reflect on some never-to-be-forgotten experiences on this front later in this chapter.

The preceding paragraph raises an interesting question. Is it reasonable to assume that a dean of undergraduate admissions at Stanford who is not an athlete, or even necessarily a fan, can make fair and evenhanded decisions on the applications of varsity athletes? I hope that most reasonable people would agree that the selection of a dean should not be determined by his or her athletic prowess or record as a sports fan. This is not to say that an appreciation of the importance of varsity athletics at a university like Stanford is irrelevant. When I was first appointed dean, I heard a rumor that a zealous Stanford alumnus was incensed to discover (I don't know how) that I had never bought a football season ticket. I was equally incensed, reasons of privacy aside, that I was already prejudged to be a nonsupporter of the football team. This argument could be extended to the relevance of gender in selecting a dean of undergraduate admissions. Again, some of the most ardent Stanford fans have argued that the job is not well suited to a woman and have questioned whether the judgment of a female dean of admissions could possibly be in the best interest of Stanford athletics. Fortunately for me, I had heard this kind of argument before; when I was appointed as the first female assistant to the president at Stanford, one older alumnus was heard to remark, "That is not a job for a lady." Times and attitudes, I hope, have changed, although the domain of athletics may be one of the last holdouts.

Though the selection of student-athletes at Stanford University follows essentially the same procedures as the selection of other undergraduates, there are a few notable differences. One is that the process occurs earlier in the year, which means some supplementary information cannot be included in the review of each student-athlete's file.

It is important to explain why the difference in timing exists. As noted earlier, Stanford plays in the Pacific-10 Conference of the National Collegiate Athletic Association (NCAA), an organization with more than 800 college and university members. The rules governing the individual divisions of the NCAA are complex, to say the least, as evidenced by the NCAA manual, which runs to more than 450 pages of bylaws, special rules of order, and policies and procedures. (I don't recommend this manual as light reading, and the family lawyer will probably be needed for help with interpretations.) Schools compete in one of three divisions (I, II, and III); according to the NCAA manual they are distinguished as follows: "A member of Division I strives for regional and national excellence and prominence . . . recognizes the dual objective in its athletic program of serving both the university or college community (participants, student-body, faculty-staff, alumni) and the general public (community, area, state, nation); . . . athletics contests are scheduled primarily with other members of Division I, especially in the emphasized spectator sports." By contrast, Division III institutions "place highest priority on the overall quality of the educational experience . . . and place special importance on the impact of athletics on the participants rather than on the general public and its entertainment needs."[3] Stanford participates in Division I along with 294 other colleges and universities.

Institutions that participate in Divisions I and II, but not those in Division III, may award athletic scholarships that are based on athletic ability and not on need. The NCAA specifies the maximum number of such awards that may be made for each sport. An "award" covers room and board, tuition, fees, and books. Some schools, Stanford included, give partial awards in selected sports to extend the number of student-athletes who receive scholarships—for example, 30 half scholarships rather than 15 full scholarships. There are two subdivisions of Division I, called I-A and I-AA, to allow for the "differences in institutional objectives in support of football." These distinctions are determined by qualities such as the number of Division I varsity sports sponsored; the average attendance at home football games over a four-year period; and the seating capacity of the football stadium. According to rules in the 1991–92 NCAA manual, members of Division I-A must maintain an average paid attendance of 17,000 per home game over a four-year period or have a home stadium with at least 30,000 permanent seats. There are 106 colleges and universities currently playing Division I-A football; Division I-AA, the less costly and less visible competitive level in football, has 115 members. In 1992, each Division I-A school was subject to annual limits of 25 initial financial aid awards and 95 total financial aid awards to student-athletes in football. Similarly, in Division I men's and women's basketball, the 1992 annual limits on awards were fifteen for men and fifteen for women. (Incidentally, because these rules seem to change regularly, they will undoubtedly be out of date when these words appear in print.)

I mention football and basketball because they are generally recognized as the primary revenue-producing sports in college athletics; they certainly earn the most media attention. The other NCAA Division I sports are allowed fewer awards; for example, baseball has thirteen, men's cross-country and track has fourteen, both men's and women's soccer have eleven, and women's swimming has fourteen. Associated with these awards, and with each varsity sport, is one day, set by the NCAA, when student-athletes across the country sign their "letters of intent." Letters of intent are precisely what the name implies; they are letters signed by the recruited student-athletes, and their parents or legal guardians, to confirm the students' intentions to enroll, with the support of athletic scholarships, at specific colleges or universities.

This essential background on college athletic scholarships and letters of intent enables me to explain the timing differences in the admissions office's review of applications from prospective varsity athletes. The earliest official signing day, for men's and women's basketball and several other Division I varsity sports, falls in mid-November of a high school student's senior year. The football signing period begins on February 5 of the senior year and extends through April 1. In a typical year, the decisions on all freshman applications to Stanford are mailed around March 31. The difference between the signing dates and the normal schedule for the review of applications is apparent.

To illustrate the issues, I will focus on one major sport for the freshman (as opposed to the transfer student) admissions process. Imagine that you are a prospective varsity basketball player at Stanford, and the coach is recruiting you for a basketball scholarship; you must submit all your application materials to Stanford no later than the first week in November of your senior year in high school so that your application can be assembled and reviewed by the staff in Undergraduate Admissions before the mid-November letter-of-intent date. The basketball coaches must also provide the admissions office with details of your past achievements and an assessment of your potential in basketball, emphasizing the importance of your anticipated contribution to the varsity basketball program at Stanford. The first assignment calls for careful organization and planning during the busy fall quarter of your senior year of high school; the latter task requires significant advance preparation and careful scouting by the basketball coaches to seek out the best talent in the country, and sometimes the world. (For example, one recent, and inspirational, basketball player on the men's team at Stanford, Andrew Vlahov, came from Perth, Australia, where he now plays professional basketball.) The coaches' preparatory work must extend beyond the assessment of athletic talent. There is no point in finding great high school basketball players with academic records that preclude academic success at Stanford. Consequently the coaches' work involves a steady paring down of candidates on the basis of both academic and athletic assessments. When they have prepared their final list, the coaches submit what we called an Athletic Rating Form (commonly known as an ARF) for each prospective varsity basketball freshman applicant. These ARFs are added to the applicants' files so that they can be considered when the admissions staff members read the applications.

At this point, an exercise that is already complex and intense becomes even more so. If both the men's and women's head basketball coaches have three scholarships to offer this year, they may try to encourage applications from six to ten candidates. For several reasons, the number of candidates often exceeds the number of available scholarships. First and most important, at Stanford the coach never has a guarantee that the dean of admissions will admit all the applicants; there is usually some preliminary discussion of transcripts and test scores before an application is completed, but only when all the required application materials—essays, references, current transcript, and official test scores—are assembled does the admissions staff have sufficient information for a decision. On occasion, the coach's preliminary information is unfortunately not confirmed by the student's official record.

Second, in any team sport, some positions may be more critical in a given year than others; the basketball coach must decide on the priorities for forwards, centers, and guards. At the same time, no coach wants to lose a stellar talent, regardless of position. Finally, even if a star varsity basketball player meets the approval of the admissions office and the coach subsequently offers the scholarship, this student-athlete may choose not to sign a Stanford letter of intent. Such talents will have caught the eye of many other college basketball coaches, who will also be poised with offers of scholarships; the young basketball player can sign only one letter of intent. The whole exercise resembles an intricate, transcontinental chess game, played in more than two dimensions, under the ever-watchful eye of applicants, parents, high schools, admissions officers, coaches, other players, the NCAA officials with that 450-page rule book, and (last but not least) the press.

But let us say all goes well. The dean approves the applications of three or more varsity basketball players, and the basketball coach is successful in signing the top three recruits. What next? This exercise for basketball must be carried out simultaneously for all the other sports with November signing dates for letters of intent. At the same time, all the details associated with the applications of thousands of other high school seniors must be dealt with. The fall quarter is the busiest time in an admissions office for high school visits; the two major meetings for admissions professionals are held in October and November; the mail is at its peak; and the telephone never stops ringing. The applications from varsity athletes are very important, but they must be kept in perspective. We expect some 14,000–15,000 applications to be completed by mid-January, by which time we have approved the admission of a dozen or so varsity athletes to enable them to sign the November letters of intent. And the most intensely scrutinized athletic admission process is still ahead: football.

I was talking recently to a Stanford alumnus who now works at the university about the remarkable success of both men's and women's athletics at Stanford. To my surprise, he commented, "Well, all the teams can do as well as any school in the country, but that pales in comparison with the success of the football team. For me, that's the only sport that really counts." This is not, unfortunately, an atypical view—at least, it is one that I have heard more times than I care to count, with all due respect to our fine football program. For reasons that I leave to sociologists to debate, varsity football is generally acknowledged as the premier sport at most colleges and universities in the United States; it is certainly the sport in which admissions decisions become most public. Football also has the most abuses nationally, partly because of the size of football programs (remember that Division I-A teams can award 95 athletic scholarships for the overall football program, whereas men's and women's basketball have only 15 each). The other reason for the dominance of football in college programs is, alas, money; I say "alas" because it strikes me as an irony that institutions that pride themselves on their altruistic and primary missions of teaching, learning, and research and that have the tax-exempt definition of nonprofit organizations should be caught up in the win-loss records of football teams. However, the revenue generated by a football program in a Division I-A institution may, for better or for worse, determine the general financial health of an athletic department. A good season with a football stadium filled to capacity can create a surplus to contribute to the support of other sports and the following year's budget; a bad year can cause a deficit.

The process for admitting football players to Stanford mirrors the basketball scenario I described earlier, except that it is more intense. There are a greater number of files to be read, the pressure of timing is more acute, and the accompanying articles in the press seem to report every nuance in blow-by-blow accounts. In the late 1980's, for example, I opened our local evening paper and read that a young football player, a high school senior from southern California, was planning to attend Stanford. This was news to me—I had neither known he was applying nor read his application, much less made a decision on it. But this was a highly recruited athlete with potential to play professional football, and when a reporter talked to this inexperienced-with-the-press high school senior, the rest was news.

There will always be the unexpected story, but the following scenario is more typical. The high school football player completes his Stanford application, it is reviewed by the admissions officers, and the student is approved for admission. This word is passed on to the football recruiting coordinator, who tells the football coach, who then decides whether to offer a scholarship. (Incidentally, the scholarship is not always offered at this point. The football coach decides on the best strategy for each case according to the need in that player's position, the pressure of competition from other schools, and the likelihood of the student's enrolling at Stanford, all of which involve an element of uncertainty.) Let us assume that the student is told that his application has been approved and that the football coach is offering him an athletic scholarship. Ideally, the student-athlete then commits verbally to Stanford. (He still has until the letter-of-intent signing date in early February to make this official, but for the most part, verbal commitments are honored.)

At this point the press has a field day reporting on the latest coups, usually comparing how UC Berkeley, UCLA, and the University of Washington are faring in their recruiting battles with Stanford. This is a potentially difficult time from the viewpoint of the admissions office. When I followed up the student's verbal commitment with a written confirmation of Stanford's offer of admission, I also made it clear that the offer (like all offers of admission) was contingent on the student's maintaining an academic record comparable to what we had seen at the time of the admissions decision. In seven years, I subsequently withdrew only one offer (I think the student involved would agree that he earned what he received), and I deferred one offer until the student had made up some academic deficiencies.

I also pointed out in the confirmation letter that the news of acceptance should be handled with sensitivity. Many varsity athletes receive their admissions decisions earlier than the rest of Stanford's applicants because of the NCAA regulations concerning letters of intent. Consequently, we ask student-athletes to be sensitive to the feelings of their classmates and to be discreet about their news. The requirements for early signing dates, however, are not well known to the public at large, and some students and parents consider it unfair that acclaimed varsity athletes at their high school hear from Stanford and other universities in the late fall or winter while regular applicants do not hear until the first week in April. The admitted football player may be discreet, but this does not stop an understandably proud coach or parent from sharing the scholarship offer with a reporter, and the next thing they know the story is front-page news in the sports section of the local, and sometimes national, press. The athletic department, justifiably proud of its recruiting successes, also does not shy away from press attention at this juncture.

Other critical information feeds sports rumor mills as well—particularly the academic credentials of varsity athletes at Stanford and how they compare with those of the non–varsity athletes. The underlying question is, How much do we compromise in making admissions decisions to try to enroll a winning football team? Of course, I cannot provide information that would identify specific individuals, but I can answer the question directly in a general way. In Chapter 1, I presented an academic profile of all applicants, admitted students, and enrolling students at Stanford for the year 1991. All the varsity athletes are included in these data. (Some colleges omit varsity athletes, and sometimes minority students, from such tables in order to improve the numbers they give the public.) So the next obvious question is, Are the varsity athletes all in the bottom sections of the ranges of SAT and grade-point average? The answer is no; however, even if varsity athletes were overrepresented in the lower parts of the table, the Stanford ranges are significantly higher than the national norms and confirm the degree of selectivity for *all* admitted students. In my seven years as dean, no football player (to cite the most competitive athletic case) at Stanford came even close to being what is technically known as "a Prop. 48 athlete." (Proposal 48 is discussed more fully later in this chapter.) I am sure my predecessors and successor could make similar claims.

A related question is, Do we "stretch" more for football players than for other varsity athletes? The answer is probably yes; the qualification is prudent because I must admit that I never actually made comparative calculations for each of the varsity sports, but I do have an institutional, impressionistic memory. (When a colleague once asked me, in a public forum, the point-blank question, "Does Stanford lower standards for football players?" it was only half in jest that I said if we did, we would have a team with a better win-loss record, and the football coach might be angry at me less often.) As I have already mentioned, the pressure is certainly the most intense in football. It is also fair to say, however, that we take note of any extraordinary talents in athletics, irrespective of sport. The critical tests that we always apply in admission decisions about athletes, with football players no exception, are similar to those applied in minority admissions: Can the student successfully complete a degree course at Stanford? Has she earned a place? Is he well supported by his high school in applying to Stanford? In considering these questions, we take it as a given that the applicant has more than met the secondary criterion for admission, evidence of achievement outside the classroom; on this measure the readers in the admissions office rely upon the judgment of the experienced coaches at Stanford. The coaches' considerable records of success justify this trust, and the coaches have more to lose than to gain by strongly supporting the application of a student-athlete who would be ill matched with Stanford.

It should be clear at this point that the success of athletics programs at Stanford is itself an extended team process. The team encompasses more than the players, the coaches, and the other staff in the Department of Athletics; it includes the staff in Undergraduate Admissions as well. The essential mutual trust and agreement on principles and goals are not easily developed. Teamwork requires constant good communication, response to constructive criticism from both offices, and ongoing programs to ensure that the process works as well as it can. The hiring of new coaches or admissions directors calls for a regular program of education.

A new coach can be taken by surprise by the rigorous demands of the Stanford admissions office, just as a new admissions officer can be surprised by some of the decisions made on varsity athletes. Both perspectives involve comparative judgments, and the Stanford process can seem somewhat bewildering to the newcomer—admissions officer or coach. I look back, now with some amusement after the benefit of experience, on my own initiation. No one is born knowing how to master this "Hindu rope trick."

Incorporating the goal of enrolling the best student-athletes in the country into admissions practice admittedly took some trial runs, with some fine tuning en route. What seemed to work effectively was the assignment of two associate deans of admissions (the senior staff members) to serve as liaisons with the coaches. One associate dean, the director of freshman admissions, was assigned to deal with the November and April letters of intent; the other associate dean, who was also the director of transfer admissions, handled the February letters of intent. In addition, a special assistant to the deans was responsible for coordinating the recruitment of all special talents, including all the varsity athletes. Each of these experienced staff members developed quite close working relationships with the individual coaches (the balance between the personal and the professional has never been more delicate), as well as with the recruiting coordinator in the Department of Athletics. Each of the liaison deans was the second reader for every application that fell within his area of responsibility. The first reader was usually an experienced associate director in admissions; in the case of minority applicants, one of the minority directors was also involved in reviewing the file. Each of these readers made a recommendation for or against admission before the file was passed on to me for a final decision.

One of our in-house ground rules was that every reader exercised an independent judgment on the file; as might be expected, reasonable people sometimes disagreed. In the vast majority of cases, I concurred in the associate deans' recommendations, but not always. I was confident that when I was wavering, they had significant doubts too. Even after six years, the decisions on these tough files never got any easier, but each year once they were made I managed to forget how hard they were. This is no doubt a prime example of the human instinct for self-preservation! On these most difficult of files, there would always be some extended (and often lively) discussions and more follow-up with the high school teachers, guidance counselors, or even the principal, before I felt confident that I had all the necessary information. When I was wavering most, I often picked up the telephone and called a teacher myself. These are obviously not easy calls for a teacher to receive; who would want to share the responsibility for denying a scholarship to a promising young athlete? I always began by reassuring the teacher or counselor of the confidentiality of our conversation and by confirming that their comments would be but one aspect of what I would consider in making the final decision. I was always impressed by the sensitivity and thoughtfulness of the teachers and counselors to whom I spoke, and they were unquestionably helpful. The buck then stopped at my desk, a responsibility that was not without its discomfort and often meant the loss of sleep. In the end, one has to be able to live with the final decision, to feel confident that the best possible effort has been made to reach a conclusion that is as fair as possible to all, and to accept that any human process is fallible. When the decision was finally passed on to the respective coach, any internal disagreements were history; I was fortunate that the admissions staff respected both the integrity of the team process and my final responsibility as dean.

The assignment of the two associate deans as liaisons with the athletics department and the appointment of a special talent coordinator in Undergraduate Admissions had some obvious advantages. Individual responsibilities were unambiguously defined and fit well with the calendar of remaining responsibilities. This way of organizing things also promoted close working relationships between the designated staff members in admissions and individual coaches, and the majority of my communication with coaches took place through these three colleagues. Every fall we jointly planned a special program in the athletics department, which was attended by the senior admissions staff, all the coaches, the recruiting coordinator, and all the directors in undergraduate admissions. The purpose of this program was to introduce members of both staffs to one another, to review the full process of freshman and transfer admissions (including the academic profiles of the newly admitted classes), to discuss any problems of the past season and their proposed solutions, and to allow questions to be answered. For the very experienced coaches, this must have seemed an unnecessary annual repetition; they know better than anyone how to do their jobs, and they do them very well. But their presence provided some essential stability, a source of information and credibility, not to mention a confirmation that the extended team of admissions and athletics could, and did, work.

This is not to say that all was unfailingly well between the coaches and the staff of Undergraduate Admissions. I can recall at least one decision of mine each year that left one or another coach disappointed or frustrated at best, and plain angry at worst. These were the occasions for a personal, often not-too-pleasant visit, or an intemperate letter or telephone call across campus. It would be unreasonable to assume that such difficulties would *not* occur since the best coaches are inevitably highly competitive. There is an inevitable tension between athletics and admissions in a process such as ours. The coaches here are not handed the keys to prospective winning seasons with only minimal limitations on offers of admission; they must work within the well-established ground rules of a highly selective university. I hope, in the long run, that the varsity coaches at Stanford would agree that they, their student-athletes, their programs, and the university all benefit from the existing process. At the risk of sounding both self-congratulatory and self-righteous, I believe that the process places a high value on the ideals of integrity, honesty, trust, and hard work. What remains foremost is a commitment to the long-term best interests of the student-athletes themselves.

THE COMPETITION

As mentioned earlier, in a typical year Stanford offers almost 2,600 applicants admission in order to enroll approximately 1,550 freshmen. Of the 1,000 or so students who chose not to enroll at Stanford each year in the period 1984–91, more than half enrolled at one of four other institutions. Their choices, in order, were Harvard, Yale, Princeton, and MIT; usually UC Berkeley was fifth. With the exception of UC Berkeley, none of these universities plays Division I-A athletics. Stanford's academic competition for undergraduates, perhaps not surprisingly, lies predominantly in East Coast, Ivy League, and highly selective institutions outside the big-time football circuits.

Stanford's athletic conference is the Pac-10, whose other members are UC Berkeley, UCLA, USC, Arizona, Arizona State, Oregon, Oregon State, Washington, and Washington State. The contrasts between Stanford's academic and athletic competitors appear even more striking if we examine the graduation rates of all freshmen, freshmen athletes, and football recruits at Stanford and those two groups of institutions (see Table 9). (MIT is omitted because it does not play Division I athletics.)

An examination of any one year's data, of course, can lead to unfounded conclusions. For example, at Stanford the graduation rate of the football players is generally much closer to that of the Stanford student body as a whole. Nevertheless, some striking differences are readily apparent. Perhaps most obvious, the graduation rate of freshmen in the Pac-10 schools (Stanford excepted) is much lower than those at Harvard, Princeton, and Yale—the universities with which Stanford generally competes most for admitted freshmen. Second, and reassuringly, the graduation rates of varsity athletes at most of the schools listed are not much different from those of their classmates; in some cases, the varsity athletes actually graduate at a *higher* rate. Finally, in some Division I-A institutions, the graduation rate for football players falls significantly below that of their freshman cohort. While this fact is cause for concern, the most glaring disparities of this sort do not occur at Pac-10 schools; at a few Division I-A schools elsewhere, the graduation rate of the football players is below 10 percent.

Circumstances similar to Stanford's can be found at Rice University, also a member of Division I-A of the NCAA. In a 1992 report commissioned by the then president of Rice, George Rupp, the sports program was praised for its "high integrity, honesty and strict

TABLE 9

Graduation Rates at Selected Division I-AA and I-A Institutions, 1989

	1984 freshmen graduating by Aug. 1989	1984 freshman athletes graduating by Aug. 1989	1984 freshman football recruits graduating by Aug. 1989
Division I-AA institutions			
Harvard	93.3%	96.4%	94.3%
Princeton	93.3	97.4	96.6
Yale	92.3	93.7	89.2
Division I-A institutions (Pac-10)			
Arizona St.	37.6	30.5	27.3
Oregon St.	26.3	28.1	31.6
Stanford	88.8	84.1	71.4
Arizona	36.0	43.9	n.a.[a]
UC Berkeley	65.0	62.4	51.6
UCLA	62.6	54.6	50.0
Oregon	44.2	50.0	40.0
USC	53.5	46.6	25.0
Washington	51.4	45.9	31.0
Washington St.	43.2	53.1	61.9

SOURCE: "Graduation Rates of Athletes and Other Students at Division I Colleges," *Chronicle of Higher Education,* Mar. 27, 1991.

[a] This information was withheld.

adherence to the rules"; it was also noted, though, that intercollegiate sports at Rice have operated with a multimillion-dollar deficit in recent years and at the same time have lowered the institution's academic standards. Although the standards and graduation rates for Rice athletes were far higher than those of other universities in the Southwest Athletic Conference, and though the standards for athletes had improved over the previous eight years, the authors of the report found that admissions standards and graduation rates for scholarship athletes were much lower than those for regularly admitted students. The panel's report discussed several possible responses, including abandoning intercollegiate sports altogether or moving Rice to a level of competition at which no scholarships would be offered. The director of athletics considered both these options nonviable. In April 1994, after the collapse of the Southwest

Conference, the Rice University Board of Governors announced Rice's intention to proceed with discussions about joining the Western Athletic Conference, the largest Division I-A conference in the nation. President Malcolm Gillis affirmed Rice's commitment to managing the revenues and costs of intercollegiate athletics so that academic programs would not suffer.

With evidence of low graduation rates and other problems now widely available, it is not surprising to see newspaper articles declare that "local campuses fail many athletes."[4] Despite the hopes of most varsity athletes, very few actually make it to the pros; the chances are about 1 in 100 in football and 1 in 500 in basketball. Even more troublesome is the abuse of black student-athletes in varsity athletics. UC Berkeley sports sociologist Harry Edwards claims that 65 to 75 percent of black athletes never graduate from the school they represent in sports. They are exploited for their entertainment and money-making value and then cast adrift. Stanford, I am glad to say, is among the exceptions; we have stood firm in making the tough calls in admissions, and the university subsequently provides good support throughout the undergraduate years to all student-athletes. The success of varsity athletics depends on maintaining a firm resistance to compromising basic standards, in spite of the relentless pressures for, and temptations of, a championship record.

Occasionally, we do receive assistance from a higher power. A few years ago, I was giving a talk at a national meeting of college admissions counselors about the challenges of selecting the freshman class at a university that plays Division I-A football. As it happened, Stanford was scheduled to play the nationally ranked Notre Dame football team that very weekend, and I concluded my talk with that piece of news and the request that everyone please pray for us. The weekend arrived and, to the amazement of even Stanford's staunchest fans, the football team beat Notre Dame. In my mail the following week arrived a set of letters from my colleagues at the conference, extolling the power of collective prayer!

PITFALLS AND PLAINTIFFS

As I have stated elsewhere in this book (and it cannot be said too often), the practice of selective admissions is, among other things, an imperfect art and a constant balancing act; the balancing can seem particularly delicate in athletics. The pitfalls of the process are demonstrated annually in the large volume of mail that the dean receives from disappointed and often angry parents. Here are two typical, real examples that focus on questions related to athletics. The following letter is from Mrs. P, the mother of a denied applicant:

I have followed with interest the series of articles appearing in [the local press] concerning the college application process. My son spent considerable effort completing the Stanford application, so I was able to relate to the families and students who were also going through the application process to the colleges of their choice. . . .

Having visited several college campuses last summer and hearing admission officers explain the admission process, this business of how an admissions committee chooses certain students over others still remains a mystery to me. It certainly is sad that a motivated, talented, well-rounded student who has a thirst for knowledge and has taken the most challenging course of study the high school has to offer (five advanced placement subjects . . .), plus taken an active interest in a variety of school and out-of-school activities, a friendly person who has lots of friends and gets along well with everybody should receive an impersonal form letter rejecting him from attending the college of his choice. Although a college may not be able to accommodate all qualified applicants, a student who has invested considerable time and energy in the application process—and who has maintained straight A's in a challenging program of study—deserves an explanation.

It was stated in [the local paper] that the admissions office at Stanford is adamantly opposed to early action decisions to Stanford, as this may interfere with the motivational drive to achieve his highest level of achievement to the end of high school. Why does this viewpoint not apply to athletes? According to articles appearing in [the local paper], two students from [the local] high school not only were accepted for admission to Stanford in December, thereby forgoing the grueling application procedures, but they were actually guaranteed scholarships. Both these students stated they were lucky to have football talent, that they did not take the most challenging course of study, and they did not put as much effort into their high school academics as they should have. . . .

I find it difficult to have respect for a college that builds its athletics program by rejecting highly talented students who have demonstrated academic curiosity and have a keen desire to develop their intellectual potential. Stanford University needs to get its priorities in order.

This was not an easy letter to answer; the parental bond is strong and protective, and it is not surprising to see mothers and fathers represent their young sons and daughters with ferocity and pride. In this case, the student was ranked second in his large high school senior class, the mother was justifiably proud of his achievements, and little I could say would mitigate her disappointment, although I tried. The question of institutional "priorities" raised by Mrs. P is often extended to challenge Stanford's award of athletic scholarships when it awards no scholarships solely for academic merit. The answer has to be one based on pragmatism; we *do* play college athletics in the Pac-10, and we could not compete without following the same basic rules that our athletic competitors do. In times of limited resources, need-based aid is considered more important than non-need-based merit scholarships. Having made the case, I can also understand why this argument does not satisfy many parents such as Mrs. P.

Parental disappointment directly related to athletics appears in this second example from a father, Mr. D, who wrote to Donald Kennedy, then president of Stanford:

While attending Stanford had been my son's top priority for several years, he didn't put all of his eggs in that basket. He applied to all the other top academic institutions to assure himself the opportunity to maximize his talents. As of this writing, he has been accepted to every institution to which he has applied. This includes the Army, Navy, Air Force academies, UC Berkeley, UCLA and Harvard. Given his credentials, this does not come as a surprise to anyone, probably not even to Stanford admissions. After all, what better way to prove that Stanford is more selective than anyone else.

The high point in my son's portended relationship with Stanford was in January of this year. At that time, he was a highly recruited football player who had ambitions of receiving a football scholarship to Stanford. He was invited to and attended an official football weekend visit. We considered it an interesting but perfunctory event since we were told that Stanford football does not invite prospects unless it was intended to offer them scholarships. The only potential pitfall was the possibility that the Admissions Office would not accept his academic and extracurricular credentials. This seemed remote since M has been a 4.0 student throughout high school and president of his class. And indeed, he was told during the visit that he had been accepted. From that point on, Stanford hit him with every slight imaginable.

He was subsequently advised that he would not be extended a football scholarship. Worse than that, he was told that he had been de-accepted by the Admissions Office. . . . While it was a blow, we thought the situation was far from terminal. With his academic and extra-curricular history, he was sure to be accepted through normal channels, or so we thought. Besides that, M was being recruited by Stanford baseball. The baseball staff assured me . . . they didn't see much of a problem, given M's credentials. On top of that, they put him on their blue chip list lending as much weight as they could. Well the terminal blow came in the mail last week.

After having experienced all of this, a metamorphosis occurred. M doesn't seem disappointed that he will not be attending Stanford. Notwithstanding the shoddy manner in which he was treated, he discovered that Stanford did not match up to his expectations of integrity. He will be attending Harvard in the fall.

This unfortunate case provides graphic illustration of some of the pitfalls of recruiting varsity athletes. M was indeed recruited by the football program; Undergraduate Admissions reviewed his file and approved his admission (in precisely the manner described earlier in this chapter). Owing to the number of other talented football recruits, the coaches decided not to offer M a scholarship, a decision that nullified the admissions office's preliminary approval, although M and his father clearly thought that M's admission had been definitively approved. The recruiting coordinator denied having misled them, but, as often happens in such cases, what is said and what is heard may have been very different. Parents and students are not familiar with the intricacies of the process (for example, what a campus visitation implies); the coaches are working under considerable pressure and time constraints; and the amount of time they spend on the road hinders communication. In spite of good intentions on the coaches' part, misunderstandings are common and perhaps not surprising, considering the complexities. In a memo describing the circumstances of M's case, the recruiting coordinator explained to me, "It is unfortunate that our lines of communication somehow got tangled, and that we presented Admissions' decision in a manner that probably should have been better left unsaid." My office was left to explain as best we could how the events unfolded and to clarify the procedures.

The unavoidable early notification of scholarship athletes seems to be a particularly sensitive issue in the Bay Area. Stanford typically received 40–70 applications a year from each of the large local high schools. When one of those applicants was a football or basketball recruit, the local press would inevitably announce the scholarship awards months before the first week in April, the regular mailing date for admissions decisions. High school seniors are quite savvy and generally accepting and pragmatic, but I always wondered how other students felt when such announcements were emblazoned on the sports pages while their own applications were still under review.

One of my worst memories involving the early notification of an athletic decision resulted from a coincidence. It is not unusual, in an applicant pool of 14,000, to have candidates with precisely the same name. The credentials staff would mark such files "careful"; this was an alert to double-check social security numbers and birthdates when filing test scores and reference materials. In this case, two young women with the same name were being recruited for the same sport; we approved one of them and—you can guess—the wrong student was informed by one of her prospective team members (who had been told of our decision by the coach). Such inadvertent damage is hard to repair. In the normal admissions process, the admissions staff completely controls the information applicants receive, and essential decisions are conveyed by letter. In the awarding of athletic scholarships, we need to share the information and, by default, immediately lose control.

Another kind of difficulty, although not one near the top of my worry list, comes from the uncertainty of predicting athletic success. The teamwork between the athletics and undergraduate admissions staffs involves, beyond the essentials of honesty and integrity, cooperation based on mutual trust: the admissions office makes the academic judgments and the coaches make the athletic ones. (This reminds me of a spirited conversation I once had with football coach Jack Elway. He said firmly, "It's my job to see that my team doesn't get beaten up on the field," to which I replied, "And it's my job to see that they don't get beaten up in the classroom.") When, for compelling athletic reasons, we make a stretch decision on the admissions side, we reason that the prospective undergraduate will not only benefit from coming to Stanford but will also contribute to the university community through his or her considerable athletic prowess.

But coaches, like admissions officers, are not infallible, and they cannot guarantee that potential at the age of seventeen or eighteen will meet expectations during the next four years. It must be a devastating experience, for example, for a young student-athlete to enroll at a university, full of promise on the national scene, only to suffer a debilitating injury during the freshman or sophomore year; at least such a student can still work on an undergraduate degree, more than a modest consolation. One of my most poignant memories of Stanford undergraduates is of "Ted," a brilliant young man whose college guidance counselor wrote of him, "His forehead has been touched by the finger of God." Ted was recognized as an all-American athlete, he came to Stanford on an athletic scholarship, and almost immediately he fell apart on all fronts. He not only found himself burned out academically from the pressures of high school, but the higher level of competition in his sport proved more than he could cope with. It did not help matters that his family had serious troubles during Ted's freshman year. Ted finally "stopped out" of Stanford and wandered around for a year; the last I saw of him, he had disengaged from his sport and somewhat unenthusiastically re-enrolled at Stanford to complete his classes.

THE POWER OF THE PRESS

The previous anecdotes come from private correspondence, or privileged information, and in each instance I was able to respond in a detailed manner that treated the situation and the individuals involved with the seriousness and attention they deserved. Although time-consuming, these were relatively easy cases in comparison with those that were played out in public. Charges leveled in a public forum, particularly the press, are nearly impossible to respond to adequately. The misperceptions and inaccuracies seem unlimited, and the opinions or perceptions of parties outside the admissions process are often difficult to refute without compromising confidentiality. My first press "controversy" came early in my career as dean and was played out on the sports pages of many Bay Area newspapers. It offers a striking example of the complexity, challenges, and cost of balancing the aspirations of the Department of Athletics in the admissions process, and it also conveys an accurate idea of how serious the stakes involved can be. The incident provided me and the admissions staff with painful though invaluable lessons, and the news clippings and correspondence the episode generated now fill a fat file in my cabinet. Since the subject was publicly discussed at the time, I will not be violating anyone's privacy in recounting the details.

First, some facts (not always to be assumed when reading the press, as I was to discover). In March 1986, the men's basketball coach at Stanford, Tom Davis, asked that I review, once again, the application of a young black basketball player from Riordan High School in San Francisco; the young man's name was Chris Munk. Coach Davis considered this high school senior a potentially singular force in varsity basketball, someone who could propel men's basketball at Stanford to the forefront of NCAA competition, heights untouched since 1942, when the team won its only national championship. We had already evaluated Chris's file before the November letter-of-intent date and had not been optimistic about approving admission. In March, we had additional academic information to consider, and I acceded to Tom Davis's request for another look. I think it is fair to say that I spent more time on this one file than on almost any other in seven years as dean. I read and reread the complete application; discussed it with my colleagues in Undergraduate Admissions; slept on it; discussed it with a specially convened group of faculty who were well informed on athletics, including a law professor who was the faculty athletic representative; and slept on it again. But consultation and reflection have their limits, and the final decision clearly rested with me. The time had come, and it was not a pleasant moment. I continued to have strong reservations about the academic preparation of this promising basketball player and decided against approving his admission. Chris Munk subsequently was awarded a basketball scholarship at USC, and Tom Davis left Stanford a few weeks later, to be basketball coach at the University of Iowa.

Those are the bare facts of the case. A sample of what subsequently appeared in the press may now be judged on its own merits. The newspaper articles are interspersed with a sampling of letters to emphasize, as if there is any doubt, the strength of public feeling about varsity athletics. (I was told that the president's office at Stanford received more mail on this subject than on Stanford's divestment of its holdings in South Africa, another critical subject of that year.)

A few years ago, Stanford was playing football against USC. This was during USC's best days, and from the first snap it was apparent that the Cards were taking a pounding.

As the score climbed, the USC students began to taunt the Stanford section, until the locals pulled out their ultimate weapon, a sign which read: "But we're smarter."

This academic pose is Stanford's last refuge when it fails athletically. The little scholars can't be expected, after all, to compete at a high athletic level.

Now with the chance of losing Tom Davis as basketball coach, there can only be one piece of advice for Stanford fans—make lots more signs. . . .

Davis and his assistants began to work with Munk three years ago, when he was a sophomore. Munk changed his curriculum and improved his grades to a C+ to B– level. . . . He took the SAT four times.

He was still, by all indications, a borderline admission although as Geiger [Stanford's then athletic director] says, "There isn't anybody in Division I-A that wouldn't accept that young man." There are even those who believe that if Munk had been admitted, it would have been possible to find students in his class with lower qualifications.

Davis was asking the Stanford admissions board to trust him. Davis' point was that this was no dumb jock the school would have to hold its nose and accept, but a highly motivated player who had worked hard to get in and would be an asset to the university. Davis put his integrity on the line, investing three extensive years in choosing and building a case.

Munk was turned down for reasons that will never be explained. There are no written or spoken criteria for admission to Stanford. . . .

Munk is out and Davis appears to be on his way. You have to wonder, if Davis leaves, what coach will believe he can win under the circumstances. . . .

This time Stanford looks a little too smart for its own good.

C. W. Nevius, *San Francisco Chronicle*, Mar. 28, 1986. © *San Francisco Chronicle*. Reprinted by permission.

Dean Jean Fetter, known nationally among scholar-athletes as "The Hammer," has been named UPI's "Rejector of the Year." The Welsh-born, Oxford-educated neophyte is a devastating blocker who in her first varsity season (as Stanford's admissions director) has personally destroyed Stanford's comeback in basketball. "Eliminating football may take more time," Fetter enthused. . . .

Steve Williams, San Jose
Letter to the editor, *San Francisco Chronicle*, Apr. 12, 1986

Many of the alumni that I've talked to are concerned about Munk's rejection. One, for instance, worried that Stanford is returning to the rigid standards of the '60s, when the school got the straight A students and wound up with a very dull student body.

Certainly, basketball coach Tom Davis left because he was convinced he couldn't get enough basketball players into school to make a national impact. . . .

"I don't know that the admissions office has changed directions," says John James, a past president of the Buck Club [an alumni group that supports athletics at Stanford], "but if they have, they have to understand that this impacts on the kinds of teams we'll have, which impacts on the gate, which impacts on our whole program. People don't like to hear this, but I think if our admission standards are going to be tougher, we'll have to get out of the Pac-10. We won't be able to compete."

Nobody can be sure whether the standards will be higher; the decisions coming out of the Stanford admissions office are often as cloaked in secrecy as anything coming out of the Kremlin.

But I must say that I respect the Stanford attempt to balance athletics and academics. It is a special school.

Glenn Dickey, *San Francisco Chronicle*, Apr. 22, 1986. ©*San Francisco Chronicle*. Reprinted by permission.

All I can say in closing is that somewhere along the line this process went terribly, terribly wrong. The benefits of admission so enormously outweighed the detriment as to render its rationality—and even its bona fides—suspect. It is impossible to avoid the suspicion that Munk and Davis' credibility were sacrificed to some other-worldly, Montsalvian fantasy of academic purity. If so, this is Stanford University at its worst, exhibiting the maddeningly effete, Ivy-League type arrogance that seems to permeate the atmosphere of institutions with selective admissions standards. . . .

I don't think there is any question that Munk deserved his chance, or of Davis' basic commitment to the academic standards of Stanford. However, the competence of those who participated in this disgraceful decision is open to serious question.

A Palo Alto attorney   Letter to President Donald Kennedy, Mar. 28, 1986

I wish to thank you for your recent support and help you have given the Athletic Department in their efforts to recruit student athletes for the University's interscholastic programs.

I am enclosing the Buck Club's annual request for funds to provide financial support of these student athletes. Since you have been so helpful it seems appropriate that you should take over this responsibility as well. The envelope is self-addressed in case you do not know where the Athletic Department is located on campus.

Also please check your schedule as the way things are developing, you may have to coach these teams.

An alum (class of 1949)   Letter to the dean of admissions, Mar. 27, 1986

Up until about two weeks ago, the Stanford basketball program looked to be solidly on its way to respectability. Coach Tom Davis' young, exciting team challenged for a berth in a postseason tournament right up to the end of February, and with another crop of blue chippers expected to enter the Farm in the fall, Stanford's hoop future looked rosier than it had in decades.

And then, on March 21, Dean of Admissions Jean Fetter stuffed Davis' best shot. . . .

But we feel it is not our place to pass judgement on decisions made by the Department of Admissions. The Stanford admissions process is a careful and comprehensive procedure, one that considers many things besides grade points, SAT scores and athletic talent. There are many things we do not know about Munk's candidacy for admission. . . .

Fetter's decision was a brave one. No one would have thrown a fit if she had let Munk in, and Stanford's basketball team would probably have benefitted tremendously. Instead, she did the unpopular thing: she applied Stanford's rigorous academic standards to athletics. We have faith that her decision was made carefully and for a good reason.

"Respect Fetter's Choice," *Stanford Daily*, Apr. 1, 1986

A number of conclusions may be drawn from these press items and letters, but I will restrict mine to two: the role of varsity athletics is a volatile subject on which few are neutral in their views; and the uninformed are amazingly uninhibited in voicing their opinions as fact. The latter judgment holds for the press as well; in all the outcry associated with the Chris Munk case, only one reporter ever called me to check the facts (he is not one quoted here, although I owe him a debt of gratitude). Instead, the admissions process is declared incomprehensible and "cloaked in secrecy." The public information presented in Chapter 1, and available to anyone for the asking, would immediately dispel the putative mystery for anyone interested in learning the facts, but as a wiser dean than I has said before, "Never underestimate the difficulty of changing false beliefs with facts."

The sports press, of course, writes on more general subjects in college athletics as well as the admission and denial of individual athletes. Some aspect of the Stanford sports program is an almost daily item in the Bay Area press, an occurrence that is both a compliment and an occasional hazard. Usually, minor inaccuracies are more easily swallowed than protested, but on two particular occasions I was moved to object. The most egregious example prompting a protest appeared in the *Peninsula Times Tribune* (a newspaper serving the communities adjoining Stanford), under the provocative title, "Can Stanford Rise Again?" A local reporter reflected on "the good old days" of Stanford football, 1964–81, when Stanford never once had a losing record.[5] This time, I will quote my letter to the editor, written in response.

"Can Stanford rise again?" questioned Rick La Plante about Stanford football. For those pessimistic observers of the Stanford sporting scene who hold such a bleak view of our considerable talent, the result of the Colorado game should provide a contrary answer.

It is not on this subject, however, that I want to question Mr. La Plante, but on a more fundamental topic: the accuracy of his reporting on undergraduate admissions at Stanford. The September 5 article provides some immediate and provocative examples, of which I will cite two. Based on the assumption that both Bill Walsh and Jack Elway were correctly quoted, I'm surprised by the following: Walsh implies that one or more B's on a prospective football player's transcript would be reason for him not to be admitted. He should know better. No one on my staff would ever claim that we admit only straight 'A' students (although it is true that we could more than fill the freshman class with students who earned such records). Admissions decisions simply are not based on such elementary criteria. Elway claims that "You can't get kids in who you know can do the work." Leaving aside the dubious grounds for this assertion, we are also concerned, among other things, that a student has earned the right to attend Stanford, not simply be able to survive academically here.

Elway also recalls the denial of some of his recruited quarterbacks. Our records contradict the reasons and data reported by La Plante—which brings me to my basic point. At no time during the past six years has Rick La Plante called our office to check the accuracy of his reporting, although admissions has been cited many times to "confirm" a range of claims. I would think that the checking of primary sources was a fundamental principle in journalism.

While, for obvious reasons, I am not free to reveal confidential information on any one applicant, I could confirm or deny general claims such as these. On a subject as volatile as football and college admissions, the damage is extensive when a reporter makes no effort to verify controversial factual claims. Good stories and correct information are not mutually exclusive. I hope Stanford can continue to provide you and your readers with an abundance of sports excitement through the achievements of our student-athletes.

In fairness to sportswriters, I should note that I have also written at least one fan letter. Leonard Koppett, a former sportswriter for the *New York Times* and editor emeritus of the *Peninsula Times Tribune*, seems to me a voice of sanity as well as an admirably talented writer on a wide range of social and political issues. Just after Tom Davis's departure from Stanford in April 1986, Mr. Koppett wrote an article describing Stanford's coaching needs:

A Stanford coach must measure up in character and flexibility as well as in technical proficiency, and the best interests at Stanford (and any good school) are served when a head coach remains for many years and establishes stability. A young, brilliant man on the make, with all these qualities, will move on as soon as he succeeds here; a mere producer of victories, without the other teaching and leadership qualities, has no place here to begin with.

So in seeking coaches, Stanford must always choose character first and "winning" second—not to play down winning, or to accept losing, but to keep priorities straight. . . . Stanford needs to be lucky again, in seeking a basketball coach. It's not easy to find the combination of brilliance and character this job requires.

But national rankings, in today's world, aren't attained by coaching magic. They require a totality of effort that Stanford is not likely to—and, in my opinion, should not—make. If Stanford ever does, it won't be because the "right" coach came along; a long line of coaches will be lined up begging to be hired.[6]

Well, fortune smiled on us in April 1986, when Director of Athletics Andy Geiger hired Mike Montgomery to succeed Tom Davis. Under Montgomery's leadership, the men's basketball team has made its only two appearances at the NCAA championship tournament since 1942, and the team won the National Invitational Tournament in 1991.

PRIORITIES, PRESSURES, AND PROBLEMS

It is not difficult to make a case for the substantial advantages of a strong college athletics program, such as the one offered at Stanford. In addition to Juvenal's time-tested motto, "A sound mind in a sound body," college athletics bring the benefits of discipline; development of a work ethic; promotion of selflessness; contributions to team spirit; development of pride in doing one's best and pride in the institution; and a unifying element and rallying point for the whole college community. In short, college athletics can foster and exemplify much that is noble about the human spirit.

In June 1991, the Faculty Senate of the Academic Council established the ad hoc Committee on Education and Scholarship at Stanford to provide greater faculty involvement in the budget-cutting process that was then under way. The report of this committee, describing its goals and guidelines, began with a quote from Stanford's first president, David Starr Jordan: "Mr. Stanford wants me to get the best." This was as true at Stanford in 1891 as it was in 1991; indeed it is appropriate to any discussion of athletics at the university. In affirming the unique qualities of Stanford, the faculty report stated:

The University remains committed to the aims of the Founders to create a university open to both men and women, both rich and poor, to educate its students in both moral character and pragmatic skills, and to place its resources in the service of society at large. Stanford educates its students to live thoughtfully and courageously in a plural and ethnically diverse society. We wish our students to value and contribute to public service. We endorse the tradition of excellence not only in academic studies but also in other endeavors—the tradition of the scholar-artist and the scholar-athlete. We are proud that this tradition is embraced and realized with such success at Stanford.[7]

This statement, I think, would be endorsed by almost every member of the Stanford community, but the question of the university's priorities in attracting, recruiting, and enrolling the very best scholar-athletes is more debatable. Indeed, when the Committee on Education and Scholarship published some preliminary recommendations in October 1991, it noted specifically that activities supported by the Department of Athletics and Physical Education, while "valuable and highly visible," are not at the core of undergraduate education at Stanford. It continued, "Protection of those programs supported by general funds should have a lower priority than in the case of central academic programs."[8] This is just as it should be at a university of Stanford's academic caliber; indeed, I would argue that the first priority at any educational institution, without question, should be the support of teaching, learning, and (where appropriate, as at major universities) research.

I have already outlined some of the challenges involving priorities from the perspective of the admissions office. Not surprisingly or inappropriately, some members of the Stanford faculty could not care less about Stanford's successes in athletics; some of them may not even know the location of the football stadium, much less the rules of the game. When the president of MIT gave an address at Stanford's centennial convocation in September 1991, he noted, somewhat tongue-in-cheek, that MIT had soundly defeated Stanford in sailing in 1953, but added, "Unfortunately, I cannot find a more recent reference." For many scholars, there is something slightly unbecoming about a major research university's having nationally ranked athletic teams.

The views among students are perhaps more mixed, although there was no doubt in the mind of the Stanford junior who wrote to the *Stanford Daily* in October 1991 about prospective cutbacks resulting from Stanford's budget deficit. Praising Stanford's established commitment to academic excellence, she proposed that "the Department of Athletics should be the starting point of budget cuts." But as the director of athletics knows only too well, any move to cut or reduce a program (fencing, wrestling, and field hockey all had their spot on this lineup) immediately brings howls of protest from affected students and alumni supporters. The *Daily* letter writer was even so bold as to propose that athletic scholarships be eliminated, suggesting:

Those athletes who met academic requirements and were dedicated to Stanford's goal of academic excellence would come to Stanford regardless. Thus student-athletes would be on the same level as other students who have to choose between other schools which offer academic scholarships and Stanford with its policy of need-blind financial aid. . . . The women's soccer team is an example of a team without athletic scholarships, but with an excellent program and excellent student-athletes. It is time to put other athletic programs to the test.[9]

Leonard Koppett has been even more critical of the system of awarding athletic scholarships, leveling the blame for the distortion of educational priorities on the NCAA. Koppett notes that each year, the top 100 "major sports" colleges allot the equivalent of about $100 million for scholarship aid exclusively on the basis of football-playing ability. This amounts to $400 million per four-year class—$1 billion over the course of a decade. These scholarships are divorced from any economic need on the part of the recipient; students who are exceptionally gifted in academic subjects receive no such awards. Koppett is savvy enough to know the counterarguments. Statistically, the number of students receiving athletic scholarships is insignificant, and, in any case, the athletic scholarship money is mostly donated by alumni interested in athletics who consequently subsidize the financial aid budget of an institution. Statistically, while this is a legitimate point, Koppett's argument on principle is both valid and important: the message sent to students is that becoming skilled at football or basketball can get you through college free; in a time of national concern for the provision of financial aid for college students, top priority is given to athletes, a message that degrades educational performance and motivation and distorts the national system of values. The fundamental question to be answered, of course, is why does the American system of higher education support the awarding of athletic scholarships at all? In placing blame on the NCAA for maintaining such a system, Koppett goes so far as to suggest that, since there is no hope of reforming the NCAA from within, "decent schools can cut loose from this misguided organization to which they lend respectability, and set about building a more rational system." [10]

Such a proposition would demand enormous energy and time from university presidents, who are bombarded with other urgent matters (diminished research support, competition in faculty hiring, declining enrollments, and an economic recession, to name a few). With the nation facing a difficult period in higher education, athletic scholarships are not only lower on the priority list but also run the risk of raising the wrath of many loyal, and often powerful, alumni. The president of the American Council on Education, Robert Atwell, writing in 1992 on the problems of intercollegiate athletics, extended the responsibility beyond that of college presidents. Atwell claimed that in recent years the faculty have been among the most negligent members of the academic community in addressing reforms and that a stronger faculty role is necessary.[11] I believe Stanford is less in need of reform than almost any other institution of higher education in the country that offers athletic scholarships, but the question of institutional priorities is more of a given than a subject for periodic debate—and any issue of substance benefits from the latter. The university, however, is certainly well positioned to assume the mantle of a pacesetter on the national level. During the 1970's, Stanford's president Richard Lyman once led the way in proposing that the NCAA abolish athletic scholarships, but the proposal was defeated.

The priority placed on college athletics in the United States is unique. The Japanese, the Germans, the British, and others all have their sports manias and associated problems at the professional level, but only in the United States is athletics such a high priority in the system of higher education and in so many other spheres of national life. It is hard to imagine reading, for example, a description of a Japanese or British politician in the national press such as the one that appeared in the *New York Times* to describe the faltering presidential candidacy of Senator Bob Kerrey: "My sense of Kerrey is of a guy who hit .385 in triple-A ball, is proclaimed by all the scouts as the next phenom, comes up to the Major Leagues and so far hasn't really shown that he'll be a star in the World Series."[12] While I will leave it to the social scientists to explain this intriguing cultural difference, three important points relevant to the U.S. educational system are significant here: the establishment of priorities, the role of ethnicity, and the role of gender in college athletics.

The priority of athletics is established at an early stage in the national educational program. Though atypical, the compelling and disquieting story of the 1988 season of the Permian High School Panthers in Odessa, Texas, provides a vivid portrayal of the importance placed on a high school football team.[13] A *New York Times* review described this "football-obsessed" community, where "the school spent $70,000 on chartered jets for the team's road games, $6,400 on rushed film prints of the games, and $5,040 on teaching materials for the English department."[14] This narrative provides a telling example of the distorted role of sports in the education of young people in this nation and the misplaced priorities involved in producing "the winningest" high school football team.

Unfortunately, abuses in athletics programs are not restricted to high schools. The *Chronicle of Higher Education* provides regular updates on the number of institutions under NCAA sanctions for violations of its principles, along with the details of the violations. A sampling includes: unethical conduct by a former coach; lack of institutional control; misleading investigators; improper recruiting; cash payments to football players; improper offers to recruits; unethical conduct by three staff members; academic fraud; allowing academically ineligible football players to compete; improper benefits to men's ice hockey players by boosters; and improper financial aid. In a recent issue, 34 colleges and universities were listed as having committed one or more of these violations; inclusion on the list is not only an embarrassment to the schools involved but reflects the shameful state of affairs in some of our colleges and universities.[15] In May 1991, we heard that lawyers for the Federal Trade Commission had subpoenaed a decade's worth of records from the 106 universities that play big-time football in an attempt to prove that the sport has primarily commercial, not educational, objectives.[16] Again, I believe that Stanford is among those with an exemplary program, but we suffer some guilt by association in belonging to the same national organization as the offenders. More important, teams such as Stanford's sometimes compete with institutions that operate under a very different code of ethics and priorities—a situation that can scarcely be defended as a level playing field (pun intended). Such inequity puts pressure on the coaches, who in turn put more pressure on the admissions officers—and the outcomes are combustible.

An analysis of the ethnic composition of football and basketball teams at Division I colleges is also revealing, and the conclusions are cause for concern of a different kind. A recent study on college sports showed that over 50 percent of football players and 70 percent of men's basketball players are black; 1990 college enrollment data show that blacks make up just over 8 percent of all college students.[17] A *New York Times* reporter tried his hand at estimating the ethnic representations during the "Sweet Sixteen" stage of the 1992 NCAA basketball tournament and concluded that the sixteen colleges, whose student bodies are more than 90 percent white, have basketball teams that are 80 percent black. The writer went on to offer another disturbing set of statistics provided by the Center for the Study of Sport in Society: at NCAA Division I schools, 56 percent of the varsity basketball players are black, 7 percent of the students on campus are black, and less than 2 percent of the faculty is black. White athletes are twice as likely to graduate as black athletes; the dropout rate after four years of eligibility is 28.5 percent for blacks, 10 percent for whites.[18] What tragic ironies of desegregation! Such data are good reason to heed the criticisms of leading blacks, such as former Wimbledon champion Arthur Ashe and UC Berkeley professor of sociology Harry Edwards, that young blacks are valued for their potential as athletes, but not as students; Edwards calls them "black gladiators," who are paid to entertain and then are cast out, without completing their education. Yet even in the athletic arena there are glaring inequities between blacks and whites. In 1987, an analysis of head coaches in football, basketball, baseball, and men's track at 278 Division I schools showed that only 4.2 percent were black; of athletic directors, only two were not white males. As Murray Sperber observes, "One of the myths of college sports is that it provides opportunities for poor blacks to make good in American society. If success is defined as brief moments of glory while carrying a football or shooting a basketball, then the myth is true for a small number of blacks. If being able to earn a lifelong living from college sports is the definition, the myth shatters."[19] I would go even further; lifelong success for young blacks depends more on good education and graduation from college than on athletic prowess on the football field or basketball court. This message, I fear, sometimes falls on deaf ears; one alumnus wrote to me a few years ago to complain that Stanford didn't have enough black players on its football team.

No discussion of college athletics and minority student-athletes would be complete without some mention of Proposal 48, although this is not the place for the thorough analysis the subject merits. This proposal was passed by the NCAA in 1983, became effective in 1986, and resulted from the concerns of a number of university and college presidents about the stringency, or lack thereof, of academic admissions standards and grant rules for varsity athletes. Before 1986, the only NCAA rule in effect for college admission and eligibility for an athletic scholarship involved the overall high school grade-point average, which was required to be at least a C (or 2.0). Proposal 48 kept the 2.0 rule but applied it to eleven core courses in high school, including three English and two mathematics courses. In addition, the proposal required that a varsity athlete achieve either a combined verbal and math score of 700 on the SAT or a composite score of 15 on the ACT. The stringency of this testing requirement at Stanford can be measured by reviewing Table 1, which makes it clear that no varsity athlete comes close to failing the Proposal 48 standard; to judge the potential effect on other major football powers, Sperber provides some sobering examples of the low levels of academic achievement of some college athletes. These cases should be an embarrassment to any institution of higher education. Unfortunately, a more prevalent view is evidenced in the following comment about one Division I school: "If you could walk and chew ice, you were eligible to play basketball and football." [20]

In the autumn of 1986, 206 incoming athletes in Division I-A football programs failed to meet the Proposal 48 standard; 85 percent of them were black. Options such as sitting out the freshman year and losing a year of eligibility were open to those who partially qualified but who were unable to meet the full standards. Rumors of cheating on Proposal 48 (such as arranging surrogate test takers) circulated, and consequently, the NCAA amended the standard in 1989 with Proposal 42, which disallowed athletic awards in the freshman year to partial qualifiers. Details aside, the important point is that supporters of both proposals argued for upholding educational standards; opponents, though they may have supported the principle of standards, charged that the proposals are racist and discriminate against black athletes, in particular, through the use of standardized tests that are considered culturally biased. Sperber has suggested, instead, testing athletic scholarship holders at the end of four years of college using the Graduate Record Examination, arguing that such a plan answers the demands and objections of both proponents and opponents of the proposals. He concludes: "For the NCAA, the plan has one major drawback—it calls the bluff of all NCAA members on the question of whether their athletes are truly receiving a college education. . . . The NCAA will never accept the GRE plan or anything similar to it. It would reveal to the world that 'student-athletes' have no academic clothes."[21] This is a harsh assessment and one that certainly has no legitimacy at numerous Division I colleges and universities, including Stanford, but it does have an unfortunate element of truth for schools where violations of the rules are the norm.

Another area of dramatic change has been in the status of women's sports in college athletics. Before commenting on the advances made in the past twenty years, I want to make some more personal observations on the role of women in higher education, particularly as it relates to varsity athletics. As mentioned earlier, some men continue to be skeptical that women can care for, understand, or support athletics programs. I was the target of some of that skepticism, as these stories illustrate.

In 1986, I was appointed to the search committee for the appointment of a new Stanford football coach, a search that culminated in the successful appointment of Denny Green, now the head coach for the Minnesota Vikings. The appointment was notable because Mr. Green was Stanford's first black football coach and one of few nationwide. There were two other women on the committee, both distinguished faculty members at Stanford, one in political science and the other in neurosurgery. The former probably knew at least as much about professional football as anyone else on the committee; the latter was an athlete of note herself and was also married to a former Olympic javelin thrower; and I had captained a varsity team at Oxford and played three sports in high school. In short, personal modesty aside, we made quite a high-powered athletic female trio. In the midst of the search, a member of the committee reported that he had been jogging on the Stanford track when he overheard two alumni absorbed in conversation. "Have you heard about the search committee for the new football coach? I heard that there are two broads on that committee," said one. "*Two* broads?" replied the companion, "*Three* broads!"

I guess I should be reassured that a male member of the committee was willing to tell us that story, one that I admit to finding funny—at least in my more charitable moments. My role in the search was to ask the tough questions about admissions standards and academic values, an important but, considering my position at Stanford, not difficult assignment. There were some discomforting moments when I pushed the finalists; answers from prospective coaches can be very different in theory than in practice, and it is crucial to distinguish between theory and practice in an interview.

In a similar vein, a female colleague of mine in undergraduate admissions who also works at a Division I-A school told me of her first encounter with their varsity baseball coach. He patiently began, "You see, in this sport we have left-handed pitchers and right-handed pitchers." Not the most promising of starts for a strong, collaborative professional relationship and (fortunately for me) very different from my own encounters with the Stanford baseball coach. My own relations with the coaches at Stanford were, for the most part, great—at least from my perspective. Of course there were tensions; they pushed, and I did not always give. The important factor, however, was that I respected their talents, professionalism, and commitment, not to mention their understanding and acceptance (most of the time) of the decisions that were made in undergraduate admissions. I was also genuinely enthusiastic about their mission. What I did not like was the occasional behind-the-scene complaining and rumormongering and the occasional plain untruths that were generated and distributed by some of the more single-minded alumni supporters. I would much prefer, as any human being would, to be told directly what was bothering someone, but expressions of discontent sometimes came secondhand. One day, for example, a faculty friend called me to say that he had heard a tale from a coach and an alumnus; because he could not believe it sounded like me, he was calling to get my version. The rumor was that I had denied admission to a highly touted recruit just because we had turned down the valedictorian at the same high school. I had a hard time figuring out where this complete myth came from, but I was glad to have the chance to set the record straight. Would things have been different if I were a male dean? The reader can answer that one; yes, maybe, and no are all possible (and plausible) answers.

Other encounters were perhaps a consequence of my British background or humor, which compounded the issues of gender. I laugh about the story supposedly told by football coach Elway that the first time he met with me he planned to serve tea and crumpets. As I remember it, we had an intense, five-hour session in my office, with not even a glass of water offered as refreshment. Coach Elway was, as I remember him, a great wit. After a humiliating 49–0 loss, a reporter asked the coach, "When would you say was the turning point in the game?" To which Elway quipped, "Well I guess it came just after the playing of the Star-Spangled Banner." Another more personal story originated in a conversation I had with a Stanford alumnus on the sideline of a home football game; when the Stanford placekicker bungled a field goal and hit the uprights in the process, I joked, "It must be very difficult to do that!" Those who know me recognize the humor, but this line subsequently made the rounds as an example of my ignorance of the game. I was amazed that a faculty member actually asked me, in all seriousness, a few months later whether the attribution was correct.

When Congress enacted Title IX in 1972, it became illegal for institutions receiving federal financial assistance to discriminate on the basis of sex in any educational program or activity. The deadline for schools to comply with the new regulations was set for July 1978, and it produced significant changes in athletic departments as a whole and specifically in women's athletics. At Stanford, for example, there are currently three levels of varsity sports teams. Varsity I sports are fully funded by the athletic department, athletic scholarships are given, and the coaches are on the university payroll; these sports are baseball (men only), basketball, football (men only), gymnastics, swimming and diving, tennis, volleyball, and water polo (men only). Varsity II sports are partially funded by the athletic department, limited scholarships are given, and the coaches are on the university payroll; these sports are crew, cross country and track, fencing, golf, and soccer. Varsity III sports are administered and partially funded through Club Sports, and the coaches are hired and paid by the teams; the associated sports are field hockey (women only), lacrosse (men only), sailing, skiing, softball (women only), synchronized swimming (women only), and wrestling (men only). The successes of the women's teams at the national level have been extraordinary, particularly in winning five successive NCAA championships in tennis. The Cardinal women have also won championships in swimming and, more recently, in basketball, where under Tara VanDerveer's capable and determined leadership, the Stanford women moved out of the Pac-10 basement to win five consecutive conference championships and their first NCAA championship in 1990, followed by a repeat in 1992. While the merger of the Buck Club (supporters of men's sports) and the Cardinal Club (supporters of women's sports) at Stanford was not without its detractors, relatively speaking the support for women's athletics has been exemplary, although a glance at the Varsity I sports reveals an ongoing emphasis on the revenue producers.

Across the nation, the picture is not quite as hopeful as it is at Stanford. While women make up slightly more than 50 percent of the total college enrollment nationwide, male athletes outnumber females two to one and receive twice as many athletic scholarships. Similarly, men's teams get three-fourths of the operating funds and more than 80 percent of the recruiting funds. The NCAA's executive director, Richard Schultz, has acknowledged that some colleges may have "dragged their feet" and that others may have "done some things to avoid compliance" with the federal laws. Schultz also noted, as we approached the twentieth anniversary of Title IX, that "this is more than a financial issue. It's a moral issue as well." [22] One of the key elements in the discrepancies is football, a sport for which there is no female equivalent. Yet even when football is discounted, discrepancies in basketball expenditures continue; in a Division I college, an average of $167,000 is spent in operating costs for men's basketball and just $60,000 for women's basketball.[23] The differences in football and basketball reflect the status of professional sports in the United States, in which women, even in the very best interpretation, are minor players. An article about the Stanford women's basketball team accentuated the importance of academic success to these women players.[24] With far fewer opportunities open to women on the professional circuit, women college players concentrate on their degrees; it is not surprising that the graduation rate of women athletes in Division I programs is close to 60 percent and that the rate for their male counterparts is 46 percent. On the larger question of equity for women, as with issues of affirmative action, there are limits to the responsibilities that colleges and universities can assume in addressing societal concerns and cultural norms, but we should at least set a good example.

THE FUTURE

The challenges associated with college athletics are increasingly complex. I have touched on some of the major issues—appropriate priorities in higher education, admissions standards, graduation records of athletes, violations of NCAA rules, budgetary concerns, abuse of minority athletes, and unequal treatment of women—but only superficially. Any reader interested in more detail can turn to Sperber's book and the Knight Foundation Commission's report on intercollegiate athletics.[25] Both provide excellent background for better understanding the vast array of articles on current issues in varsity sports that appear in the press.

While Stanford maintains its high standards, indeed sets an example on these matters, by virtue of participation it cannot be considered immune to the pressures of the system. As the competition in intercollegiate football and basketball escalates, it becomes more and more difficult for institutions like Stanford to be among the very best in all things. In fact, when newly reappointed Bill Walsh, former head coach of the San Francisco 49ers, began his initial spring practice with the Stanford football team in April 1992, he said of the players he'd inherited, "This team is so much better than any of the teams I coached here [in 1977–78], no comparison. Unfortunately, the teams we're playing are much better too."[26] Football, the sport that has been described as driving the college sports machine, presents the most formidable challenges in making the choices between academic integrity and a winning season. Even in other sports, amateur status is becoming a relic of the past, and more pressure is put on college tennis players and baseball players, for example, to turn professional at an early age. For Stanford teams that are ranked in the top five in the country, the pressure is always on to be number one. Ironically, the pressures do not stop when a team *does* win a national championship; the coaches and players then feel added pressure to repeat the triumph. The circles of anxiety and discontent, produced by the pressures to win, spread from the coaches, to the players, to the admissions office, to the administration and faculty, and to the alumni. Costs are becoming prohibitive, and budget limitations add to the stresses within the university. Under such circumstances, priorities run an increased risk of distortion.

I once heard someone say that Stanford is among the very few universities that has successfully managed the balance between excellence in academics and excellence in athletics but that if one more university attempted the same, the selective university system would become unstable and self-destruct. That may be something of an exaggeration, but it serves to illustrate the point: Stanford has indeed been managing what many consider an impossible undertaking.

Ethical Dilemmas

From that moment in our lives at which we learn to speak we are
taught that what we say must be true. What does this mean?
What is meant by "telling the truth?" What does it demand of us?
—Dietrich Bonhoeffer, *What Is Meant by "Telling the Truth?"*

COMMON CONCERNS

There seems to be no professional group in the country that does
not gather annually to discuss the members' latest news, current
practices, and common concerns. The profession of college admissions is no exception, and the responsibility for organizing the two
major national meetings has fallen to the National Association of
College Admissions Counselors (NACAC) and the College Board.
Many high school guidance counselors and college admissions
officers try to attend at least one national or regional meeting each
year, where the common theme is always lively and informed conversation with committed colleagues. I found that the informal networks that developed through these meetings were both professionally helpful and personally sustaining. The formal agenda, reflecting
common concerns, inevitably included topics related to ethical

dilemmas: for example, honesty in college admissions; admissions as ministry; why we select the way we do; ethics in admissions; and the role of subjective admissions criteria.

The reason such subjects were always on the agenda is simple: virtually every action or decision concerning the admission of young people to college involves some kind of ethical dilemma on which guidance is hard to come by. Few admissions professionals are trained as moral philosophers, and in any case, even professional moral philosophers cannot always provide satisfactory answers to the many questions about the practice of life. As I see it, the common goal of such panels and discussions is to ensure, in particular, the protection of students and, in general, the integrity of the college admissions process. In fact, one of the first actions taken by the founders of NACAC in 1937 was the creation of a code of ethics. This code undergoes regular review and forms the current "Statement of Principles of Good Practice," which was jointly developed by the American Association of Collegiate Registrars and Admissions Officers and the College Board and is endorsed by a number of associated secondary school and college associations. The current statement, which runs to a densely packed four pages, covers admission promotion and recruitment, admission procedures, standardized testing, financial aid, and advanced standing and the awarding of credit.[1] Each section of the statement also focuses on the responsibilities of the college and university, the secondary school, and independent counselors (guidance counselors not affiliated with any particular school who advise high school students and their families about college). A number of challenging situations present themselves in each sector, at best, involving conflicts of interest and at worst fundamental moral choices with no easy answers. The subject of moral choice has been debated since well before the establishment of the first college in this country, and modern philosophers and writers have extended the discussions to modern-day quandaries.[2] In the process of college admissions, there are at least three perspectives on the associated dilemmas: those of the applicant, the high school, and the college.

THE VIEW FROM THE APPLICANT

Months before high school seniors begin work on their college applications, they take the standardized tests that are required for admission to more than 90 percent of public and private colleges in the country.[3] On a typical Saturday test day in the spring, one of six throughout the year, almost 350,000 high school students sharpen their no. 2 pencils for the Scholastic Aptitude Test administered by the Educational Testing Service (ETS). In the course of a year, more than 1.5 million students take the tests. In many colleges, admissions decisions turn on the combination of high school grades and standardized test scores (although, as has been shown, the most selective colleges use much more subjective admissions processes). And because an athlete's eligibility to play NCAA sports now hinges on those standardized test scores, the pressure on high school students who take them is great. Under conditions of stress, human beings act in uncharacteristic and unpredictable ways; reports and rumors of cheating on standardized tests are, alas, annual occurrences.

Paying an impostor to take the SAT in a student's place is a well-known method of cheating. Until recently, I had not heard of a more novel system, in which test takers use different-colored M&M candies to signal answers. According to an article in the *New York Times*, about 450 students are caught cheating on the SAT every year, and two of the most recent cases have resulted in lawsuits.[4] A spate of such incidents occurred a few years ago at a high school not far from Stanford, and they were reported in some detail in the local press. A few days later, I received a call from an agitated senior at the same high school to ask if Stanford would be penalizing all applicants from that high school because we knew of the cheating. I tried to reassure him that our basic principle of operation was an honor code (a system in which we believed all applicants were acting honestly until we had evidence that they were not), and unless we received specific names from the high school principal or counselor concerning such incidents, we would certainly not impose a general penalty. The circle of anxiety that began with a few dishonest students subsequently spread to the concerned high school administration, to innocent students, and out to the colleges to which they were applying, so that many more than the guilty were affected.

The Educational Testing Service anticipates modest changes in scores on the SAT from one sitting to another; there is, after all, a standard error in measurement of plus or minus 30 points, and one would hope that after, say, a six-month period, any high school student would improve his or her scores. But an increase of more than 350 points on the combined math and verbal score (out of a possible 1,600) prompts an investigation by ETS. If ETS finds substantial evidence to support a suspicion of cheating, the student in question is notified and given a number of options: to retake the test, to submit to arbitration, to produce additional information, to cancel the score, or to have colleges receive the questioned score with a note explaining why it is being questioned. (Incidentally, a score gain of 350 points or more is not, in and of itself, considered sufficient reason by ETS for withholding scores.) A guidance counselor at a small private school once explained to me the dilemma of one of her students, a Chinese-American senior, who received one of these letters; as a matter of personal honor, he was unwilling to accept any of the options given him. Under these circumstances, ETS exercised its right to cancel the score, and the student was unable to provide test scores for his college applications. I made a few telephone calls to try to confirm the situation and to help formulate an acceptable alternative, but I was unsuccessful in adding to the existing information. (The example serves, among other things, to illustrate differences in codes of ethics for different ethnic populations. In our increasingly multicultural society, a traditional Western perspective is not always understood and may even be offensive.)

These events create dilemmas for both the individual students and for the ETS; the rights of the former need to be protected, and the latter needs not only to ensure a just and credible process but also to protect the privacy of test takers. In a typical year, ETS looks at about 2,000 questionable cases. Half of these come from increases of 350 points or more in verbal and math scores combined; the other half are triggered by letters from counselors, students, and others. About half of the 2,000 cases are cleared in the initial investigation. Of the 450 students with whom ETS corresponds or for whom scores are withheld, more than half choose to take the test again. Of the 30 cases that have gone to court, ETS has never lost a case, and has won 20, with the others being settled in their favor or withdrawn.

Assuming that successful test taking is now behind our high school senior, the next step is completing the college application forms. There were two questions on the 1992 Stanford application that presented ethical dilemmas (apart from those associated with self-identification by ethnicity, which were considered in Chapter 5). The Supplementary Information Form asks:

1. Have you ever been placed on probation, suspended, or expelled from any school? (If so, please explain fully on separate sheet.)
2. Have you ever been convicted of a criminal offense? (If so, please explain fully on separate sheet.)

Our purpose, of course, is to learn whether the personal qualities of the applicant may adversely affect either the applicant's career at Stanford or the lives of fellow students and others.

The vast majority of applicants answer no to both questions; the yes answers can be very revealing both in content and in tone. How serious is the misdemeanor? And how does the applicant tell us about it? The most scrupulously honest seniors sometimes take a page to tell us about relatively minor suspensions of a day for involvement in a scuffle in seventh grade, or even elementary school, for the causes of social justice or moral outrage: "He insulted my best friend by calling him names," or "He pushed me and called me a tattle-tale for saying that he'd cheated on a test, so I pushed him back." Others are more serious: "In tenth grade, I got drunk at a school dance and was put on probation for the quarter." Others have admitted being expelled for drug use or repeated plagiarism. Sometimes the confessions are accompanied by a mature admission of having learned from the experience, or an indication of regret for injudicious actions; sometimes there is no sign of remorse; occasionally there are obvious signs of defensiveness and belligerence.

The question about probation is also asked of the college guidance counselor, so the admissions officer has the advantage of two versions of the story. The reader in the admissions office is, however, in a difficult position when the two answers conflict; for example, sometimes the counselor will tell us about a suspension that the applicant fails to mention. Obviously, such discrepancies have to be pursued with care and sensitivity.

The Supplementary Information Form also contains the following statement:

Stanford's Honor Code has been fundamental in fostering an atmosphere of trust and respect among students and faculty. It provides for a standard of honesty and integrity in all aspects of academic life. Your signature below embraces the spirit of the Honor Code and signifies that ALL of the information you have provided in your application is your own work and, to the best of your knowledge, complete and accurate.

On the following page, the applicant is asked to provide a summary of involvement, talents, and achievements outside the classroom during the tenth, eleventh, and twelfth grades, including the number of hours spent per week, weeks per year, and positions held or honors won. Again, we cross-check the accuracy of this information with the college guidance counselor's form, but for the most part we rely on the applicant's adherence to the honor code. Unfortunately, some evidence exists to confirm the comment, "Students don't join the French Club to experience French culture but because Yale will be impressed."[5] It may be just a white lie to claim a more-active-participation-than-was-realistic in the French Club, but the white lies can add up.

The essay questions give rise to a different set of ethical dilemmas. The essay provides an opportunity to see whether an applicant thinks critically and writes effectively and also can give some inkling of a student's personality. In general, the essay allows some basis for subjective judgment beyond the measures of the scores and transcript. A fundamental premise in reading essays is contained in a closing statement of the instructions: "[We] trust that the essay will be your own work." Some twelfth-grade English teachers routinely assign college essay questions as a fall quarter assignment. Is the corrected version, strictly speaking, the applicant's own work? What about the words of advice from mother or father? It is very difficult to ensure the same interpretation of "your own work." Another possibility is that an independent guidance counselor has written the whole thing. I include this example at the risk of offending most of the scrupulous counselors who work with high school students; unfortunately, it happens to be a real-life occurrence that I heard about from the principal of a local high school who called to ask me what he could or should do about such practices. Again, these are sensitive issues to investigate, and I could offer only the reassurance that we relied on the signed statement to be true, and also that an excellent essay could not compensate for a mediocre academic record and lukewarm references from two teachers and a counselor. In general, good writing in the essay is corroborated somewhere else in the application materials, and part of the art of admissions is interweaving all the information from different sources to compile a coherent portrait of the applicant.

The other kinds of ethical dilemmas raised by the essay question arise from an injudicious choice of subject by the admissions office or intemperate opinion by the applicant. One year, we selected an essay topic that invited trivial responses from the less mature adolescents, but at least it helped to sort them out: "If you could choose to spend the day with anyone, who would it be and how would you spend your time?" The most obviously immature responses were usually corroborated by other parts of the application, such as the opinions of the high school teachers or counselor. However, in one troubling case, an exceptionally talented transfer student with uniformly strong references applied from a highly selective college; the applicant was a minority student in the sciences, rare potential not easily passed up, but he chose to write his essay about Marilyn Monroe, and the details are best left to the reader's imagination. Now why would a bright young man *do* that? And how were we to factor his poor judgment into our decision? After considerable debate among the directors, we decided to offer him admission but agreed that the letter of admission should be accompanied by a handwritten note from me regretting his injudicious choice of essay. I did precisely that; the student accepted and enrolled, and eventually (to the best of my knowledge) was graduated with an unblemished record. I never heard from him again. A variation on this theme came in response to the essay question, "What person or event has influenced your life and why?" One freshman applicant (male), who was again a splendid candidate in terms of our formal criteria, chose to write (and he wrote very well) about his seduction by the family maid. The outcome on this one was not easily decided. Some of us felt that he was simply a rather young man answering the question honestly; others argued that the topic was absolutely unsuitable for a college application. We hedged on the outcome by agreeing to wait-list him—and that year ended up not admitting anyone from the wait list.

The other class of problem essays—ones that express intemperate opinion—can occur in response to even the most serious of topics. Here are a few memorable examples: a well-written essay on the Holocaust that contained unambiguous expressions of admiration for Hitler; a sensitive essay on modern literature that was offensively homophobic; a moving essay about life in the rural Midwest that was blatantly sexist; a strong essay about a new stepfather that was terrifying in its hatred; a poignant essay about a seriously drug-addicted brother, a member of a deeply troubled family, who was serving a third term in prison. Now we state clearly in our essay instructions that there is no "right" choice of answer; we also advise, "Choose a subject you know and feel strongly about; use specific concrete details." No one could argue that the applicants quoted above did not follow our advice, but they left the readers with a number of uncertainties. What *kind* of people were they? What effect would they have on other students in their dormitories? And who were we to be passing judgment on them based on a single piece of paper? Fortunately, of course, the single piece of paper is one of many elements to be considered in the application; the hard calls come when all the rest of the application materials point to an admit decision.

Another kind of worry is about all those other applicants who may have been less honest in their essays, choosing topics that they thought would go over well with the readers, telling us what they thought we wanted to hear. How are we to distinguish the good from the bad? And are not "good" and "bad" hopelessly subjective labels anyway? As is probably clear by now, readers in admissions offices can be tortured by such debates. My own strategy was to focus on the larger array of information, to assume that people were for the most part honest, and to accept that all one can do is to make one's best judgment in difficult and uncertain circumstances. I am convinced that in spite of the inherent challenges it is far better to incorporate subjective judgments into an admissions process than to base decisions on quantitative measures alone. Fortunately, in a selective admissions process, one has the luxury of doing just that. Even so, not even the most selective college has so perfect a process that all its admitted and enrolled students prove to be estimable human beings. I worry even more about the institutions whose very survival depends upon maintaining a specific enrollment to generate tuition; for them, such judgment calls may be moot.

One further ethical dilemma associated with the essay merits mention. That is the unavoidable emotional impact that some essays have on the reader and consequently on the recommendation on admission. (I discount the ones that make us laugh, such as the applicant who appealed, and also contributed to, some of the myths in Chapter 3: "I feel that the Stanford Office of Admissions should know that I'm pale, have brown hair and am fairly sickly looking. I have been told that everyone at Stanford is tanned, blonde and healthy looking. So I'm hoping to get in as some part of a minority quota.") As before, real examples best make the point. One otherwise unremarkable applicant used the essay to talk about her sexual abuse by her father; this was powerful reading that left those of us who read the essay aghast. Another gave a horrifying account of finding her suicidal aunt hanging from a tree. Stories of family tragedies abound: the beloved grandfather with Alzheimer's disease; the twin sister with inoperable cancer; the sibling who died at birth;

and (perhaps most frequent of all) the trauma of parental divorce. I decided to eliminate the request that applicants provide a small photograph after I looked with anguish at the photo of a seventeen-year-old who had been severely burned on the face and neck. One cannot forget that applicants are very much individual human beings involved in life's tragedies. How appropriately to factor such experiences into the final decision on an application for admission is another matter. One applicant bravely concluded her essay, "Thus, owing to my resilient nature, I have been able to emerge relatively unscathed from the vicissitudinous seas of life."

Not all the examples of ethical dilemmas, however, evoke sympathy. Every so often, there are incidents of maliciousness from high school students that promote anger. In the late 1980's, I received a letter from a high school senior in response to an alleged letter from me asking questions about the help he had received in writing his essay. I was confused by the letter because I had never written to this student. To shorten a long and complicated story, after some inquiries, it turned out that a "friend" of the senior had decided to play a joke on him by writing a forged letter on our official stationery (how he obtained this remains a mystery). Eventually, I asked the school principal to intervene and help resolve the situation, which she gladly did. In return, I received a highly offensive and angry letter from the initiator of the joke, telling me what he thought of me and my deplorable lack of a sense of humor. Fortunately, he was not an applicant to Stanford; unfortunately, the victim of the joke was, for legitimate reasons, denied admission. On another occasion, after the decision letters had been mailed, we received a call from a senior who had been denied admission saying that she had misplaced her decision letter and asking for another one. When my secretary passed on this request, I was suspicious; why would anyone want a second copy of a denial letter? When we called the applicant back to ask about the circumstances, we learned that she had not telephoned our office in the first place. We were left wondering why someone would want to do such a mean thing to a classmate.

THE VIEW FROM THE HIGH SCHOOL

The college application process has the general reputation of being grueling and fraught with anxiety, but fortunately it is a one-time experience for high school seniors. Yet for the teachers, principals, and high school guidance counselors who write references, fill out forms, and provide official transcripts, it is an annual responsibility; indeed, admissions officers could not function without their help. In addition to playing an important role in the education of young people, the high school teachers, principals, and counselors inevitably get involved in ethical dilemmas concerning students; they also face a number of more personal dilemmas in the college admissions process. It will be helpful here to begin with some of the specific questions that Stanford asked of teachers and counselors in 1992. Incidentally, we call the relevant forms "references" rather than "recommendations"; we do not expect all the information we receive to necessarily serve as a recommendation.

The counselor is asked to provide an official high school transcript, a list of current courses, an assessment of the level of difficulty of the program taken, and a rank in class for the applicant. Most of this is straightforward, but a few high schools give no grades, and a much larger number do not provide a specific rank in class. (The alternatives offered are grade distributions by subject or overall grade ranges for the senior class, both of which leave it to the admissions officer to estimate rank.) Beyond some other specific academic questions, the counselor is also asked:

What do you like best about this student? In what ways has the student made an impact either in your school or in the community? Are there any factors that might interfere with the candidate's academic performance and/or personal relationships at Stanford? Is there anything else we should know about this student (e.g., personal circumstances, unusual accomplishments)? Has this student ever been placed on probation, suspended, or expelled from your school? If yes, please explain fully on a separate sheet.

(Incidentally, all of the required reference forms are sent to the applicants so that they have an opportunity to read the questions that are asked of both the counselor and the teachers.) Clearly, the answers to these questions are most helpful to admissions officers when they are specific, detailed, and honest; as we tell the counselors and teachers on the forms provided, "we read and re-read every last one of them." The letters often reveal the wonderful wit of the counseling professionals; in response to our question asking how well she knew the applicant, one counselor replied, "Less well than his mother, but better than his mailman."

The sensitivity of the questions on the reference forms is immediately apparent, as, I think, are the ethical considerations. I received an early lesson in this at one of the first national conferences I attended, when I listened attentively to a presentation by an experienced guidance counselor at a select private high school. He described how he had reported an incident of plagiarism on one such reference form and was subsequently sued by the applicant's lawyer father. Although the father ultimately lost the case, the experience was not a pleasant one for the counselor and did not encourage new counselors to be as honest. In such circumstances, the high school counselor faces an unenviable dilemma: whether to tell the truth and perhaps jeopardize the applicant's chances of admission, not to mention risk incurring a lawsuit; or to conceal the truth and mislead the college admissions officer. Many other circumstances produce similar dilemmas: alcohol and drug abuse; eating disorders; pregnancies; violent behavior patterns; suicide attempts; cheating incidents; difficult or abusive family situations; learning and physical disabilities. Are these relevant considerations in the college admissions process? And if not, why not? What are the rights, responsibilities, legal limitations, and privileges of all concerned?

As a way of reassuring principals, counselors, and teachers about the forms they complete, during my tenure as dean of admissions we stated on the Stanford application materials: "This form is a confidential report written on behalf of the applicant . . . and will be used solely for purposes of admissions. Should the applicant be admitted to and enroll at Stanford, this report will be removed from our files prior to such enrollment and will not become part of the student's cumulative file at the University." (Why we did this will become clear in the next section, "The View from the College.") In spite of such reassurances, it is understandable that the respondents to the questions posed by colleges face some difficult decisions in deciding what information to include.

The guiding legal principles are incorporated in the Family Educational Rights and Privacy Act passed by Congress in 1974, in a section commonly known as the Buckley Amendment. In brief, the statute grants to students and former students the following:

1. the right, unless specifically waived, of access to "education records";
2. the right to challenge and rebut misleading and/or inaccurate information contained in the education records; and
3. the right to control the release to third parties of their education records and other personally identifiable information.

To comply with the act, each educational institution is required to take three basic steps: to provide a written institutional policy, to inform students of their privacy rights, and to give students access to their educational records. While it takes a good lawyer to consider, defend, and argue all the nuances, my understanding, based on professional advice, is that high schools bound by the Buckley Amendment are permitted to disclose anything from the student's record if

1. the disclosure is initiated by the parent (or a student who is at least eighteen), as by sending in a request to provide information; or
2. the high school policy (which is supposed to be published to all students every year) includes a notice that the school forwards records to other schools that ask for them in connection with a student's application or enrollment. The high school must give the parent (or eligible student), on request, a copy of the record that was disclosed.[6]

Of course, the guidance counselor, principal, or teacher may have personal knowledge of the student that is not included in the student's record in the literal sense. Communication of personal knowledge is not covered by the Buckley rules, but passing on such personal information could well get the counselor, and the school, in trouble; most human beings prefer to avoid trouble, and many schools prefer their employees to follow the safest path. In short, it is clear, and not surprising, that high school staff may be reluctant to provide all the information they have. The responsibility of the college is to solicit only relevant information and to use the information provided in proper ways. For example, colleges should obviously not use health or handicap information to discriminate against qualified applicants. At the same time, what *is* relevant to the college application is not always obvious. Alcoholism may be considered a disability, but violent behavior of students under the influence of alcohol seriously affects the lives of other students. If an applicant has had an illegitimate child, this is private information, but it will have consequences for any freshman who wants to live in a dormitory with her child or any freshman who wants his partner and child to accompany him to a residential university. Occasionally, counselors conclude the required form with a note saying, "Please call me." Such notes suggest that the counselors have further important information that they are reluctant to put in writing; sometimes, the added note is simply provocative, as it was one time when I *did* call a counselor to ask what he wanted to say and he replied, "I was just curious whether you ever read what I wrote."

Every year NACAC and the College Board arrange programs for new high school guidance counselors and college admissions officers on the writing of effective reference letters. This activity is certainly an acquired art; it is also a demanding assignment. From the point of view of the college, there are a number of hazards in reviewing these required letters. For example, the letters we receive from a guidance counselor who has responsibility for a public high school graduating class of 400 differ greatly from those we receive from a counselor in a small private school who has to write only 40 letters. The former tend to be more general, brief, and formulaic, often revealing that the counselor does not know the applicant well: "Chris was an exceptionally gifted and motivated student. She was consistently at the top of her class, thrived on difficult problems, and was a joy to have in class." The latter go to the other extreme in their embellished detail, length, and intimate knowledge. How does the college admissions officer assess "the truth" when such applicants, by sheer accident of circumstance, are represented so differently? How can we compensate for unequal counseling resources? This problem has become an increasingly difficult one as public schools continue to cut counseling services.

I have already mentioned the ethical and legal problems associated with honest and appropriate disclosures of personal circumstances. Another very different ethical issue regarding letters of reference came to my attention a few years ago. A staff member in a local public high school called to tell me that the guidance counselor was asking the seniors to write their own letters of reference; after being shown a draft, the counselor then signed the edited final version. When I called the principal about this conversation, I learned there was some truth to it; the guidance counselor involved was new and inexperienced. I was also assured, however, that Stanford had not been sent any such letters (not quite so reassuring for colleges that *had* been on the receiving end). This was not the first time that I had heard of students being involved in the writing of their own reference letters. The procedure successfully skirts such difficulties as the counselor's lack of specific knowledge of the students and the applicants' Buckley Amendment rights, but the value of the references is seriously compromised.

One challenge for admissions officers is to recognize their own biases in the reading of applications. These come in many forms: the jock bias, the nerd bias, the cheerleader bias, and the dungeons-and-dragons bias, to mention a few from a much larger set. We could, I suppose, make some attempt to balance out the biases among the readers by judicious distribution of applications. Instead, we rely on the openness and honesty of individual readers to declare a specific bias on the work-card. And all readers know that they are not to evaluate the applications of students that they know well or are related to. On the other side of the process is the bias, or (a different matter) stereotyping, by the teacher or guidance counselor who has provided a letter of reference. This is a particular hazard for the reader of applicants' files because our mental portraits of the applicants are often drawn by the writers of such letters. Here is an unconscious, classic example of stereotyping from a math teacher: "Stephen has the standard virtues we have come to expect in an Oriental: he is industrious, gentle and self-motivated. But he is also something that has not been seen until recently among Asiatics: a recognized leader and an eager contributor to life at the School. He is also something that is still more rare among Orientals: a student who is gifted in more than sciences (although he is superb in mathematics and all the sciences)." A variation on the theme comes from the physics teacher who describes a female student as "not bad for a woman in physics." Comments such as these do the applicants a disservice by minimizing, or detracting from, their accomplishments. In any letter of recommendation the choice of adjectives by the writer contributes to the potential bias of the reader: naive; industrious; young; all-American; assertive (especially when applied to women); dogged; self-confident; shy. The writer of letters is an essential filter for the reader and, as such, carries significant responsibility. The admissions officer must be on constant guard not to hold a poorly written or unhelpful letter against the applicant; the letter was not, after all, the responsibility of the student. Some high schools, particularly private ones, use a committee to write college application letters, a process that safeguards against individual idiosyncrasies. More often than not, though, these committees produce bland, "milk-toast" recommendations that are not very helpful to the admissions staff; and the process is practically impossible to carry out well in a large public high school.

A final kind of dilemma from the high school side is infrequent. It arises when a college receives two completely contradictory reference letters from teachers. In the extreme case, the eleventh-grade science teacher is very high on the applicant and urges admission in the strongest possible terms, while the twelfth-grade history teacher compares the applicant unfavorably with others who have been admitted in the past. The dilemma is compounded when two teachers agree but are contradicted by the high school principal in the third required reference. Clearly, even assuming that all the letter writers are trying to be fair and honest, the admissions officer needs to follow up on such discrepancies for a competitive applicant. But who should be called? And how should the questions be phrased? And what was the cause of the contradictions in the first place? Again, as always, what is "the truth"?

The above examples illustrate many of the points made in Sissela Bok's splendid book on lying, but this discussion has not done justice to the larger issues. Bok provides a fitting, if not entirely reassuring, point of reflection:

All deceptive messages, whether or not they are lies, can also be more or less affected by self-deception, by error, and by variations in the actual intention to deceive. These three factors can be looked at as filters of irregular thickness, distortion, and color that alter the ways in which a message is experienced by both deceived and deceivers. To complicate matters further, someone who intends to deceive can work *with* these filters and manipulate them; he can play on the biases of some persons, the imagination of others and on errors and confusion throughout the system.

The interaction of these filters through which communication passes and is perceived is immensely complex. . . . We see the intricate capacities of each person for denial, deflection, distortion, and loss of memory; but also for accuracy, regeneration, and invention. Add the fact that communication takes place over a period of time, sometimes long, and often between more than two persons. The many experiments on rumors show how information can be distorted, added to, partially lost, when passed from one person to another, until it is almost unrecognizable even though no one may have intended to deceive.[7]

THE VIEW FROM THE COLLEGE

As I think is apparent, the perspectives of the applicant and the high school are intertwined in the ultimate goal of developing as accurate a portrait as possible of the applicant. Many of the questions raised in the previous two sections are relevant from the college's perspective, too: incidents of cheating on the standardized tests; personal qualities of the applicants; factors that might affect academic progress in college; assessment of unequal opportunities. None of these issues appeared for the first time in the 1990's. In his frequently cited text from 1966, for example, the director of admissions emeritus at MIT wrote:

At its lowest and least imaginative level, exchange between high school counselors and admissions people constitutes a kind of brokerage operation. At this level, the job is one of negotiation: the high school counselor tries to make the best possible bargain on behalf of his "client" for admission to a strong college. In an independent school, the student is quite literally a client, and in the eyes of status conscious parents, a school's reputation may, to an embarrassing degree, depend on its success in getting graduates into the particular colleges favored by its parent group, an objective often only remotely related to the genuine educational worth of the processes carried on in these colleges, or their suitability for the students concerned.[8]

Although many of the ethical issues in college admissions are not new, the increased competition for students in recent years has put formidable new pressures on colleges to attract and recruit the most talented students. Not surprisingly, as colleges have become more businesslike in their approach to admissions, introducing new positions such as director of enrollment management, some of the consequent competitive marketing strategies have encountered justifiable criticism. The dean of admissions and financial aid at Harvard has described this competition as analogous to "an international arms race. Both sides allocate more and more resources to their respective campaigns, at times losing sight of larger purposes."[9]

In their attempts to attract more applicants, for example, colleges have produced eye-catching and sophisticated publications; it is not unusual for high school seniors with high scores on the SAT to receive, with no expression of interest on their part and at no cost, 30 or 40 glossy brochures from colleges hoping to entice them to apply. If students have taken the PSAT (Preliminary Scholastic Aptitude Test) during their sophomore or junior years and scored well, the deluge of mail begins earlier, and by their senior year, hundreds of colleges will have sent them information. (The names of any specified set of test takers can be bought from the Student Search Service of the College Board and the American College Test offices.) Many colleges now extend their marketing technique to the electronic media, producing videos. The accuracy with which colleges represent their campuses, programs, and students in these media varies significantly, as do the quality and accuracy of content. Although most colleges provide some measure of their selectivity by publishing the average test scores of their applicants, admitted students, and enrolling students, some colleges provide information on limited sets of mean SAT scores, omitting all athletes or specially targeted minorities, consequently distorting the measure to prospective applicants. (The way Stanford presents this information, with a discussion of the reasons, is presented in Chapter 1.)

Admissions officers suspect that the offending institutions in these cases are tempted by the college-ranking lists that seem to have become an addiction of some national media, an addiction that is no doubt fueled by a desire for increased sales and profits by magazine producers. Since the rankings depend on, among other things, measures of selectivity in admissions, the more selective a college can appear, the higher it will place on the nationally publicized list and the more applicants it will attract—or so the reasoning goes. Although the media deserve some blame for their sometimes misguided efforts and enthusiasm to compile ranked lists, the fault is not entirely theirs. The simple question from a prospective applicant, "How many applications did your college receive last year?" can be answered in various and creative ways. Some colleges define an "applicant" as any student who writes a letter of inquiry; others count all those who are sent an application form; some count just those who pay the application fee; and some define an applicant as a student who has submitted a complete application. The choice of definition obviously affects the apparent selectivity of the college. The 32 colleges and universities in the Consortium on Financing Higher Education (COFHE) define "applicants" as those students to whom letters are sent when notifications of decisions are made. Interestingly, even within COFHE, six institutions have exceptions to this definition. The "truth" on this score is known only to the individual deans of admission and their staff members. I do not know of any agreement on such a definition other than the one developed by COFHE. The public should receive, and has a right to receive, accurate information about college admissions, but the two potential sources must meet critical tests in providing it: colleges must be honest and helpful in presenting the information, and the media must place higher priority on a full understanding and analysis of the relevant data than they do on selling their wares. Not surprisingly, at least one director of admissions has written on how the media's "rating game" affects college admissions.[10] She concludes that the most effective way to guide students to the best college match is through a network of colleges, students, parents, and secondary school counselors, with the media assisting en route through the transmission of full and accurate information.

Another misleading way of counting has to do with the reported "yield" of admitted students—that is, the fraction of those students *offered* admission who *accept* it. At first glance, it would seem that the higher the yield, the more desirable the college. There is some truth to this if a college attracts and admits the very best students, but it is possible to have a yield of 100 percent if a college admits only those students who have no other options! Some very selective colleges have yields of 55 percent or less, precisely because they offer admission to students who are also accepted at other very selective schools. In short, the apparently simple measure of yield can be misleading to the uninitiated. For cosmetic purposes, a college may also consciously enhance its yield in various ways. If, for example, a college goes to its waiting list to admit students, it might first call the prospective admittees to ask whether they will accept. A guaranteed acceptance helps to boost the yield, whereas playing the process straight may lower the yield. The former strategy seems ethically questionable to me. One year, for example, I received a call from a high school guidance counselor who wanted to know whether Stanford planned to admit a particular student I will call Sam. At this point, we had not mailed the decision letters, and so I asked why the counselor needed to know the decision early. He replied, to my amazement, that selective college Z had overadmitted freshmen for that region and wanted to pull back on some admit decisions; if Stanford planned to offer admission to Sam, college Z would drop Sam because it was known that Sam would rather attend Stanford than Z. (In the language of this section, a positive decision by Stanford meant that Sam would lower Z's yield.) I replied that Sam would have his decision from Stanford in a few days and that college Z would have to solve its problem without knowing Stanford's decision on the unsuspecting Sam. (He *was* admitted to Stanford.)

I now regret, with the benefit of hindsight, that I was not more consistent in raising private or public objections to such unprofessional behavior.

Once the students are admitted, offers of financial aid can strongly influence the final choice of college, particularly in middle-income families who would not qualify for need-based aid. So-called merit awards offering financial support above and beyond the computed need have proliferated during the past decade. A 1985 survey showed that close to 80 percent of all four-year institutions offer no-need scholarships.[11] Merit awards are not inherently unethical in a time of financial constraints for both families and institutions, but their use for purposes of recruitment is certainly debatable and raises serious questions about institutional priorities. Some institutions offer inducements in the form of free trips to campus during the decision month of April to selected students. Stanford developed such a program of free visits, too—but only for a small number of students from families with demonstrated need. Ideally one would like to provide all needy students the opportunity of a visit to help them make an informed choice (more affluent families often pay for such trips), but the associated financial costs would be very high.

I would like to add two final examples of ethical dilemmas for the college. The first is associated with a relative newcomer to the scene of college admissions, the independent guidance counselor, who provides advice and assistance to college applicants, usually for a substantial fee. Since the late 1980's, the number of independent college guidance counselors has grown considerably, both because of the decline in the number of high school counselors, often victims of school district budget cuts, and because of the increased pressures that applicants and their parents apparently have felt to gain entrance to selective colleges. (This anxiety is somewhat paradoxical in a time of declining high school enrollment, when admission to colleges and universities should be less competitive.) One plausible explanation is the natural instinct of parents to want to provide their children with every advantage, particularly advantages the parents were denied. Educational advantages provide more reassurance of a place in the apparent security of the upper middle class. A number of fine independent counselors are well trained for the college guidance profession; their work meets the highest ethical standards. These counselors provide a valuable service for high school students and parents new to the world of college admissions, and some of the independent counselors (those who are members of NACAC) provide services free of charge to disadvantaged students.

Some tension has developed, though, between independent counselors and high school counselors, and (for different reasons) between independent counselors and college admissions officers. The high school guidance counselor may sometimes be slightly offended when a family seeks a second opinion from an independent counselor, especially when the latter is not well informed about the high school's curriculum, grading system, or other factors relevant to the college admissions process. From the point of view of the college admissions staff, a reference letter from an independent counselor who is in the applicant's employ may not be entirely objective. For that very reason, some independent counselors do not write references for their clients. Others, however, submit a student's whole application in an elaborate folder, including background information, supporting documents, details about the family, and anything else they think relevant. Speaking from experience, I know that admissions directors receive these packets unenthusiastically and do not take kindly to the follow-up telephone call or special note to inquire about the admissions decision. Fortunately, these practices seem to be on the decline; nevertheless, the independent guidance counselor is alive and well, and stories of unethical methods still make the rounds. Independent counselors who become members of NACAC agree to honor the same code of ethics that the rest of the profession does. I support all who help students better prepare for college, but I am bothered by the rather steep fee (as high as $2,500) that independent counselors charge those who need it least: students from middle- and upper-income families, generally in good school districts, and with well-educated parents. Unfortunately, the overzealous parents are ultimately responsible for packaging their children for college admissions. Some begin this mission before their sons and daughters have finished elementary school.

The second recent ethical dilemma from the college perspective is the whole question of the confidentiality of what Stanford calls the work-card. As explained in Chapter 2, the readers of freshman applications summarize their findings on a work-card that is placed at the front of the applicant's file. The work-card provides a quick and useful summary for the readers of the file and facilitates subsequent reviews of the file's contents. At the end of the admissions period, the work-cards are pulled from the files of enrolling students, and the documents relevant to the student's educational record at Stanford (such as the high school transcript) are passed along to the Office of the Registrar.

We assumed, until the spring of 1992, that the work-cards were not covered by the Buckley Amendment because they were not a part of the student's permanent academic record and did not affect students once they were enrolled. All this changed after a recent Harvard graduate, a former editor of the student newspaper, the *Harvard Crimson*, tried to gain access to comments made about his own application to Harvard. After Harvard balked at his request, on the same grounds as those just given, the U.S. Department of Education ruled in his favor, citing the 1974 federal Family Educational Rights and Privacy Act. The Harvard student then contacted students across the country, including the staff of the *Stanford Daily*, who subsequently asked to see their own work-cards. Although my successor as the dean of undergraduate admissions, James Montoya, also disagreed with the Department of Education's decision, he honored it and made work-cards available to students who asked to see them. Before this happened, however, the admissions office taped over comments taken from confidential reference letters. In the future, Stanford will not retain work-cards after the admissions process is complete and will not keep work-cards from previous years that have not been requested for viewing by a specified date.

Several ethical issues surface here. How does a college admissions office, which is dependent on the honest and frank assessments of teachers and high school guidance counselors, guarantee the confidentiality of their comments? Would admissions officers write different summaries if they thought their comments would be read by the admitted students? (The ruling does not apply to applicants who are *denied* admission.) Why would an admitted student be eager to see the comments of admissions officers? Plain curiosity? Simple reassurance? Checking the system? And what, beyond personal satisfaction, is to be gained by such a request? These students were, after all, admitted to the university. (In 1992, more than 700 Stanford undergraduates asked to review their work-cards.) According to an article in the *Chronicle of Higher Education,* the Harvard student who initiated the practice argued that the information gleaned from the work-cards (or their equivalents at other colleges) could shed new light on how leading universities decide whom to admit in general, and on the validity of charges that Asian-American applicants in particular face discrimination in the admissions process.[12] However worthy these issues may be of fuller discussion, I am not convinced that an undergraduate's review of his or her own work-card would contribute, in any notable way, to those debates. Moreover, the fact that some students were hurt by the comments made about them on the work-cards illustrates the difficulty of interpreting information out of context. In a process where candor is essential, the ruling encourages all participants (counselors, teachers, and admissions officers) to be *less* candid. The situation is not only an unfortunate example of insecurity and deep-seated mistrust, but one in which individual rights must be weighed against the effective operation of a large-scale process. As one who was responsible for the latter, I believe there are other important measures to ensure the protection of individuals; in the admissions process at Stanford, the faculty and student oversight committee of the Faculty Senate serves to guard the integrity of the process.

Examples of the preceding dilemmas are best illustrated by some actual case studies of freshman applicants. They have of course been disguised in small but important ways, to protect individuals' privacy.

CASE STUDIES

The cases that follow are examples I encountered at Stanford between 1984 and 1991. I preface these with one case from the same period but from another selective university. It merits inclusion here simply because it is an example that engenders fear in every admissions officer, and because it has some Stanford connections. All the cases share a common theme in varying guises: misrepresentation. The non-Stanford example was reported in an issue of the *Princeton Alumni Weekly*. In early 1991, the Princeton police arrested a Princeton undergraduate, Alexi Indris-Santana, in his geology lab. The report went as follows:

When Princeton first heard from Santana, a self-educated ranch hand from Utah with a great potential for long-distance running, it believed it was getting a diamond in the rough. What it got was the cleverest imitation in Princeton history.

Santana, who claimed to devour great literature while tending cattle, had one of the shortest applications on record: a list of the books he had read, authentic SAT scores above 1400, a reference from a Utah ranch, and newspaper clippings of track results that evidenced outstanding speed for an eighteen-year-old. On the basis of his application and an on-campus interview, Dean of Admission Anthony M. Cummings admitted him in the spring of 1988.

Santana, fatherless, asked for a year's deferral to care for his dying mother in Switzerland. The university assented, and a year later Santana, now calling himself Indris-Santana, matriculated with the class of 1993. For two years, no one found out that "Indris-Santana" was a pseudonym for James Arthur Hogue, a youthful twenty-nine-year-old college dropout who needed the deferral to serve ten months of a five-year prison sentence in Utah for possession of stolen property. On February 26, acting on information provided by the university, Princeton police confronted Hogue with his past and arrested him for breaking parole. The University voided his matriculation.[13]

The way Hogue was caught provides another example (as do the following cases B and C) of the amazing role that coincidences can play in college admissions life. At a Harvard-Yale-Princeton track meet, a Yale senior recognized Hogue from another of his deceptions, this one in California, where he had briefly posed as a sixteen-year-old to enroll in a Palo Alto high school. (He had told school authorities that he wanted to qualify for admission to Stanford, and during this time he actually ran in the Stanford Invitational Open cross-country race and posted the fastest time.) The Yale student alerted authorities in California, who then notified Princeton. Hogue was charged with five crimes, including theft by deception (his acceptance of $40,000 in financial aid). In 1992, after pleading guilty, Hogue was sentenced to nine months in jail and five years' probation. He served 134 days at the Mercer County Work House before being released to Massachusetts. In May 1993, Hogue was charged with receiving stolen radio equipment and with the theft of $50,000 worth of precious stones from Harvard University.

Case A: The Scholar-Athlete with a Past

This was perhaps the most extraordinary example of an ethical dilemma in my seven-year experience and, according to colleagues with two decades of experience, one of the most complex cases ever.

When I was away from campus making high school visits one fall, my secretary referred one of my telephone calls to an associate dean. The caller, "Ted," disconcerted my colleague by asking if Stanford had any intention of admitting a convicted felon. Ted then went on to say that young "Joey" was applying to Stanford and that he, Ted, had evidence that Joey had committed a criminal offense. After the associate dean reported this conversation to me, I returned the call and confirmed that Ted was making a serious charge; I could only pursue the matter if he were willing to submit the claim in writing. To my surprise, Ted not only agreed to do so, but, in response to my further questions, said he had no objection to my sharing a copy of his promised letter with Joey. This second telephone conversation also revealed that Ted was an attorney and a graduate of an Ivy League school for which he was a college admissions interviewer.

A few days later, the promised letter arrived from Ted, informing me of a robbery at his house with which Joey was charged. After some careful thought, I wrote to Joey to explain that I had received information about him, as detailed in the enclosed letter, and said that I would appreciate hearing his response to the allegations. At this point, the story became even more complicated. Joey took the letter to his high school guidance counselor, who immediately called me to expand on the details. Apparently, Joey lived with his divorced mother. Ted lived close to the high school and had taken an unusual interest in the welfare of many of the young men who attended the school; because of Joey's family circumstances, Ted had taken a particular interest in him, an interest that had homosexual overtones. Ted had subsequently given Joey both a car and the key to his house, which Ted encouraged him to visit whenever Joey wished. One day, when Ted was away on a business trip, Joey took a group of his friends to Ted's house for a party; since Joey had forgotten his key, the young people entered the house through a window. When Ted returned, some items were missing from the house, and Joey was subsequently charged with their theft.

At this point, it became very difficult to decide which reports to believe, and I told the guidance counselor that I wanted to discuss the matter with my colleagues and think about it further. I did not want to pursue the matter with the local police, hoping that I had sufficient information from the immediate sources. Meanwhile, I received a letter from Joey's uncle, also a lawyer, repeating the high school counselor's version of Joey's position. A call soon followed from the school principal, urging me to believe that Joey was not entirely responsible for the circumstances. I wrote up reports on all these conversations for Joey's file. His file already contained an enthusiastic athletic rating form from a varsity coach at Stanford, enumerating Joey's significant achievements at the state level in his sport. In addition, it was clear from Joey's transcript and high school references that he was a fine student, not only in the context of his high school, but in the Stanford applicant pool. If we had not heard from Ted, Joey would easily have gained an offer of admission.

The dilemmas were multiple, and the time to decide on them was limited. How to sort out the facts? In what way was Joey responsible for what had happened? How should it all affect the decision on admission? Should I alert my counterparts at the other colleges to which I knew Joey to be applying? How could I explain the situation to the Stanford varsity coach? In the end, we decided to let every one of the twelve directors in our office read the file, complete with all the notes and correspondence, and have everyone cast a private vote; I said that I would go with a majority decision. In fact, the decision turned out to be straightforward because the votes were overwhelmingly for a denial of admission. (If the reader thinks this an unreasonable outcome, it is because I am unable to do justice to all aspects of the story without revealing confidential details and supporting documents.) I did *not* alert my colleagues at other colleges, reasoning that they too should reach an independent decision based on the information available to them, although I did not know whether Ted had provided them with the same information that he had given Stanford. (Calling them to check this point would have just added to the complexities.) As for the Stanford coach, I arranged a special meeting to tell him that I knew he would be surprised by the decision on Joey, but that he was going to have to trust my judgment, which was based on information I could not share with him. To his credit, the coach took the news very well, owing, I hope, to our previous good working relationship. As for the high school, the counselor and the principal were not happy, and I spent a good hour with them when I visited the school the following fall, trying to explain our position. Following our principle that decisions should be conveyed to the applicant only (although we do share them, upon request, with high school guidance counselors), Ted was not informed of the decision on Joey's application. As for Joey, I understand that he enrolled at a large state university.

Case B: Mistaken Identity

The Basic Information Form contained in the freshman application requests information about an applicant's ethnicity. Stanford strongly encourages all applicants to self-identify and to provide any related information they care to offer.

A few years ago during the month of April, after decision letters had been mailed out but before the common reply date, "Bob," an admitted high school senior from out of state, visited our office. Bob asked to talk to one of the directors and during the conversation mentioned that he wondered why he was receiving publications from the black student organizations at Stanford. The director, who saw that Bob did not look black, offered to pull Bob's application file to see if it contained any information that might provide an explanation. To the director's surprise, the optional self-identification section was completed, with a tiny mark in the box opposite the Black / African-American designation. He pointed this out to Bob, who made no comment and soon afterward left the office. The incident struck the director as odd, and he dropped by my office to tell me about it. By sheer coincidence, my mail that day contained a rare item, an anonymous letter. (In seven years, I don't think I received more than three or four anonymous letters, for which I am grateful. Anyone who does not have the courage to associate his or her name with a strongly expressed opinion should not offer it.) The letter was written by another senior, who identified himself as a classmate of Bob's. He wanted me to know that Bob was bragging about his admission to Stanford, claiming that he had been admitted after identifying himself as black. Normally, anonymous accusations present a quandary; by definition, there is no way to check the source and one's instinct is to disregard them, but serious charges, anonymous or not, make us feel uneasy. In this case, the coincidence of Bob's visit and the content of the letter prompted some action.

Fortunately, there are ways to check ethnicity short of calling the high school counselor for confirmation. When high school students take national standardized tests, the associated forms ask them to identify themselves by ethnicity, and this information is passed on to the colleges that receive the required scores. When we cross-checked the standardized test information, Bob was again identified as black. So with three independent sources pointing to mistaken ethnicity, I decided to write to Bob. As I reviewed his file, I couldn't help but note that Bob's father was an attorney. In my letter to Bob, I reported all that I had learned related to the question of his ethnicity, including the anonymous letter, and asked simply if he could provide a response that would be helpful to the Office of Undergraduate Admissions in understanding the situation.

A few days later, I received a telephone call from Bob. He had a few questions, he said. Was he admitted to Stanford simply because he had identified himself as black? And would he *not* have been admitted if he had self-identified as white? I replied that he was not focusing on the relevant issue. He had signed his application to confirm "ALL of the information . . . provided in your application is . . . complete and accurate." Deliberate misrepresentation was grounds for withdrawal of his offer of admission. At this point, with all the evidence pointing to misrepresentation, Bob had little to say. I told him that I regretted that I had no option but to withdraw his offer of admission to Stanford, and I subsequently confirmed this action in writing. Bob did not contact Stanford again. What the circumstances were with his other applications I do not know, but I decided he had received adequate retribution from Stanford. Why he alerted us to his own misrepresentation in the first place is difficult to understand, except that perhaps he was worried about being found out if he enrolled at Stanford.

The question of misrepresentation by ethnicity in the case of American Indians has recently received attention in the national press.[14] Most colleges and universities ask students to self-identify, but they seldom check whether the declarations are true. Since the U.S. Bureau of Indian Affairs provides many millions of dollars in undergraduate financial aid to Native American students, and some states set reduced tuition rates for these students, an applicant acknowledging some American Indian heritage has a significant advantage. Many colleges now require students to prove their claims to Native American Indian heritage before they are made eligible for financial aid, but there is no standard procedure in place. Such proof includes providing information on tribal affiliation, tribal number, or a certificate-of-blood card.

Case C: Missing Records

For reasons that the previous case made clear, admissions officers are constantly on the alert for possible false information in an application. At least twice a year, we uncovered examples of falsified transcripts or letters of recommendation, and we probably did not discover them all. In a variation on this theme, an applicant does not actually provide false information but instead conveniently omits selected parts of the academic record.

One such omission involved "Caitlin," a young woman who was actually enrolled at Stanford. The omission was discovered through another set of coincidences. Caitlin's application as a transfer student was very impressive. Her academic record was uniformly strong, she was talented in an array of extracurricular activities, and she came well supported from the college in which she had enrolled as a freshman. After Caitlin enrolled at Stanford, she happened to be spotted on campus by an administrator who was visiting from another selective college outside California. When this administrator met with a dean at Stanford to discuss other business, he remarked on his surprise at seeing Caitlin. Apparently, her somewhat troubled record was well known to him at his home institution, and he was interested to learn that she was now enrolled at Stanford. The Stanford dean subsequently mentioned this conversation to me, and I pulled the application file. On close examination, we noted a gap of one year between Caitlin's graduation from high school and enrollment at the college from which she was admitted to Stanford. On her application, Caitlin had explained this year by saying she had taken time off to help out with some family problems at home, all of which seemed both reasonable and noble to us at the time. But her college transcript did show an unusual number of transfer credits from an unspecified college. A call to the registrar of her transfer college confirmed our growing suspicions: Caitlin had previously been enrolled at yet another undergraduate institution, from which she had been expelled for a variety of academic problems. She had omitted this part of her academic record when applying to Stanford.

The question at Stanford then became an interesting one of jurisdiction. Which dean was responsible for handling such a violation? Ultimately, it fell to Undergraduate Admissions to rescind her admission because of misrepresentation. Caitlin was dismissed from the university, and the last I heard she had enrolled elsewhere. It was a painful experience for all concerned.

Case D: The Summer Tragedy

Because even a single admissions season has so many memorable individuals, I usually resist characterizing stories about them as "the most poignant ever." However, I will never forget a tragic case from my second year as dean, one in which the issue of ethical dilemmas extended far beyond the decision on admission. This case received national attention—including front-page reporting in the *New York Times*—and later became a book and a television movie, so it would be pointless to camouflage the student's identity. Edmund (known as Eddie) Perry was a talented young African-American who was admitted to Phillips Exeter Academy, an elite boarding school, through a special minority recruitment program. The transition cannot have been an easy one for Eddie; any adolescent would experience understandable culture shock in going from a public school in a poor rural or poor urban neighborhood to an exclusive private school with some of the most advantaged students in the nation.

Nevertheless, by his senior year, Eddie had earned a solid academic record, and we were sufficiently impressed with his potential to offer him a place at Stanford. He accepted the offer of admission and was all set to enroll at Stanford the following fall. That summer, Eddie returned to New York for a summer job and lived at home with his mother and an older brother who was already enrolled in college. One evening, after a pickup basketball game near their house, for reasons not entirely clear, Eddie and his brother attempted to rob a passerby. The man happened to be a plainclothes detective with a gun strapped to his leg; in self-defense, he pulled out the gun and shot Eddie in the stomach. Eddie died at a local hospital a few hours later.

All of us in Undergraduate Admissions were stunned and horrified to read the story reported in the national press. Details of Eddie's life were printed, including his impending enrollment at Stanford. A national reporter wanted me to release Eddie's application essay for publication; he could not understand either my refusal or my objections.

I soon started receiving letters from parents of denied applicants asking why Stanford would admit muggers and deny admission to their virtuous children. Based on details subsequently reported in the press about Eddie's life at Exeter, other questions arose about whether we had been fully informed of his high school record. The questions about what activities (legal and illegal) students pursue could be applied to any high school, public or private, in this country. The very experienced guidance counselor assured me that some of the information had been unknown to him too, and that Exeter had been honest in the references it had sent Stanford. Whatever "the truth," the fact remained that a tragedy of many dimensions had occurred, and a talented young black man with a promising future was dead.

Case E: The Terminal Illness

This is not, strictly speaking, a case study. I have chosen instead to present the ethical dilemma in general terms because any one specific example could be identified. Privacy takes precedence over the more compelling illustration by case study. The case of Eddie Perry produces a permanent tug at the heartstrings, but such a feeling is, unfortunately, not unique during the course of an admissions season. In any given year there are other cases, involving terminal illnesses, in which students actually enroll at Stanford with both student and university knowing that they will probably not live to graduate. I mentioned earlier how difficult it is for admissions officers to divorce their feelings from individual circumstances. Making a rational decision on an application from a young woman battling cystic fibrosis or inoperable cancer, or from a young man coping with the consequences of an accident that has left him quadriplegic, I found to be close to impossible. We have no standard measures in admissions to weigh personal courage or the ability to triumph against the consequences of a debilitating accident. We do have, however, memorable examples among Stanford's undergraduates of the capacity to overcome improbable odds. The effect of the presence of such young men and women on their classmates is inspirational. One of my favorite Stanford photos is of a student happily riding his bicycle, towing along his paraplegic roommate in his wheelchair.

There are no specific ethical decisions involved in admitting qualified students with serious illnesses (we claim, after all, not to discriminate on the basis of handicap in implementing our admissions policies, and I believe we live up to that claim). The hard part comes in deciding exactly how to factor in all the extenuating circumstances. There is no formula to apply, there are no tables to refer to; the whole process is irreducibly subjective. How does, and how should, the heart rule the head in such decisions? I know I was inconsistent in making some final decisions. Some decisions came from the heart; others were definitely from the head. Often, the various readers disagreed on the decision. I don't think another seven years in the job would have made me any more consistent on these very difficult decisions, and one tries to accept the inevitable fallibility of a subjective process.

Buying a Place

Though somewhat unusual, this case does illustrate one end of the range of approaches to applying for a space in the freshman class. One day when I was away from campus, two formally dressed foreign gentlemen arrived in our office with a request to speak to the dean. They were invited to meet with an assistant dean who would answer their questions. The businessmen explained that they were visiting Stanford on behalf of their corporate director, whose son was soon to be a high school senior. The director was very eager to have his son attend Stanford. "Would $10,000," they politely asked, "be sufficient?"

It soon became clear that the financial question dealt with the cost of gaining admission rather than the cost of attending Stanford. The somewhat surprised assistant dean attempted to explain that the selection of the freshman class was not conducted that way, and she patiently described the selection criteria and process. Undaunted, the two businessmen pulled out a checkbook and persisted, "Well, how much *does* it cost?" When again rebuffed, the representatives replied that they had not had this kind of problem at the other colleges they had visited, a claim I find difficult to believe.

Postsecondary institutions enroll a freshman class in a variety of ways. Many junior colleges have "open admissions," simply requiring graduation from high school. Many four-year state colleges and universities require national standardized test scores (SAT or ACT) and the completion of required high school courses with a prescribed passing grade. The most selective four-year colleges and universities admit a freshman class on the basis of a more complex, subjective process, such as that described in this book. As I have mentioned earlier, more than one faculty member at Stanford, and elsewhere, has suggested that the class might be selected by some kind of random process. The reader can undoubtedly suggest further ingenious alternatives for a college admissions office. Of these four stated possibilities, it is only the subjective process that directly involves ethical dilemmas. The examination of high school transcripts and standardized test scores can be completed by a computer, and the admissions decisions can be made without involving any human beyond the persons responsible for entering the data and collecting the computer printout.

While I personally believe that the subjective process allows for better decisions because they are based on a more complete, albeit a more complex, range of considerations, the process is imperfect. The imperfection stems primarily from the inescapable fact that admissions officers are human beings, with limitations, preoccupations, and biases. Furthermore, the information they consider is always incomplete and comes through the filters (as Sissela Bok has described them) of another set of human beings—applicants, teachers, principals, and counselors. The subjective selection process is fraught with ethical dilemmas and involves vulnerable young people at an important transition point in their lives. Nevertheless, admissions officers should not despair of doing the very best they can in carrying out their responsibilities. Everyone involved in the college admissions process must constantly aim to maintain a credible and honest process. The principles of selection must be publicly explained, defended, and periodically reviewed and re-assessed, and they must be put into practice with integrity. Telling the truth demands a great deal of us—as I have been reminded again and again in writing this book.

The Changing Scene

There is a danger of America becoming a nation "split into a small educated elite and a vast under-class ill-prepared for college or the workplace."
—Donald Stewart, President of the College Board, 1991

AS THE PRESIDENT of the College Board, Donald Stewart, has pointed out:

Much of higher education stands poised on the brink of a period that is likely to result in greater adjustments of a more lasting nature than were experienced at the end of World War II or during the baby boom. . . . The current enrollment profile is a harbinger of what we should expect to come in the next decade:

- 53 percent female
- 57 percent enrolled in four-year versus 43 percent in two-year institutions
- 80 percent enrolled in public institutions
- 59 percent enrolled full-time, 41 percent part-time
- increasing ethnic and racial diversity and a declining proportion of white students

- approximately one-half of all college students are 25 and over and about 20 percent are 35 or older.[1]

Each of these changes has implications for college admissions, and people in the profession have reason to wonder whether the traditional system of admissions can meet the new demands. The College Board has addressed this issue in a series of eight monographs, whose details extend well beyond the scope of this book to include other important topics such as financial aid and school-college articulation.[2] Here I focus on a few selected issues that are most relevant to this book and weigh heavily on the minds of more than one dean of undergraduate admissions in the 1990's.

NATIONAL DEMOGRAPHICS

The factor with the most significant effect on college admissions nationally is the number of high school graduates. Without high school graduates, considerations of excellence and diversity have no content; as the number of high school graduates declines, the competition between colleges in enrolling their freshman classes becomes more intense. Recent changes in national and state demographics of high school graduates have been quite dramatic, as have the associated changes in ethnic composition. The changes will continue through the year 2000, and they will take different forms.

A detailed analysis of high school graduate projections indicates that the number of public high school graduates in the United States will decline approximately 3.5 percent between 1986 and 1995. After 1995, the number of high school graduates will rise steadily, increasing by nearly 9 percent between 1990 and the year 2000.[3] Although the 3.5 percent decline may appear small, the regional variations are much more dramatic; during this period, the western states will actually see an increase (12.8 percent) in the number of public high school graduates, whereas the Northeast can expect the largest decrease (16.3 percent). The South / South Central region has more high school graduates than any other region and is expected to retain that position through 1995.

Perhaps the more notable fluctuations are expected in the ethnic representations of the graduates. The U.S. Bureau of the Census estimates that by the year 2000, nearly one-third of the school- and college-age population (5 to 24 years old) will be nonwhite and Latino. White non-Latinos constituted nearly 78 percent of public high school graduates in the nation in 1986; their share will fall to approximately 72 percent in 1995. In the same period, the representation of Latinos in the high school graduate population will increase from 5.9 percent to more than 9 percent, while the representation of Asians and Pacific Islanders will increase from 2.6 percent to more than 4 percent. During this time, the percentage of African-Americans (13.2 percent in 1986) and American Indians / Alaskan natives (0.7 percent in 1986) is expected to remain relatively stable. Here again, when the changes are examined by region and state, the differences are striking. According to the Western Interstate Commission for Higher Education, in 1995 in five states (California, Hawaii, Mississippi, New Mexico, and Texas) and the District of Columbia, the student population enrolled in public schools (grades one through twelve) will be approximately 50 percent nonwhite and Hispanic.

These national changes in high school graduates will have a number of repercussions for college admissions. For any college that recruits nationally, a decrease in the number of high school graduates presents an immediate concern. Though the *quality* of these graduates is the primary consideration in selective admissions, the competition between colleges and universities inevitably sharpens when the absolute number of prospective applicants declines. Even a college or university that draws primarily on its home state for enrollment will soon experience the consequences of a big change in the regional or national number of high school graduates. In colleges where tuition income is the primary source of revenue, the very survival of the institution depends on filling the freshman class year after year: the fundamental consideration is the *number* of students. Furthermore, freshman enrollment is subject to fluctuations in the economy. Given the population figures cited above, it is not surprising that the University of California, for example, has seen a steady increase in applicants. Between 1978 and 1988, fall term freshman applications to UC Berkeley increased from 7,296 to 22,439. Some of this increase is due, no doubt, to a fundamental change in the application process in the University of California system. In 1978, students were allowed to apply to only one University of California campus, and the application fee was nominal. Applicants designated one campus—UC Berkeley, UCLA, or UC Davis, for example—as their first choice and then ranked their preferences for the other UC campuses. If a student's first-choice school did not accept him or her, it routed the application to the student's next preferred campus. In the early 1980's, the university began allowing simultaneous applications to several campuses; it also modified the application fee structure, linking the fee to the number of applications being submitted. Still, the increased numbers applying to Berkeley in part reflect the increase in the state's high school population.

In contrast to the University of California, colleges in the Northeast region have experienced notable decreases in their primary applicant pools. Consequently, recent years have seen some turmoil in college admissions; colleges are making admissions decisions that surprise high school guidance counselors and are also admitting more students from their waiting lists. Any isolated year in college admissions is always vulnerable to unexpected or uncontrolled perturbations, such as unfavorable press coverage of events on campus (sit-ins, budgetary problems, and incidents of violence, to name a few), or accidents of nature (tornadoes, floods, and earthquakes are some memorable recent examples). In a national system where all institutions engaged in freshman admissions are inextricably interconnected, when the unpredictable is superimposed on the unanticipated, the anxiety level of all the participants reaches unusual heights.

Beyond the number and quality of high school graduates, admissions professionals are mindful of the diversity of the student population. There is already considerable concern that selective colleges and universities are competing to admit the same, select set of talented black, Hispanic, and Native American Indian high school graduates. Colleges in regions with comparatively small numbers of ethnic minority students have greater difficulty enrolling a diverse freshman class than colleges elsewhere. As the numbers of minority high school graduates in specific states decline further, this challenge escalates. Conversely, in states with a comparatively larger number of ethnic minority students, the challenges take other forms, such as recognizing the often different quality of preparation of minority students and white students; ensuring that many different ethnic groups are fairly represented in a student body; and being prepared for the implications and future of affirmative action programs. Some campuses of the University of California already enroll more minority students than white students, a circumstance that raises questions about the meaning of affirmative action.

Effectiveness in college admissions means, among other things, the successful recruitment, admission, and enrollment of a well-qualified and diverse student population. Once students are enrolled in college, one important measure of educational success is their graduation rate. A recent study has shown that fewer students are now completing bachelor's degrees in four years.[4] Of the more than 530,000 full-time, first-time freshmen who enrolled in fall 1984 at 297 of the NCAA's Division I institutions, only 53 percent had graduated within six years. By race, these graduation rates were even more troubling: 29 percent for American Indians; 62 percent for Asians; 31 percent for blacks; 40 percent for Hispanics; 56 percent for whites. The increase in the length of time to graduation has been attributed to a number of causes. Since 1960, changes in financial aid policies have shifted much assistance from outright grants to student loans, increasing financial pressures on students. More students now work twenty hours a week or more during their college years, understandably extending the time they require to complete their degree. Moreover, in their efforts to enroll a more diverse student population, colleges and universities are admitting students who are not always well prepared for college. In institutions without adequate counseling and tutoring programs for such students, their chances of graduating are significantly diminished. While there are other social causes, the financial aid changes and the inadequate support programs undoubtedly contribute to the lower graduation rates of minority students. Both these factors will continue to be a concern throughout the next decade, as colleges and universities struggle through a period already beset by national economic recession.

AFFIRMATIVE ACTION

In 1988, there were 11.3 million students enrolled as undergraduates in two-year and four-year public and private institutions of higher education in the United States. Of these students, 8.2 million were enrolled in the 2,000 or so four-year colleges and universities; the approximate ethnic breakdown in these schools, in descending order, was 81 percent white; 8 percent black; 4 percent Asian; 4 percent Hispanic; 4 percent international; 0.5 percent American Indian. (Rounding yields a total over 100 percent.)[5] With the exception of the Asian-American students, ethnic minorities are underrepresented among college enrollments when compared with their proportions in the national population, and the proportion of minority high school graduates who enroll in college has remained essentially unchanged since the early 1980's. As with the national demographic changes presented above, however, the cumulative national data present a very different picture from that of individual states.

The state of California presents an unusual case study. Not only is it currently the most populous state, with over 30 million people, but it is also third in the nation in its proportion of college students who are ethnic minorities.[6] (Hawaii leads the way with 68 percent, followed by New Mexico with 35 percent and California with 33 percent.) It has been estimated that soon after the year 2000, non-Hispanic whites will no longer constitute a majority in California, making it the first mainland state without a majority racial group.[7] The past decade at UC Berkeley has seen significant changes in the diversity of the entering freshman class. In 1988, 37 percent of the new freshmen identified themselves as white, compared with 58 percent in 1981; the comparable numbers at Stanford (which has a more national representation among its undergraduates) were roughly 65 percent in 1988 and 75 percent in 1981. It is not surprising, given such changes, that there are critics of affirmative action in college admissions. Every dean of admissions in the country can provide some evidence of painful backlash against affirmative action decisions. A faculty member on the 1989 Committee on Admissions and Enrollment at UC Berkeley noted, "The various controversies that have surrounded the admissions process—among them, the at-times bitter conflicts over both Asian admissions and affirmative action—cannot be understood without grasping that *all* policy decisions on admissions have taken on a zero-sum character."[8] Following a year's intensive study and deliberation, the Committee on Admissions and Enrollment at Berkeley submitted a report on freshman admissions that outlined ten general principles to guide admissions, as well as six specific recommendations for changes in the existing policy. The principles included the need to "actively seek diversity—socioeconomic, cultural, ethnic, racial and geographic—in its student body," and the confirmation that the university "will not tolerate quotas or ceilings on the admissions or enrollment of any racial, ethnic, religious, or gender groups." The report also notes the continuing commitment to a "vigorous affirmative action program."[9]

This brief summary cannot do justice to the thought and hard work behind the Berkeley committee's discussion of an enormously challenging topic: how best to construct a careful and judicious decision-making process for the admission of a freshman class from a pool of 20,000 applicants, while honoring the university's mission to maintain a leadership role in "the construction of a genuinely pluralistic environment." I cite the example, however, to illustrate a challenge that all colleges and universities will need to face in the not-too-distant future. As the nation becomes more ethnically diverse, will affirmative action policies remain a factor in admissions? In institutions where the student representation of nonwhites exceeds that of the regional population from which the institution draws its freshman class, how should admissions policies be modified? These are not easy questions to answer, and they are fraught with social dilemmas and political overtones. But all admissions policies that include special considerations should receive periodic review to reassess the wisdom of their principles.

ARTICULATION BETWEEN HIGH SCHOOLS AND COLLEGES

The average parent, or high school student, would probably be hard pressed to explain the meaning of "articulation" between schools and colleges. As pointed out by the College Board, articulation is a term used "in the educational context to refer to continuity and orderly progress from one level or institution of learning to another."[10] This continuity involves several important dimensions in the arena of college admissions, including academic preparation, counseling, and financial planning. I briefly consider each of these elements, with an acknowledgment that the necessary brevity is an injustice to the subject.

Academic Preparation

The significance of institutional interdependence is apparent as students move from elementary school, to high school, to undergraduate programs, to graduate school. Although the U.S. educational system is the envy of many countries, the sheer size of this nation presents some formidable problems of scale, quality control, and diversity. With a population of 250 million people of various ethnic and cultural backgrounds, all of which are represented in roughly 26,000 high schools, 2,000 four-year colleges, 1,500 two-year colleges, and 7,000 vocational institutions, the prospect of developing national standards on which all 50 states can agree is daunting. Close to 13 million students are currently enrolled in institutions of higher education. In 1991–92 there were approximately 2.4 million new high school graduates and 2.3 million first-time freshmen enrolled in colleges. These college freshmen were not all entering immediately from high school; in fact, in 1993 only 63 percent of high school graduates went on to college directly from high school. At the opposite end, the national noncompletion rate of all high school students in 1991 was about 29 percent, ranging from a low of 9 percent (in Minnesota) to a deplorable high of 42 percent (in the District of Columbia and Florida).[11]

Reading college admissions applications provides an unparalleled opportunity to see the significant variation in educational opportunities offered to high school students, ranging from excellent to mediocre to downright embarrassing. Through no fault of their own, but rather by chance of location and socioeconomic status, many young people never have the opportunity for a good education. A few students can compensate, of course, in college. The students most affected by early disadvantages, however, cannot ever make up for not having been taught to write well, to perform simple mathematical calculations, to read and think critically, to argue rationally and persuasively—not to mention the lack of opportunities to understand and appreciate history, science, literature, and the arts. In short, many students graduate from high school without the fundamental preparation needed to benefit from a liberal arts education in college.

Given such inequities, it is no surprise that the question of national assessment and standards remains at the center of the national educational policy debate and progress reports. The publication of *A Nation at Risk* in 1983 gave impetus to the establishment of standards and minimum competency tests. President George Bush and the nation's governors met at the first education summit in 1989, and in February 1991, President Bush announced "America 2000," a strategy to help the nation move toward some newly established goals. Briefly, these goals are that, by the year 2000, all children in America will start school ready to learn; the high school graduation rate will be at least 90 percent; students will master specific subject matter and will lead the world in mathematics and science achievement; every adult will be literate and will possess the skills needed to compete in the global economy and to act as responsible citizens; and schools will be free of drugs and violence. Under the Clinton Administration, the emphasis on national standards has been retitled, "Goals 2000." [12]

Of course, such proposals primarily affect only public schools. In a typical admissions year at Stanford, 30 percent of our applicants attend private schools; many parents incorrectly assume that private schools guarantee better education than public schools and that this difference will provide the edge for their son or daughter in gaining admission to a university like Stanford. Interestingly, year after year, the acceptance rates for applicants in the public and private high schools are essentially indistinguishable. This fact prompts the reasonable conclusion that there are good private schools and there are good public schools.

The most relevant issue for this discussion is what role a college or university should play in setting the educational standards for its prospective students through the admissions process. Stanford distributes a free publication that advises, among other things, on the type of curriculum that best prepares students for a Stanford education.[13] The introduction notes the considerable debate about the appropriate role of college and university admissions requirements in influencing secondary school academic programs and explains why we do not attempt to dictate a specific curriculum for prospective applicants. "Thus, rather than require specific courses, we simply state that students ought to take the most intellectually challenging program available in courses that span the humanities, social sciences, mathematics, and sciences. In addition, we believe that exposure to the creative and performing arts enhances a student's intellectual breadth." The publication then describes the kind of secondary school preparation that students should bring to Stanford to gain the most from the university's educational resources; this includes three years of English, three years of mathematics, at least two years of history, two or more years of laboratory science, three years of a foreign language, one year in one of the creative and performing arts, and some level of computer literacy. The publication also provides three examples of high school transcripts, with an evaluative commentary, to illustrate how the recommendations may be carried out; course grades are omitted from the sample transcripts to encourage a focus on the course content. Until admissions officers can be confident that all applicants have benefited from equal educational opportunities, this nonprescriptive stance seems to be the best solution; the time of truly equal educational opportunities seems to me, alas, very far off.

The College Board is approaching its fortieth year of running the continuously expanding Advanced Placement program, and though successful completion of Advanced Placement classes and examinations in high school promotes academic success in undergraduate courses, fewer than half the nation's high schools offer Advanced Placement courses. A more recent program of the College Board, Pacesetter, was developed in response to the goals set by President Bush and the governors at their 1989 education summit. Pacesetter is described as "an integrated program of standards, teaching and assessment for educational reform at the secondary school level. Designed to bring challenging standards, higher expectations, and improved performance to all students, Pacesetter consists of course content outlines, related assessments, and teacher development opportunities."[14] The pilot program in mathematics began in 1993–94, with English and Spanish on its heels. Pacesetter differs from Advanced Placement in that it represents high school study in each subject; Advanced Placement provides opportunities for students to undertake college-level study while still in high school. Clearly many well-intentioned programs and planners are working on some enormously challenging national educational issues, but the rhetoric is as yet unmatched by action or results.

Counseling

Every fall, a new generation of students enters the postsecondary system. Almost 2.3 million students move from 26,000 high schools to redistribute themselves among 3,000 colleges and universities across the country. The process has been appropriately described as "the great sorting."[15] Apart from the obvious main characters, the students themselves, many individuals play a role in this sorting: parents, other relatives, peers, teachers, high school guidance counselors, principals, and admissions officers. The relative influence of these parties varies from student to student, but undoubtedly two of the key roles are played by the college admissions officer (the decider) and the high school counselor (the guider), who ideally should work cooperatively. The details of the interaction between this pair of professionals have been discussed elsewhere, but I would like to add some thoughts from a personal perspective.[16]

A few critical elements determine the success of an effective working relationship between college admissions officers and high school guidance counselors—the provision of essential information, clear communication, and established trust. Unfortunately, several factors impose limits on all three elements. Both college admissions officers and high school counselors operate with the constant pressures of deadlines and anxious constituents; these pressures do not allow much time for sharing information or for communication between counselor and admissions officer. In a period of increased financial constraints in education, reduced budgets result in fewer staff, who in turn find themselves under increased pressure. Furthermore, the number of possible interactions between the 3,000 colleges and universities and the 26,000 high schools presents a daunting proposition; even when the interaction is limited to the number of high schools that actually submit applications, Stanford alone would be working with more than 4,500 schools. Trying to share the responsibilities for these schools among ten or so staff members in the admissions office produces obvious problems. Beyond the pressures of numbers and deadlines, the college admissions profession is unusual in that, unlike most other professions, there is no formal preparatory training and its practitioners learn on the job. New officers are usually hired by selecting people who, beyond the formal qualifications of education and experience, are articulate, energetic, and enthusiastic about the education of young people; burnout rates are high (people typically remain in the business for three to five years), and no sooner are relationships established with a small number of high school guidance counselors than the admissions officer moves on to new professional challenges. The impression that some experienced high school guidance counselors form of the eager, inexperienced novices they typically deal with often fails to promote confidence and trust. The relationships are further complicated because most admissions officers strive to be evenhanded in working with high school counselors, avoiding even the appearance of favoritism. Unfortunately, their genuine attempts at fairness are sometimes interpreted as insensitivity and unwillingness to communicate.

As for the high school counselors, their very title may be a misnomer despite their formal training in individual counseling. High school seniors and their parents often (and understandably) appear concerned about one thing only: how to get into the best college possible. They want guarantees and unambiguous answers where few are possible, and "counseling" is not high on their immediate agenda. Independent college guidance counselors, to whom some families turn for their hoped-for guarantees, are serving more and more students, as public schools across the country eliminate counselors and counseling departments because of budget cuts. More schools are relying on "paraprofessionals" in "career centers" to assist students in the college application process, and families may see independent counselors as a guarantee of more personal representation. For all the reasons cited, the often heard criticism about the poor working relationships between college admissions officers and high school counselors is frequently valid, but unfortunate. These professions share a purpose: to contribute to the postsecondary education of the next generation and all the good that comes from that. In times of declining numbers of high school seniors and institutional budget cuts, the more aggressive enrollment strategies adopted by many colleges (along with some unfortunate and questionable ethical practices) have not won the hearts of high school counselors. The counselors are often troubled by the quality, accuracy, and adequacy of the information provided to their students through college admissions handbooks. National organizations, such as the National Association of College Admissions Counselors and the College Board, have played a helpful role in developing collaboration and colleagueship between constituents, but there is still room for improvement. New programs, such as year-long internships for high school guidance counselors in college admissions offices, or collaborative projects on special topics, could contribute to better articulation.

Financial Planning

For the twelve months that ended in January 1992, inflation, as measured by the consumer price index, stood at 2.6 percent; in the academic year 1991–92, the average tuition increased 12 percent over the previous year at public four-year colleges and 7 percent at private four-year colleges.[17] At one end of the spectrum, the University of California announced fee increases of 22 percent for the 1992–93 academic year (to $3,036), following a 40 percent increase the year before. State budget proposals in New York included undergraduate tuition increases of 23 percent for the state university system; Texas proposed an increase of 20 percent for its four-year institutions. Small wonder that the increases have been greeted with student protests and parental despair. Tuition at private four-year colleges in 1992 averaged $10,017; at public four-year colleges, the average was $2,137.

Over the decade ending in 1989, the median tuition at the 32 member institutions of the Consortium on Financing Higher Education (COFHE)—the most selective private colleges and universities—increased 196 percent, while over the same period the overall cost of living rose 90 percent.[18] Consequently, private institutions have become painfully aware of the resultant financial hardships, particularly for middle-income families. Studies by COFHE show that fewer middle-income students (who are most affected by the increases) are enrolling at selective colleges and universities.[19] Unfortunately, many parents do not know about financial aid policies at these schools. Admissions officers should explain these policies to prospective applicants, but many high school seniors are discouraged by their parents from even applying to some private colleges because of the cost. Here again, high school counselors can play a very important part in providing their seniors with information on financial aid at colleges and universities, but the information provided by the counselor can only be as good as that provided to the counselor by the college. Then too, overworked counselors can be inundated with information, and high school students need to take some personal responsibility for seeking information directly from the colleges in which they are interested.

A family's financial planning for college needs to start much earlier than high school. Today's parents need to take action that will allow them to help their children benefit from the very best education that suits their needs. Families also need to inform themselves thoroughly about the resources available to them. Many colleges can refer students to sources of advice, such as *College Costs*, which is based on data collected by the Department of Education. A number of "no-need scholarship" databanks have sprung up in the past decade, as computer technology has become more and more sophisticated. High school guidance counselors can often advise on sources of financial aid. Individual professionals and national organizations recognize their responsibilities on the financial planning; high school guidance counselors, college admissions and financial aid officers, NACAC, and the College Board have made commitments to help families improve financial planning for college, but the coming years need improved collaboration. The federal and state governments must continue to play their important parts. The affordability of higher education and the delivery of federal student financial aid are national concerns. Congress's reauthorization of the Higher Education Act (HEA) in 1992 was based on recommendations from over 100 education associations and followed by extensive hearings. One of the principal challenges of the reauthorization was to simplify the delivery of student aid while preserving equity in the distribution of dollars. To ensure that the delivery system works better for students, Congress, the Department of Education, the individual states, postsecondary institutions, and private scholarship programs must collaborate effectively.

CONSEQUENCES OF THE COLLEGE ADMISSIONS PROCESS

Clearly, the process of selecting a freshman class at any college or university has considerable implications for many offices besides Undergraduate Admissions, such as financial aid, student affairs, development, the alumni association, and the athletic department. Any change in the makeup of the freshman class also has repercussions for the undergraduate curriculum. As the class becomes more diverse by gender, ethnicity, geography, religious affiliation, political belief, and age, the faculty and students will be more likely to question how well the existing undergraduate curriculum meets their needs. A changing world requires periodic reassessments of the education best designed to meet those changes. This consideration certainly influenced the changes in the "Western Culture" distribution requirement at Stanford, a course sequence that all undergraduates were required to complete before graduation. Beginning with freshmen who entered Stanford in 1991, this distribution requirement was modified and renamed "Cultures, Ideas, and Values" (CIV). Stanford was not alone in such revisions. Beginning in 1992, UC Berkeley introduced a new undergraduate requirement entitled "American Cultures." About 40 courses have been approved to meet the UC requirement, which has two distinctive features: the courses must deal with at least three of the following five groups—African-Americans, American Indians, Asian-Americans, Chicano and Latino Americans, and European-Americans—and the courses must be comparative, placing groups in the context of American society.

In a move in a different direction, the University of Texas at Austin voted in March 1992 to reject a proposal that all undergraduates be required to take a three-hour course on minority groups or a third-world culture. According to one report, "Opponents said the proposal would have left little time for electives and was just another attempt by liberal faculty members to impose their views on students."[20] The views of other traditional, vocal critics of recent curricular changes, notably Allan Bloom and Dinesh D'Souza, have prompted many a lively debate on college campuses; former secretary of education William Bennett has added his share to the conversations.[21] The faculty on almost every campus across the country has engaged in an analysis of its curriculum in recent years, and it is no accident that such debates have coincided with changing representations of ethnic groups in college entering classes.

One Asian-American undergraduate at Berkeley reportedly commented that the "American Cultures" requirement seems fitting because the University of California tries to be "politically correct." These are the buzzwords on college campuses in the 1990's, although the roots of political correctness were planted a few decades ago. When the undergraduate population of any college campus is homogeneous, political correctness has no meaning. As campuses have become more diverse and increasingly sensitive to the associated issues, and as students have become less reluctant to speak out on controversial or formerly taboo issues, the possibility of political disagreements runs high. The scholar and cultural critic Paul Berman has compiled a collection of provocative statements on political correctness.[22] The range covers questions such as appropriate actions by college authorities in response to the use of language that offends any group or individual—such as homosexuals, minorities, or women—a subject on which the Supreme Court has recently taken a stand; the dead-white-European-male bias in college curricula; the effects of multiculturalism. In general, the white male has been under attack. The American Association of University Professors has reported that more faculty members feel intimidated about speaking out on issues of race and gender; some have referred to the phenomenon as "left-wing McCarthyism." While no moderate would deplore efforts to combat racism, sexism, and homophobia, or programs to improve the environment, immoderate efforts that involve intimidation and intolerance are not going to prove constructive in the long term. The questions that prompt debates over political correctness have no easy answers, and I suspect the turmoil will continue until campuses become better adjusted to living with their newfound diversity.

For all the policy work and larger issues I wrestled with and debated during my years as dean of undergraduate admissions, it is the impressions of individual students that leave the most lasting mark. I conclude with an example of a very different kind of consequence of the college admissions process. The example is not new to the 1990's although it is probably more intense now: the pressures that high school students experience in the application process and in making the transition to college. Among the written pieces that I have kept from my term in undergraduate admissions, one from an applicant poignantly sums up this feeling. Under the title "Elegy of a High School Senior," she included these thoughts with her formal application to Stanford. (Incidentally, this example comes from my first year as dean, at a time when we were requesting a photograph of the applicant, a request that was soon after discontinued.)

The allure, glamor, and romance of the college application process have disappeared completely. I'm tired of spending an entire day in front of a blank page because I can't word an essay properly, of being asked to share my views on the meaning of life in 250 words or less, of justifying the worth of my existence for the past four years, of agonizing over what my teachers REALLY think of me. Yesterday, I burst into tears because I had failed to tear out a "vital" form accurately along the perforations. Will this, I asked myself, be the deciding factor in my admission to Yale? Must I spend twenty minutes centering and typing an address, or can I just scribble it on the envelope in five seconds? Stanford wants a picture "to personalize the process": should I send a serious, introspective one or the smiling one which makes me look like a truly dumb blonde? Will anybody care? Do I?

I have grown disenchanted with addressing faceless masses of admissions officers in painfully, painstakingly, composed language. At some point, nestled in among the carefully worded, impeccably typed explanations of community service activities and brilliant academic accomplishments, the million dollar bake sales, and the next-step-down-from Nobel prizes, somewhere I want to write—with my bright pink pen and in my comfortable, characteristic hybrid of printing and writing—somewhere, in sprawling, shocking, wonderfully artistic and extravagant letters:

> "My life is not modeled on that of Eleanor Roosevelt. I am not Mother Theresa, or Mohandas K. Gandhi: I am *not* a viable candidate for canonization. Reading *Jude the Obscure* did NOT change my life: the columnists in *Glamour* probably influenced me more. I've goofed off a lot, I've dangled a few participles, I've gone to the beach when I should have integrated trigonometric functions. I'm often intractable, irresponsible, and utterly incapable. I'm spoiled, I spend too much time with boys, and—once, in a fit of what I know is inadmissible passion—I turned in an assignment late. Furthermore, and respectfully, o admissions staff, I have no excuse, nor will I attempt to offer any justification, 'share anything more of personal relevance,' or demonstrate outstanding musical or athletic talent to compensate for my shortcomings. I would dearly love to go to your school, and I will sink everything I have into it if admitted, but I will no longer affect pretensions of unsullied scholarly sainthood, of being the ideal 'bright, well-rounded, well-grounded, multi-faceted, focused, dedicated, productive, creative, warm, energetic, motivated, cooperative, hard-working, friendly, active,' and especially 'unique' student. I am only a person, a sixteen-year-old person dog-paddling along in the proverbially and oh-so-cliched river of life. Some day, maybe, I will write the Great American Novel, or run for President of the United States. Today, however, I am only one of the

faceless thousands of applicants whom you must consider for admission. Here I am, and good luck."

That's what I'd really like to say. Of course, I won't: I'd also really like to get accepted. But maybe some day, someone—someone who is also a veteran of three-hour fill-in-the-bubble tests and "describe your philosophy of life in the 1″ × 2″ box below—expression as well as content will be evaluated" essay questions—some iconoclastic soul will decide that the college application process is the Miss America Pageant of the mind and boycott it. In the interim, however, I am having an intimate relationship with my typewriter, attempting to fit a clearly expressed idea of who I am (somewhere between Walt Whitman and Queen Elizabeth I) in little black characters on picky little forms. I hope it's worth it.

That kind of heartfelt outpouring makes painful reading for admissions officers who try their best to make personal what unfortunately appears to some to be an impersonal, stressful, capricious, and inefficient process. Paradoxically, the move to a more effective use of technology, the impersonal computer, to complete multiple applications may help to avoid the meaningless repetition of the application process and even to improve the match of applicants with colleges. Certainly the process can be better coordinated on a national level, and the professional organizations can play a helpful role as initiator and facilitator.

Ten years ago, I was completely uninformed about college admissions in the United States. My only brief encounter with the process was as the mother of a college applicant, who I realize now received minimal help from her parents. While the past experience of others does not always prove helpful, I hope that these personal reflections about the selection of a freshman class at one university can help inform and enlighten high school students and their parents, teachers, and guidance counselors. The principles we applied at Stanford University are not very different from those in effect at many other colleges and universities in this country. The worries described in this book are also universal—or at least they *should* be. One hundred thousand applications later I am somewhat sadly, but realistically, resigned to the fact that I made many more young people unhappy than happy with the decisions for which I was responsible. Consequently, it may seem a paradox to conclude that being dean of undergraduate admissions at Stanford was unequivocally the best and most rewarding job I have ever had. I am older (certainly), wiser (probably), and humbler (unquestionably)—and persuaded that no one, including admissions officers, will ever "master the art of human assessment." And that is probably a very good thing.

Epilogue

THE EXERCISE OF WRITING this book has been a personal catharsis. I hope that it will be useful to others as well. Outside of the admissions profession, few are well informed about either the facts of the selective admissions process or the tasks involved. I hope this book explains both. More important, because writing this book was more complex than reciting facts and procedures that can be obtained directly from admissions offices, it allowed me to reflect on the underlying principles of selecting a freshman class. What factors should be taken into account and why? What issues are important and why do they give rise to disagreements? What are the pitfalls of the process?

Reporting the facts and reflecting on the issues, however, does not complete the analysis. As the philosopher Kierkegaard aptly observed, "life can only be understood backwards; but it must be lived forwards." What do I think is wrong with the process? What mistakes did I learn from? What would I now do differently with the benefit of the experience of 100,000 admissions decisions?

Fundamentally, I think the subjective process of selecting the freshman class as described in this book is sound, although it is fraught with difficulties. The primary criterion for college admissions *must* be academic achievement and promise; if institutions of higher education do not hold teaching and learning foremost among their values, we have reached a sorry state. But even at this elementary level, with the focus reduced to one primary criterion, the selection process runs into difficulties. In a country with roughly 26,000 high schools ranging from wealthy, select private schools to poor, inner-city public schools, how do we allow for the considerable variation in opportunities in estimating academic achievement and promise? How do we weigh the disadvantages of the applicant from a family with no history of attending college or from a modest socioeconomic background? Once we factor in criteria beyond the academic record, the process becomes even more complex. What could have been a scientific selection process, based on tables with weighted quantitative measures of academic achievement, now becomes a scientific art. The most obvious secondary criterion, that of achievement outside the classroom, introduces a new hierarchy of values in the selection process. Are art and music of more importance than athletics or public service? Is a team activity more valuable than a solitary one? Do cheerleaders and entrepreneurs have any place at institutions of higher education? And, of course, the dilemma of unequal opportunities so apparent in the academic criterion is ever present in these considerations too. Students from economically disadvantaged classes have many fewer opportunities to engage in extracurricular activities and, in many cases, time outside of class needs to be spent on essentials—such as supplementing the family income.

The consideration of personal qualities further complicates the subjective selection process. While achievements within and outside of class can be assigned some quantitative measure, it is hard to construct a meaningful scale of goodness or niceness or likability. Besides which, should all college students be "good," or "nice," or "likable"? Some of the most brilliant (thereby satisfying our first criterion) human beings are academically single-minded (thereby failing to meet our second criterion), and selfish and eccentric (thereby also failing the third criterion). How does one weigh out the merits? Is there any place for brilliant, selfish, single-minded eccentrics at the university? While we can all have strong opinions on the answers to these questions, there will always be a divergence of views among the readers of admissions applications. And generalizations are inevitably tested by exceptions. Who should set the standards and norms for the enrolling freshman class? How important is consensus? What recourse should an individual reader have who strongly disagrees with a decision?

The college admissions process incorporates one further general complication: a consideration of societal injustices. When we try to remedy past and present discrimination on the basis of ethnicity, we tread on exceedingly difficult terrain. Some formerly all-male colleges are attempting to compensate for past discrimination in the admission of women. Religious discrimination has played its role in the admissions process too. Being a resident of certain states may have carried a stigma: are students from the Eastern seaboard considered more sophisticated than their counterparts from the Midwest or the deep South? And, of course, the wealthy in every society have always held advantages.

Only a subjective college admissions process, with its attention to the qualities and circumstances of the individual applicant, can weigh and allow for such a range of complex considerations. Objective processes, while valuable in certain situations, are limited in their ability to take subtleties and complexities into account. The disadvantage of the subjective process, however, is that it immediately opens the door for the critics who wish to account for the world in certainties, in black-and-white terms. Inevitably people want a guarantee of admission. When such guarantees are not forthcoming, the uninformed critic is quick to judge the process as mysterious and unfathomable. Those of us who are engaged in the profession need to acknowledge that all we can hope to accomplish is to make the very best decisions we can under very difficult circumstances. This also means, however, that the appointment of the admissions staff who are responsible for making these subjective judgments is of critical importance. At the very least, such staff need themselves to meet the criteria for admission that they must apply: they must exhibit good judgment and be fair-minded, tolerant of differences, and able to read without bias. As my term as dean of undergraduate admissions progressed, I became more convinced of the importance of these personal qualities of my staff in the selection of the freshman class. With the wisdom of experience, we will all attain the humility of the former dean of admissions of Amherst, Eugene S. "Bill" Wilson, in recognizing that we can never master the art of human assessment—although there is some irony in knowing that we have to keep trying our best to do just that.

The selection process at most colleges is conducted by staff members rather than faculty. While there is usually a small faculty oversight committee for the offices of admissions and financial aid, the majority of faculty are uninvolved in the selection of the freshman class, and I suspect only a few have the vaguest notion of how it is conducted. I am not prepared to argue that this is the wrong way to do business; faculty, after all, have important priorities in teaching and research. I am prepared to argue, however, that faculty should be actively engaged in the setting of policies to guide the admissions office. This point is particularly important as it applies to the setting of criteria for admissions, and notably to important issues such as the roles that affirmative action, athletics, and alumni status should play in admissions decisions. I remember relatively few faculty discussions on these subjects that could offer guidance to the admissions staff. It is simply assumed that we, somehow, will act affirmatively, just as it is taken for granted that Stanford will continue to play football and basketball in the Pac-10. The admissions staff have to work with the consequences of these very significant assumptions, both in carrying out their responsibilities and in answering to critics of the policies.

Although many faculty may not be engaged in the discussions of affirmative action and athletics, alumni are often very vocal on these subjects. The faculty rarely hear these alumni complaints, but the president and the board of trustees are frequent recipients of criticisms of the admissions process. The criticisms are, by now for me, predictable: standards are not what they used to be; the admissions rate for alumni sons and daughters is too low; the football team is too weak; too many minority students are admitted, usually at the expense of alumni sons and daughters. Many alumni will go so far as to say that their reason for not contributing financially to their alma mater is current admissions policies; such policies are too liberal, discriminatory, and "politically correct" and therefore result in a lowering of Stanford's standards. (They are quick to forget that the competition for admission in their era was much less fierce than it is today, when only one in five applicants gains admission to the university.) Such charges have made me despair on more than one occasion. If I were dean again, I would try even harder to better inform all alumni of the facts about admissions, an assignment that could well prove to be a full-time job with no guarantee of better outcomes.

I would also make a concerted effort to ensure that alumni understand the importance and inevitability of change within a university. Many humans are uncomfortable with change; they feel more at ease with the familiar. This observation applies particularly to alumni when they consider their alma mater: nothing is as good as in the "old" days. At a recent alumni conference, I was asked to compare the class of 1948 with that of 1993. The Stanford yearbook of 1948 (which I suspect is no different from that of any other major research university of that time) contains no more than a handful of nonwhite faces, and all of those are Asian. In 1993, almost half of the undergraduate population is nonwhite, a dramatic difference. Similarly, in 1948, there was a limit on the enrollment of women, who even had to undergo a separate admissions process. In 1993, almost half of the undergraduates are female, and they are studying in all disciplines rather than concentrated in nursing (no longer offered at Stanford) and a few other fields (such as education), as they were in 1948. Furthermore, close to three-quarters of the class of 1948 came from California, a number that had decreased to 35 percent in 1993. The courses required to graduate had also changed in this period. While the Western Culture requirement of 1948 is no longer in place, the class of 1993's reading list for the Cultures, Ideas, and Values requirement is every bit as challenging, if not more so. In short, there have been many changes at the university and many (including me) believe that most of the changes have made Stanford a better place.

In 1993, Stanford's ninth president, Gerhard Casper, wrote in a personal letter to some alumni:

> I was . . . not suggesting that everything is perfect at Stanford: as is the case with any other human institution, there is considerable room for improvement. Universities in the postwar period have become very complex institutions and, like all humans, they have their shortcomings. Tensions exist at Stanford that reflect the considerable tensions and changes in American society. All of us at Stanford are trying to cope with the associated array of consequences as best we can.

This could well have been written to describe the challenges associated with the admissions process of 1990. I suspect that if my successor in 50 years writes another book on the same subject, the context will have changed again to reflect society's changes, but the description will be equally apt. It is hard to imagine a set of changes as significant as those introduced by the civil rights movement, the women's movement, and immigration movements of recent years—but historians have probably been making such comments for generations.

REFERENCE MATTER

Notes

CHAPTER 1

1. Elliott, *Stanford University*, p. 94.

2. Mitchell, *Stanford University, 1916–1941.*

3. Ibid., p. 52.

4. Ibid.

5. Ibid., p. 54.

6. Stanford University, Steering Committee of the Study of Education at Stanford, *The Study of Education at Stanford*, chap. 4.

7. Elliott, *Stanford University*, p. 574.

8. University of California, Committee on Admissions and Enrollment, *Freshman Admissions at Berkeley.*

9. Stanford University, Office of Undergraduate Admissions, *Looking Ahead to Stanford.*

CHAPTER 3

1. Stanford University, Office of Undergraduate Admissions, *Stanford Today.* This publication includes application and general information about the university.

2. Gardner, *Frames of Mind.*

3. Gardner, "Notes on Educational Implications of the Theory of Multiple Intelligences," p. 4.

4. Sternberg, "What Would Better Intelligence Tests Look Like?"

5. Crouse, "Time Has Come to Replace the SAT."

6. Wilder and Powell, *Sex Differences in Test Performance.*

7. Hiss, "Optional SATs."

8. Karen, "Toward a Political-Organizational Model of Gatekeeping."

9. In November 1994, following a recommendation from C-UAFA, the dean of undergraduate admissions announced a new calendar for 1995–96. This will include two Early Decision options. The first will have an application deadline of November 1 and an admissions notification in

mid-December, and the second will have an application deadline of December 15 and an admissions notification early in February.

10. Jean Fetter, "Behind the Dean's Door," *Stanford Alumni Magazine,* September 1989, pp. 47–51.

11. Klitgaard, *Choosing Elites.*

12. Ibid., p. 50.

13. Ibid., p. 55.

14. E. M. Yoder, Jr., "The Coins Top Colleges Flip to Select Their Students," *Washington Post National Weekly Edition,* June 24, 1985, p. 36.

15. E. S. Wilson, quoted in Klitgaard, *Choosing Elites,* p. 153.

CHAPTER 4

1. Gardner, *Frames of Mind,* pp. x–xii.

2. Tom McCann, "Dispatch from the Trenches," *Princeton Alumni Weekly* 85, no. 18, May 22, 1985, pp. 16–17.

3. Professor Julian Stanley at the Center for the Study of Mathematically Precocious Youth at Johns Hopkins University has done some interesting work on this topic. See, for example, Benbow and Stanley, eds., *Academic Precocity.*

4. Whitehead, "Mathematics," pp. 31–32.

5. "Stanford Losing Well-Rounded Atmosphere," *Stanford Review,* Nov. 19, 1990.

6. "Parents Have It Rough," *Stanford Review,* Stanford Alumni Association, October 1958.

7. "Admission Standards: Tough but Flexible," *Stanford Review,* Stanford Alumni Association, January 1958, p. 13.

8. Ibid., p. 14.

9. "Go to Harvard, Give Your Kid a Break," *New York Times,* Dec. 8, 1990.

10. Gutmann, *Democratic Education,* pp. 194–95, 202–3.

11. "Washington Update," *Chronicle of Higher Education,* Mar. 11, 1992.

12. Stanford University, C-UAFA, *Annual Report 1977–78, 1978–79,* pp. 10–12.

CHAPTER 5

1. Myrdal, *American Dilemma.*

2. Thresher, *College Admissions.*

3. Stanford University, Steering Committee of the Study of Education at Stanford, *Study of Education at Stanford,* chap. 4.

4. Stanford University, C-UAFA, *Annual Report 1985–86,* pp. 4–6.

5. Stanford University, C-UAFA, "Proposed C-UAFA Guidelines for Adding Targeted Minority Groups," pp. 3–4.

6. Stanford University, University Committee on Minority Issues, *Building a Multiracial, Multicultural University Community.*

7. Stanford University, "Responses to the Recommendations of the University Committee on Minority Issues and Institutional Standards on Cultural Diversity."

While the discussions of UCMI and the subsequent reports are important, the wealth of detail would be inappropriate to a book on undergraduate admissions. Interested readers may pursue topics of particular interest by requesting the relevant reports from the Office for Multicultural Development at Stanford.

8. Since the wording of this policy was approved in 1986, some black Americans have opted to call themselves African-Americans. Stephen Carter, and many others, have views on that subject; I will not pursue it here, but for simplicity I adhere to the original Stanford wording in the subsequent discussion. Interested readers may refer to Carter, *Reflections of an Affirmative Action Baby.*

9. Glasser, "Affirmative Action," p. 344.

10. Stanford University, University Committee on Minority Issues, *Building a Multiracial, Multicultural University Community*, p. 55.

11. Carter, *Reflections*, pp. 15–16.

12. Steele, *Content of Our Character*, p. 124.

13. Stanford University, University Committee on Minority Issues, *Building a Multiracial, Multicultural University Community.*

14. Derrick Bell is a professor of law at NYU School of Law and author of a number of books, including *Faces at the Bottom of the Well* (New York: Basic Books, 1992) and *And We Are Not Saved: The Elusive Quest for Racial Justice* (New York: Basic Books, 1989).

Stephen Carter is a professor of law at Yale Law School and the author of *The Culture of Disbelief: How American Law and Politics Trivialize Religious Devotion* (New York: Basic Books, 1993) as well as *Reflections of an Affirmative Action Baby.*

Thomas Sowell is a scholar at Stanford's Hoover Institution and the author of a number of books, including *Inside American Education* (New York: Free Press, 1993) and *Preferential Policies: An International Perspective.*

Shelby Steele is a professor of English at San Jose State University and the author of *The Content of Our Character: A New Vision of Race in America.*

Clarence Thomas is a Supreme Court Justice, whose legal written opinions when he served on the federal bench and as chair of the Equal Employment Opportunity Commission sparked debate. A sampling of his opinions is collected in *Confronting the Future: Selections from the Senate Confirmation Hearings and Prior Speeches* (Washington, D.C.: National Book Network, 1992).

15. Sowell, *Preferential Policies*, p. 108.

16. Andrew Hacker, "Affirmative Action: The New Look," *New York Review of Books*, Oct. 12, 1989, pp. 63–68.

17. Carter, *Reflections*, p. 18.

18. Rodriguez, *Hunger of Memory*, p. 170.

19. Ibid., pp. 171–72.

20. For a revealing discussion of the history of Jews at Yale University, see Oren, *Joining the Club*.

21. "A Remedy for Old Racism Has New Kind of Shackles," *New York Times*, Sept. 15, 1991.

22. Rodriguez, *Hunger of Memory*, p. 148.

23. Steele, *Content of Our Character*, p. 119.

24. Ibid., p. 4.

25. Carter, *Reflections*, p. 71.

26. McPherson and Schapiro, *Selective Admission*, p. 6.

27. Kozol, *Savage Inequalities*.

28. Steele, *Content of Our Character*, p. 111.

29. Ibid., pp. 112–13.

30. Carter, *Reflections*, p. 33.

31. Rodriguez, *Hunger of Memory*, p. 34.

32. S. A. Holmes, "Mulling the Idea of Affirmative Action for Poor Whites," *New York Times*, Aug. 18, 1991.

33. Ibid.

34. Derek C. Bok, "Admitting Success," *New Republic*, Feb. 4, 1985, p. 14.

35. There is also evidence to show the effectiveness of affirmative action in the employment of minorities. See, for example, Glazer, "Future of Preferential Affirmative Action."

36. Carter, *Reflections*, pp. 227–28.

37. Lyndon Baines Johnson, "To Fulfill These Rights," Commencement Address at Howard University, June 4, 1965. This speech is item no. 301 in Johnson, *Public Papers of the Presidents of the United States*.

38. Steele, *Content of Our Character*, p. 121.

39. Kozol, *Savage Inequalities*, frontispiece.

40. Steele, *Content of Our Character*, p. 124.

41. Some examples of interinstitutional collaboration include the group visits to high schools organized by COFHE members; the College Board's Equity 2000 program, a six-year, multimillion-dollar demonstration project aimed at erasing the difference between minority and majority students' access to and success in college; and NACAC's sponsorship of national college fairs.

42. Carter, *Reflections*, p. 221.

43. Western Interstate Commission on Higher Education and College Board, *Road to College*, pp. ix–x.

44. Stanford University, University Committee on Minority Issues, *Building a Multiracial, Multicultural University Community*, p. 59.

45. Mitchell, *Stanford University, 1916–1941*.

46. Stanford University, *Stanford: A Man, a Woman . . . and a University*, p. 61.

CHAPTER 6

1. Cavalli, *Stanford Sports*, p. 154.

2. Stanford University, Department of Athletics, *Stanford Sports Quarterly* (Summer 1991; Summer 1992).

3. National Collegiate Athletic Association, *1991–92 Manual*, pp. 350, 360.

4. "Local Campuses Fail Many Athletes," *San Francisco Examiner*, Nov. 12, 1989.

5. "Can Stanford Rise Again?" *Peninsula Times Tribune*, Sept. 5, 1990.

6. "Finding Brilliant Coach Not Answer at Stanford," *Peninsula Times Tribune*, Apr. 12, 1986.

7. Stanford University, Senate Committee on Education and Scholarship at Stanford, *Statement of Goals*, p. 6.

8. "Faculty Senate Report," *Stanford University Campus Report*, Oct. 16, 1991, p. 14.

9. "Loss of Academic Programs Would Prove Farm's Demise," *Stanford Daily*, Oct. 9, 1991.

10. "Distorting Our Educational Priorities," *Peninsula Times Tribune*, Apr. 18, 1986.

11. Robert H. Atwell, "Sports Reform: Where Is the Faculty?" *Academe* (January–February 1991): 10–12.

12. Robin Toner, "The Unfinished Politician: Nebraska Senator Bob Kerrey," *New York Times Sunday Magazine*, Apr. 14, 1991, p. 68.

13. Bissinger, *Friday Night Lights*.

14. *New York Times Book Review*, Sept. 8, 1991, p. 38.

15. "Thirty-Four Institutions Under NCAA Sanctions," *Chronicle of Higher Education*, Apr. 10, 1991.

16. "U.S. Subpoenas Data from 106 Universities in Big-Time Football," *Chronicle of Higher Education*, May 16, 1991.

17. Sperber, *College Sports, Inc.*, p. 6.

18. "Disproportion in the Sweet 16," *New York Times*, Mar. 27, 1992.

19. Sperber, *College Sports, Inc.*, p. 173.

20. Ibid., p. 217.

21. Ibid., p. 228.

22. "Men Get 70% of Money Available for Athletic Scholarships at Colleges That Play Big-Time Sports, New Study Finds," *Chronicle of Higher Education*, Mar. 18, 1992.

23. Ibid.

24. "A Degree of Success," *Peninsula Times Tribune,* Apr. 4, 1992.

25. See Sperber, *College Sports, Inc.,* and Knight Foundation Commission, *Keeping Faith with the Student-Athlete.*

26. "Coaches Will Learn, Too, During Spring Practice," *Peninsula Times Tribune,* Apr. 4, 1992.

CHAPTER 7

1. "Statement of Principles of Good Practice," National Association of College Admissions Counselors, adopted Oct. 7, 1989, New York, N.Y.

2. See, for example, Bok, *Lying.*

3. See, for example, Breland, Wilder, and Robertson, *Demographics, Standards, and Equity.*

4. "The Chase After Cheaters on College-Entry Exams," *New York Times,* May 5, 1992.

5. Boyer, *College,* p. 37.

6. "A Guide to Postsecondary Institutions for Implementation of the Family Educational Rights and Privacy Act of 1974, as Amended," American Association of Collegiate Registrars and Admissions Officers, 1976.

7. Bok, *Lying,* p. 16.

8. Thresher, *College Admissions,* p. 53.

9. William R. Fitzsimmons, "Risky Business," *Harvard Magazine,* January–February 1991, p. 23.

10. Wright, "Rating Game."

11. Breland, Wilder, and Robertson, *Demographics, Standards, and Equity,* p. 1.

12. "Students Have Right to See Comments of Admissions Officers, Education Department Rules," *Chronicle of Higher Education,* Apr. 1, 1992.

13. "The Strange Case of James Arthur Hogue," *Princeton Alumni Weekly,* Apr. 3, 1991.

14. "Campuses Ponder Who Is an American Indian," *Chronicle of Higher Education,* Apr. 29, 1992.

CHAPTER 8

1. Stewart, *College Admission Policies in the 1990s.*

2. The College Board monographs are: Ancrum, *College Application and Admission Process;* Blackburn, *Assessment and Evaluation in Admission;* Engelau, *Enrollment and Recruitment Patterns in Admission;* Healy, *School-College Articulation;* Litten, *Ivy Bound;* Loeb, *Academic Standards in Higher Education;* McPherson and Schapiro, *Selective Admission;* and Scannell, *Effect of Financial Aid Policies.*

3. Western Interstate Commission on Higher Education and College Board, *Road to College.*

4. *Chronicle of Higher Education*, July 15, 1992, p. A29.

5. *Chronicle of Higher Education Almanac*, Aug. 28, 1991.

6. Ibid.

7. California Postsecondary Education Commission, Report of the Executive Director.

8. University of California, Committee on Admissions and Enrollment, *Freshman Admissions at Berkeley*.

9. Ibid., pp. 30–31.

10. Healy, *School-College Articulation*, p. 3.

11. U.S. Department of Labor, News Bureau of Labor Statistics, no. 94-252, "College Enrollment of 1993 High School Graduates"; *Chronicle of Higher Education Almanac*, Aug. 28, 1991. The U.S. Department of Education noncompletion figures cover public schools only and are calculated by dividing the number of high school graduates by the ninth-grade enrollment four years earlier. They are adjusted for interstate migration.

12. "Update from Washington," a report from the Washington Office of the College Board (February 1992).

13. Stanford University, Office of Undergraduate Admissions, *Looking Ahead to Stanford*.

14. College Board, "Pacesetter," p. 3.

15. Thresher, *College Admissions*, p. 3.

16. For another view, see Healy, *School-College Articulation*.

17. *Chronicle of Higher Education*, Mar. 11, 1992, p. A29.

18. *National Association of College Admissions Counselors Bulletin* 28, no. 10 (December 1990).

19. McPherson, *Keeping College Affordable*.

20. *Chronicle of Higher Education*, Mar. 11, 1992, p. A12.

21. Bloom, *Closing of the American Mind*; D'Souza, *Illiberal Education*; Bennett, *De-Valuing of America* and *Our Children and Our Country*.

22. Berman, *Debating P.C.*

Bibliography

Ancrum, Ron. *The College Application and Admission Process.* New York: College Board, 1992.

Atwell, R. H. "Sports Reform: Where Is the Faculty?" *Academe* (January–February 1991): 10–12.

Benbow, C., and J. Stanley, eds. *Academic Precocity: Aspects of Its Development.* Baltimore: Johns Hopkins University Press, 1983.

Bennett, William J. *The De-Valuing of America: The Fight for Our Culture and Our Children.* New York: Summit Books, 1992.

———. *Our Children and Our Country: Improving America's Schools and Affirming the Common Culture.* New York: Simon and Schuster, 1988.

Berman, Paul, ed. *Debating P.C.: The Controversy over Political Correctness on College Campuses.* New York: Laurel/Dell, 1992.

Bissinger, H. G. *Friday Night Lights: A Town, a Team, and a Dream.* Harper Perennial, 1990.

Blackburn, J. A. *Assessment and Evaluation in Admission.* New York: College Board, 1990.

Bloom, Allan D. *The Closing of the American Mind.* New York: Simon and Schuster, 1987.

Bok, Sissela. *Lying: Moral Choice in Public and Private Life.* New York: Pantheon Books, 1978.

Boyer, Ernest L. *College: The Undergraduate Experience in America.* Carnegie Foundation for the Advancement of Teaching. New York: Harper & Row, 1987.

Breland, H. M., G. Wilder, and N. J. Robertson. *Demographics, Standards, and Equity: Challenges in College Admissions.* Report of a Survey of Undergraduate Admissions Policies, Practices, and Procedures. American Association of Collegiate Registrars and Admissions Officers et al., 1986.

California Department of Finance. Population Research Unit. "Projected Total Population for California by Race/Ethnicity." Report 88, P-4. Sacramento, Calif., February 1988.

California Postsecondary Education Commission. Report of the Executive Director to the California Postsecondary Education Commission, Agenda Item 20:1. Sacramento, Calif., January 1989.

Carter, Stephen L. *Reflections of an Affirmative Action Baby.* New York: Basic Books, 1991.

Cavalli, Gary. *Stanford Sports.* Stanford, Calif.: Stanford Alumni Association, 1982.

College Board. *Annual Report 1990–91.* New York, 1992.

———. *College Costs and Financial Aid Handbook.* New York: College Board, 1993.

———. *Measures in the College Admissions Process: A College Board Colloquium.* New York: College Board, 1986.

———. "Pacesetter: An Integrated Program of Standards, Teaching, and Assessment." New York: College Board, 1992.

Crouse, James. "The Time Has Come to Replace the SAT." In College Board, *Measures in the College Admissions Process.*

D'Souza, Dinesh. *Illiberal Education.* New York: Free Press, 1991.

Durham, G., and S. T. Syverson. "Wait Lists: The Limbo of the College Application Process." *Journal of College Admissions* (Fall 1983), pp. 3–9.

Elliott, Orrin Leslie. *Stanford University: The First Twenty-Five Years.* Stanford, Calif.: Stanford University Press, 1937.

Engelau, G. R. *Enrollment and Recruitment Patterns in Admission.* New York: College Board, 1991.

Gardner, Howard. *Frames of Mind: The Theory of Multiple Intelligences.* New York: Basic Books, 1983.

———. "Notes on Educational Implications of the Theory of Multiple Intelligences." In College Board, *Measures in the College Admissions Process.*

Glasser, Ira. "Affirmative Action and the Legacy of Racial Injustice." In *Eliminating Racism: Profiles in Controversy,* ed. Phyllis Katz and Dalmas Taylor. New York: Plenum Press, 1988.

Glazer, Nathan. "The Future of Preferential Affirmative Action." In *Eliminating Racism: Profiles in Controversy,* ed. Phyllis Katz and Dalmas Taylor. New York: Plenum Press, 1988.

Gutmann, Amy. *Democratic Education.* Princeton, N.J.: Princeton University Press, 1987.

Hayden, Thomas C. *Handbook for College Admissions: A Family Guide.* Princeton, N.J.: Peterson's Guides, 1989.

Healy, Scott F. *School-College Articulation.* New York: College Board, 1991.

Hiss, William. "Optional SATs: The First Two Years at Bates College." In College Board, *Measures in the College Admissions Process.*

Johnson, Lyndon Baines. *Public Papers of the Presidents of the United States, Book II, June 1–December 31, 1965.* Washington, D.C.: Office of the Federal Register, National Archive and Records Service, General Services Administration, 1966.

Karen, D. "Toward a Political-Organizational Model of Gatekeeping: The Case of Elite Colleges." *Sociology of Education* 63 (1990): 227–40.

Klitgaard, Robert. *Choosing Elites*. New York: Basic Books, 1985.

Knight Foundation Commission. *Keeping Faith with the Student-Athlete: A New Model for Intercollegiate Athletics*, March 1991.

Kozol, Jonathan. *Savage Inequalities*. New York: Crown Publishers, 1991.

Litten, Larry H. *Ivy Bound: High Ability Students and College Choice*. New York: College Board, 1991.

Loeb, Jane W. *Academic Standards in Higher Education*. New York: College Board, 1992.

McPherson, Michael S. *Keeping College Affordable: Government and Educational Opportunity*. Washington, D.C.: Brookings Institution, 1991.

McPherson, Michael S., and Morton O. Schapiro. *Selective Admission and the Public Interest*. New York: College Board, 1990.

Mitchell, John Pearce. *Stanford University, 1916–1941*. Stanford, Calif.: Stanford University, 1958.

Myrdal, Gunnar. *An American Dilemma: The Negro Problem and Modern Democracy*. New York: Harper & Brothers, 1944.

National Collegiate Athletic Association. *1991–92 Manual of the National Collegiate Athletic Association*. Mission, Kan.: National Collegiate Athletic Association, 1991.

Neusner, Jacob. *How to Grade Your Professors and Other Unexpected Advice*. Boston: Beacon Press, 1984.

Oren, Dan A. *Joining the Club: A History of Jews and Yale*. New Haven, Conn.: Yale University Press, 1986.

Robinson, Adam, and John Katzman, eds. *The Princeton Review, College Admissions: Cracking the System*. New York: Random House, Villard Books, 1990.

Rodriguez, Richard. *Hunger of Memory*. New York: Bantam, 1982.

Scannell, James J. *The Effect of Financial Aid Policies on Admission and Enrollment*. New York: College Board, 1992.

Schurenberg, E. "The Agony of College Admissions." *Money*, May 1989.

Sowell, Thomas. *Preferential Policies: An International Perspective*. New York: Morrow, 1990.

Sperber, Murray. *College Sports, Inc.: The Athletic Department vs. the University*. New York: Henry Holt, 1990.

Stanford University. Report to the President from the Ad Hoc Committee on Athletics at Stanford, *The Future of Athletics at Stanford*, 1991.

———. "Responses to the Recommendations of the University Committee on Minority Issues and Institutional Standards on Cultural Diversity." In *Stanford University Self-Study on Building a Multiracial, Multicultural*

University Community. Final Report of the Annual Review Panel, 1990.

———. *Stanford: A Man, a Woman . . . and a University.* Stanford, Calif.: Publications Service, 1966.

Stanford University. Committee on Undergraduate Admissions and Financial Aids (C-UAFA). *Annual Report 1977–1978, 1978–1979.*

———. *Annual Report 1985–86.*

———. "Proposed C-UAFA Guidelines for Adding Targeted Minority Groups," C-UAFA Meeting Minutes, Spring 1989.

Stanford University. Department of Athletics. *Stanford Sports Quarterly* (Summer 1991; Summer 1992).

Stanford University. Office of Undergraduate Admissions. *Looking Ahead to Stanford,* 1991.

———. *Stanford Today,* 1991.

Stanford University. Senate Committee on Education and Scholarship at Stanford. *Statement of Goals and Guidelines on the Eve of Budget Reduction,* Aug. 26, 1991.

Stanford University. Steering Committee of the Study of Education at Stanford. *The Study of Education at Stanford: Report to the University,* 1968.

Stanford University. University Committee on Minority Issues. *Building a Multiracial, Multicultural University Community: Final Report of the University Committee on Minority Issues,* 1989.

Steele, Shelby. *The Content of Our Character: A New Vision of Race in America.* New York: St. Martin's, 1990.

Sternberg, Robert, "What Would Better Intelligence Tests Look Like?" In College Board, *Measures in the College Admissions Process.*

Stewart, Donald M. *College Admission Policies in the 1990s: A Look Toward the Future.* New York: College Board, 1992.

Thresher, B. Alden. *College Admissions and the Public Interest.* New York: College Board, 1966.

University of California. Committee on Admissions and Enrollment. *Freshman Admissions at Berkeley: A Policy for the 1990s and Beyond,* 1989.

U.S. Bureau of the Census. *Current Population Reports.* Series P-60, no. 159, "Consumer Income of Households"; Series P-20, no. 431, "The Hispanic Population in the United States: March 1988"; Series P-25, no. 1022, "U.S. Population in Estimates, by Age, Sex and Race, 1980–1987." Washington, D.C.: GPO, 1988.

Wall, Edward B. *How We Do It: Student Selection at the Nation's Most Prestigious Colleges.* Alexandria, Va.: Octameron Associates, 1982.

Western Interstate Commission on Higher Education and the College Board. *The Road to College: Educational Progress by Race and Ethnicity.* Boulder, Colo., 1991.

Whitehead, Alfred North. "Mathematics." In *Science and the Modern World,*
Lowell Lectures, 1925. New York: Macmillan, 1939.

Wilder, Gita Z., and Kristin Powell. *Sex Differences in Test Performance:
A Survey of the Literature.* New York: College Board, 1989.

Wright, B. Ann. "The Rating Game: How the Media Affect College Admission." *College Board Review* 158 (Winter 1990–91).

Index

In this index an "f" after a number indicates a separate reference on the next page, and an "ff" indicates separate references on the next two pages. A continuous discussion over two or more pages is indicated by a span of page numbers, e.g., "57–59." *Passim* is used for a cluster of references in close but not consecutive sequence.

Academic achievement, 9, 23–24, 250. *See also* Grade-point average; Tests, standardized
Academic profile, 14
Academics, 5f, 136–39
Achievement Tests, 16, 41f, 45f
Admissions, vi–vii, 1–10 *passim*, 48–49, 230–35; need-blind, vi, viii, 7–8, 26, 55
Admissions criteria, 8–13, 23–25, 104–8, 111–15, 161, 249–52
Admissions process, 16–22, 32–36, 58–60, 152–64, 249–54
Admissions staff, viii, 102ff, 138–40, 161f, 163f, 193–94, 214, 239–41, 251–52. *See also* Dean of undergraduate admissions; Readers
"Admit" decision, 18–22
Admitted students, 14, 42–43, 71, 88–98 *passim*, 164–65
Advanced Placement program, 238–39
Affirmative action, 9, 77, 91–93, 101–4, 110; criticisms of, 88–91, 104–8, 111–36, 234–35

African-Americans, 9, 37, 44, 126f, 128f, 167, 184–85, 220–22, 231ff, 259n8; and affirmative action, 88–95 *passim*, 101–2, 125ff, 128f. *See also* Minorities
Alexander, Lamar, 91
Alumni, vi, vii, 47–48, 75–76, 252–54; children of, vii, 9, 30, 56, 71–79, 81–82
Alumni Association Admissions Committee, 71f
American Association of Collegiate Registrars and Admissions Officers, 194
American Association of University Professors, 245
American College Test (ACT), 41f, 210. *See also* Scholastic Aptitude Test
American Indians, *see* Native American Indians
Anti-intellectualism, 69
Applicants, 14, 35–44 *passim*, 63, 71, 195–202, 211
Application process, 35–36

Applications, 17–22, 103–4, 197–98;
    computerized, 247
Aptitude test, 4–5
Arizona, University of, 148, 165f
Arizona State University, 148, 165f
Armed services, 5
Art, 21, 57, 62–63
Articulation, 236–43
Ashe, Arthur, 185
Asian-Americans, 37, 96–98, 118–19,
    233; admission rates of, 76–77, 88,
    90f, 96–98. See also Minorities
Athletes, see Student-athletes
Athletic Rating Form (ARF), 156
Athletics, 146–49, 179–91 passim;
    Division I, 147, 154–55, 165–67,
    184ff. See also Student-athletes
Atwell, Robert, 182–83
Azzi, Jennifer, 151

Basketball, 155–57, 173–77, 184–85,
    190–91
Bates College, 46
Bell, Derrick, 111, 257n14
Bennett, William, 244
Berman, Paul, 245
Blacks, see African-Americans
Bloom, Allan, 244
Bok, Derek, 131
Bok, Sissela, 209
Bonhoeffer, Dietrich, 193
Booker, Cory, 150
Bribery, 226–27
Brown University, 50, 91
Buck Club, 190
Buckley Amendment, 205, 215–16
Bunnell, John, 32, 107
Bush, George, 237, 239

California, 54, 90, 234–35
California, University of, 8, 232f,
    241–42; at Berkeley, 66, 76, 91, 115,
    141, 148, 165f, 232, 234f, 244; at Los
    Angeles (UCLA), 91, 148, 165f
California Institute of Technology, 66

Campus visits, 37, 46
Cardinal Club, 190
Carter, Stephen, 88, 103, 111, 115, 125,
    129, 132, 140, 259n14
Casper, Gerhard, 254
Cavazos, Lauro F., 76
Cheating, 195–97, 204
Chicago, University of, 66
Chicanos, see Mexican-Americans
Children, 134–36; of alumni, vii, 9, 30,
    56, 71–79; of faculty and staff, 9,
    83–87; of wealthy, vii, 55–56
Choosing Elites (Klitgaard), 41, 58ff, 61
City University of New York, 141
Class, socioeconomic, 125–31
Club sports, 148
Coaches, 151–52, 161f, 163f, 179
Code of ethics (NACAC), 194, 214
College admissions officers, see
    Admissions staff
College Board, 193f, 206, 241, 243;
    Achievement Tests of, 16, 41–46
    passim; monographs of, 230,
    262n2; programs of, 138, 210,
    238–39, 260n41
College enrollment projections,
    229–32
Colleges, see Universities
Collegiality, of admissions work,
    34–35
Committee on Undergraduate
    Admissions and Financial Aids
    (C-UAFA), 91, 93, 96–99
Committees, 48–49
Common reply date, 28, 36
Confidentiality, 204–6, 215–16,
    224–25
Consortium on Financing Higher
    Education (COFHE), 30, 138, 211,
    242, 260n41
Correspondence, see Letters
Cost of college, 2, 5, 7, 55, 241–42
Counselors: high school, 51–52, 87,
    203–10, 214, 239–41; independent
    guidance, 199, 213–14

Criminal record, 217–20
Criteria for admissions, *see* Admissions criteria
Crouse, James, 44
Curriculum: college, 243–45; high school, 5–6, 10–11, 238

Dance, 21, 57, 62–63
Dartmouth College, 95
Davis, Tom, 173ff, 176, 179
Dean of undergraduate admissions, 7, 9, 12f, 18f, 82, 152
Demographics, 230–34
"Deny" decision, 18f, 21f, 32
Dickey, Glenn, 175–76
Director of admissions, *see* Dean of undergraduate admissions
Discrimination, reverse, 115–20. *See also* Affirmative action; Racism
Diversity, 243–45. *See also* Ethnicity; Minorities
Division I athletics, *see* Athletics
Dole, Bob, 91
Donors, 81–83. *See also* Alumni
Drama, 21, 57, 62–63
D'Souza, Dinesh, 244

Early admission, 49–53, 168, 257n9
Early notification of athletes, 169–71
Educational Testing Service (ETS), 195ff
Edwards, Harry, 167, 185
Elliott, O. L., 1
Elway, Jack, 172, 178, 189
Elway, John, 151
Emeriti, 32
Enrolled students, 14, 43, 96, 229–30, 234
Enrollment projections, 229–32
Equity Project, 138, 260n41
Essay questions, 9, 16, 198–202, 224–25, 245–47
Ethics, NACAC code of, 194, 214
Ethnicity, 6–11 *passim*, 88ff, 102–3, 142–43, 220–22, 243. *See also* Minorities

Evans, Janet, 151
Extracurricular activities, 9, 11, 24–25, 250–51
"Extreme talents," 68–69. *See also* Special talents

Faculty, 1, 13, 32, 65–70 *passim*, 252; children of, 9, 83–87
Family Educational Rights and Privacy Act, 205
Fendick, Patty, 151
Fetter, Jean, 7, 69, 153, 175
Financial aid, viii, 9, 26, 50, 55, 108–9, 181–83, 213, 242–43
Financial planning, 242–43
Football, 157–61, 169–71, 184–85, 191–92
Frankfurter, Felix, 78
Freshman class, 14, 20, 27, 71f, 90, 94, 164–65

Gardner, David, 118
Gardner, Howard, 44f, 62, 67
Geiger, Andy, 174, 179
Gender, 2ff, 5, 44–45, 91–92, 100, 119, 187–91, 229
Geographical distribution, 21, 54, 230ff, 236–37
Gilligan, Carol, 4
Gillis, Malcolm, 167
Gimmicks, 31–32, 56–57
Glasser, Ira, 100–101
"Goals 2000," 237
Grade-point average, 17, 23f, 44–45, 55, 160
Graduation rates, 109, 121, 132, 165ff, 191, 233–34
Graham, Debbie, 151
Green, Denny, 187
Grommon, Alfred, 5
Gutmann, Amy, 78

Hacker, Andrew, 113–14
Hargadon, Fred, 7
Harvard University, 26, 50, 58–60,

66, 165f, 215; minorities at, 76ff, 91, 95, 131
Higher education, 229–30, 234
Higher Education Act (HEA), 243
High school, viii, 14, 16–17, 54–55, 183–84, 203–9, 230–43 passim; curriculum, 5–6, 10–11, 238; seniors, vi, 30–32, 36–38, 51–52, 245–47
Hispanics, 90, 95, 141, 231–33. See also Mexican-Americans
Hiss, William, 46
Hogue, James Arthur, 217–18
Honor code, 195, 198
Housing, of athletes, 151

Illness, 48–49, 225–26
Income, 44, 125–27, 130–31
Indris-Santana, Alexi, 217–18
Information sessions, 57
Institutions, see Universities
Intelligences, 44, 62, 67
International students, 25–27, 37, 90
Interviews, 46–47, 48, 57
Intramural sports, 148

Johnson, Lyndon, 133
Jordan, David Starr, 10, 180
Juvenal, 146, 179

Karabel, Jerome, 77
Karen, David, 77
Katchadourian, Herant, 1
Keefe, Adam, 151
Kennedy, Donald, 13, 169, 176
Kerrey, Bob, 183
Klitgaard, Robert, 41, 58ff, 61
Knight Foundation Commission, 191
Koppett, Leonard, 178f, 181–82
Kozol, Jonathan, 126, 134–35

La Plante, Rick, 178
Latinos, see Hispanics
"Legacies," 30, 71–79

Letters, 28–29, 38–40, 101–2; of intent, 155, 159–60, 162. See also References
Lichti, Todd, 151
Lyman, Richard, 147, 183

McDowell, Jack, 151
McEnroe, Patrick, 151
McPherson, Michael S., 126
Major, 13, 63
Marketing, 210–11
Mascot, 143–44
Massachusetts Institute of Technology (MIT), 50, 66, 95, 165, 181
Mathematical Society of America, 67
Mathematics, 13, 65–69, 239
Mayotte, Tim, 151
Media, 158–59, 173–79, 211–12, 224–25
Merit awards, 213
Mexican-Americans, 9, 37, 44, 88–95 passim, 101–2, 126, 130, 136–42 passim. See also Hispanics; Minorities
Minorities, 37, 44, 134–43 passim, 184–87, 231–34, 244–45; and affirmative action, 55, 96–104 passim, 108–15 passim, 120–25 passim, 131–33, 234f; enrollment of, 95, 100, 131–33, 141, 229, 234; targeted, 93–95, 103–4, 108–9, 117, 136–38. See also African-Americans; Asian-Americans; Ethnicity; Mexican-Americans; Native American Indians
Misrepresentation, 217–23
Mitchell, Pearce, 4
Montgomery, Mike, 179
Montoya, James, 7, 215
Mooki, Oomphemetse, 150
Multiculturalism, see Diversity
Multiple intelligences, 44, 62, 67
Munk, Chris, 173–77
Music, 21, 57, 62–65
Mussina, Mike, 151

Muster, Brad, 151
Myrdal, Gunnar, 92
Myths, vii, 29–30, 54–58

National Association of College Admissions Counselors (NACAC), 28, 138, 193f, 206, 214, 241, 243, 260n41
National Collegiate Athletic Association (NCAA), 48, 149, 153–60 passim, 181–87 passim, 195
National demographics, changes in, 230–33
National Science Foundation fellowships, 66
National standards, 237
Native American Indians, 9, 37, 88–95 passim, 101–2, 124, 130, 143–44, 222, 231ff. See also Minorities
Native Hawaiians, 98, 137
Need-blind admissions, vi, viii, 7–8, 26, 55
Nevius, C. W., 174–75
Norton, Eleanor Holmes, 130f

Oregon, University of, 148, 165f
Oregon State University, 148, 165f
Oxford University, 69

Pacesetter program, 239
Pacific-10 conference, 148, 153, 165f
Parents, vi, 35–40 passim, 44, 168–70. See also Children
Percy, Walker, 42
Perry, Edmund, 224–25
Personal achievement, 9, 11, 24–25, 250–51
Personal questions, 6
Personal statement, see Essay questions
Photographs, 6, 202, 245–46
Plumer, PattiSue, 151
"Political correctness," 244–45
Portfolio, student, 44

Preliminary Scholastic Aptitude Test (PSAT), 210
Princeton University, 50, 66, 72, 95, 165f, 217–18
Pro Fro Week, 37, 68
Proposal 48, 160, 185–87
Puerto Ricans, 44, 98, 137
Putnam math exam, 66f

Questions, see Essay questions; Personal questions
Quotas, 123–25

Race, see Ethnicity; Minorities
Racism, 125, 127ff. See also Affirmative action; Discrimination, reverse
Ramirez, Raul, 147
Rating scale, 23–25
Readers, 17–22, 32–35, 103–4, 162–63, 207–8. See also Admissions staff
Readings, of applications, 17–22, 103–4
Recommendations, see References
Recruitment, 36–38, 63–65, 101–2, 155–57
References, 5, 9, 16f, 22, 203–9, 214
Rice University, 165–67
Rodriguez, Richard, 115–16, 121–22, 130
Rupp, George, 165–66

Schapiro, Morton O., 126
Scholarships, see Financial aid
Scholastic Aptitude Test (SAT), 41–45 passim, 56, 195–97; scores on, 13f, 23f, 42–46 passim, 112–13, 160, 210–11
Schultz, Richard, 190
Selection, random, 58
Selection process, see Admissions process
Self-identification, 142–43, 222

Self-presentation, *see* Essay questions
Siblings, 79–80
Snyder, Rixford, 7, 72–73
Social problems, 134–36, 251
Socioeconomic class, 125–31
Southern California, University of
    (USC), 148, 165f
Sowell, Thomas, 111ff, 259n14
Special talents, 62–71
Sperber, Murray, 185ff, 191
Sports, *see* Athletics
Staff, children of, 83–87. *See also*
    Admissions staff
Standardized tests, *see* Tests,
    standardized
Stanford, Jane, 3
Stanford Indian, 143–44
Steele, Shelby, 108, 111, 122, 124,
    128–29, 134ff, 259n14
Sternberg, Robert, 44
Sternfels, Bob, 150
Stewart, Donald, 229–30
Student-athletes, 9, 76–77, 150–80
    passim, 191, 218–20
Students, *see* Admitted students;
    Enrolled students; Freshman class;
    International students; Transfer
    students
Study of Education at Stanford, 6–7,
    92–93
Supplementary Information Form,
    197–98
Supplementary materials, 57, 62–65
"Swim" decision, 18f, 20f

Tanner, Roscoe, 147
Telephoning, 37–38, 163
Test of English as a Foreign Language
    (TOEFL), 41
Tests, standardized, 4–5, 9, 16, 41f,
    45f, 55, 210. *See also* Scholastic
    Aptitude Test
Thomas, Clarence, 111, 259n14
Thomas, Debi, 151
Thresher, B. Alden, 16, 92

Title IX of Education Amendments,
    119, 189f
Transcripts, 16f, 222–23
Transfer students, 6f, 27, 30, 57
Triplets, 80–81
Tuition, 2, 5, 7, 241–42
Tuition benefit plan, 83–84, 86
Twins, 80

Universities, 8, 78, 209–16, 233–43
    passim
University Committee on Minority
    Issues (UCMI) report, 99, 101, 143
U.S. Commission on Civil Rights, 78
U.S. Department of Education, 78

VanDerveer, Tara, 190
Varsity athletes, *see* Student-athletes
Visits: campus, 37, 46, 68; high
    school, viii
Vlahov, Andrew, 156

"Wait list" decision, 21–22, 27–32
Walsh, Bill, 178, 191–92
Washington, University of, 148, 165f
Washington State University, 148, 165f
Wealthy, children of, vii, 55–56, 126
Western Interstate Commission for
    Higher Education, 231
Westinghouse Science competition,
    67
Whitehead, Alfred North, 68
Whites, 52, 90, 115–20, 126, 233
Wilder, Douglas, 119
Williams, Steve, 175
Williams, T. M., 144
Wilson, Eugene S. "Bill," 60, 252
Women: and affirmative action,
    91–92; and athletics, 187–91
Work-card, 17, 21, 215–16
Writing, 48, 69–70. *See also* Essay
    questions

Yale University, 50, 95, 116, 165f
Yield, 20, 27–28, 94ff, 212–13

Library of Congress Cataloging-in-Publication Data

Fetter, Jean.
  Questions and admissions : reflections on 100,000 admissions
decisions at Stanford / Jean Fetter.
      p.   cm.
  Includes bibliographical references and index.
  ISBN 0-8047-2398-2 (cloth)
  1. Universities and colleges—United States—Admission—Case
studies.   2. Universities and colleges—United States—Entrance
requirements—Case studies.   3. Stanford University—Admission.
I. Title.
LB2351.2.F48 1995
378.1'05'0973—dc20   94-23098
                                                            CIP

⊗   This book is printed on acid-free paper.